Microsoft® Internet Information Server 4 For

MW01170344

What's in the Windows NT 4.0 Option Pack?

The following descibes the available components in the Windows NT 4.0 Option Pack.

Component	What It Does
Certificate Server	Creates digital certificates for authentication via SSL (Secure Sockets Layer).
FrontPage Server Extensions	Supports the use of Microsoft FrontPage to manage your Web site as well as create the site content.
Internet Connection Services for RAS	Includes a set of core Windows NT remote access services that facilitate the creation of secure, seamless virtual private networks (VPN) and improved dial-up networking connections.
Internet Information Server	Comprises the complete Web and FTP server software package that includes Internet Service Manager.
Microsoft Data Access Components	Includes tools for enabling the use of databases with your Web sites.
Microsoft Index Server	Creates a search engine for your Web and Network News sites to enable users to search for specific information.
Microsoft Management Console	Allows you to manage a variety of software tools using a single integrated interface. The console hosts programs called snap-ins, of which Internet Information Server is one.
Microsoft Message Queue	Allows applications to pass along transaction notification and continue processing without waiting for confirmation that the transaction has completed.
Microsoft Script Debugger	Provides a comprehensive debugging environment for testing and correcting errors in Web document client and server scripts. Supports VBScript and JScript.
Microsoft Site Server Express	Includes site analysis and usage analysis tools for managing your Web sites.
NT Option Pack Common Files	Includes the core program files needed by all components.
Transaction Server	Supports the creation of Microsoft Transaction Server (MTS) applications. A *transaction* is a server operation that suceeds or fails as a whole, even if the operation involves many steps. MTS supports process isolation of applications.
Visual InterDev RAD Remote Deployment Support	Enables the remote deployment of applications on your Web server using Microsoft Visual InterDev.
Windows Scripting Host	Supports the creation and use of scripts written at the command line to manage server properties.

...For Dummies: #1 Computer Book Series for Beginners

Microsoft® Internet Information Server 4 For Dummies®

Cheat Sheet

Web Site Capacity Recommendations

Application Load	Document Requests per Minute	Processor and Memory Requirements
Low	Light (60 or less)	Pentium-166 with 32MB of RAM
Low	Medium (less than 600)	Pentium-200 with 64MB of RAM
Low	Heavy (up to 6000)	Pentium-200 with 64MB of RAM up to a dual Pentium-200 machine with 128MB of RAM
Medium	Light (60 or less)	Pentium-200 with 64MB of RAM
Medium	Medium (less than 600)	Pentium-200 with 64MB of RAM up to a dual Pentium-200 machine with 128MB of RAM
Medium	Heavy (up to 6000)	Pentium-200 with 64MB of RAM up to a dual Pentium-200 machine with 128MB of RAM
Heavy	Light (60 or less)	Pentium-200 with 64MB of RAM up to a dual Pentium-200 machine with 128MB of RAM
Heavy	Medium (less than 600)	Pentium-200 with 64MB of RAM or upper-end multiple servers
Heavy	Heavy (up to 6000)	Pentium-200 with 64MB of RAM, a dual Pentium-200 machine with 128MB of RAM, or upper-end multiple servers

IIS Preinstallation Software Checklist

The following software must be installed on your computer before installing Internet Information Server:

- ✔ Windows NT Server version 4.0
- ✔ Windows NT Service Pack 3
- ✔ Internet Explorer version 4.01 or later
- ✔ Windows NT Server's TCP/IP network protocol stack
- ✔ Windows NT File System

Number of Simultaneous Web Users Supported by Different Connection Capacities

Connection Bandwidth	Maximum Number of Users
28.8/33.6 Kbps	3 to 5
56 Kbps	10 to 15
128 Kbps	10 to 30
384 Kbps	25 to 100
1.54 Mbps	100 to 300

Microsoft Tools and Resources

FrontPage 98: www.microsoft.com/frontpage/

Internet Information Server: www.micrsoft.com/iis/

BackOffice: backoffice.microsoft.com

Microsoft Support Online: support.microsoft.com/support/

Microsoft Site Builder: www.microsoft.com/sitebuilder/

Microsoft Interactive Developer: www.microsoft.com/mind/

Microsoft Visual InterDev: www.microsoft.com/vinterdev/

Microsoft SQL Server: www.microsoft.com/sql/

Microsoft Exchange Server: www.microsoft.com/exchange/

Microsoft Windows NT Server: www.microsoft.com/ntserver/

Microsoft Proxy Server: www.microsoft.com/proxy/

Microsoft Site Server: www.microsoft.com/Site Server/

Microsoft BackOffice Small Business Server: www.microsoft.com/backofficesmallbiz/

COMPUTER BOOK SERIES FROM IDG

References for the Rest of Us!®

Are you intimidated and confused by computers? Do you find that traditional manuals are overloaded with technical details you'll never use? Do your friends and family always call you to fix simple problems on their PCs? Then the *...For Dummies*® computer book series from IDG Books Worldwide is for you.

...For Dummies books are written for those frustrated computer users who know they aren't really dumb but find that PC hardware, software, and indeed the unique vocabulary of computing make them feel helpless. *...For Dummies* books use a lighthearted approach, a down-to-earth style, and even cartoons and humorous icons to diffuse computer novices' fears and build their confidence. Lighthearted but not lightweight, these books are a perfect survival guide for anyone forced to use a computer.

> "I like my copy so much I told friends; now they bought copies."
>
> Irene C., Orwell, Ohio

> "Quick, concise, nontechnical, and humorous."
>
> Jay A., Elburn, Illinois

> "Thanks, I needed this book. Now I can sleep at night."
>
> Robin F., British Columbia, Canada

Already, millions of satisfied readers agree. They have made *...For Dummies* books the #1 introductory level computer book series and have written asking for more. So, if you're looking for the most fun and easy way to learn about computers, look to *...For Dummies* books to give you a helping hand.

IDG
BOOKS
WORLDWIDE

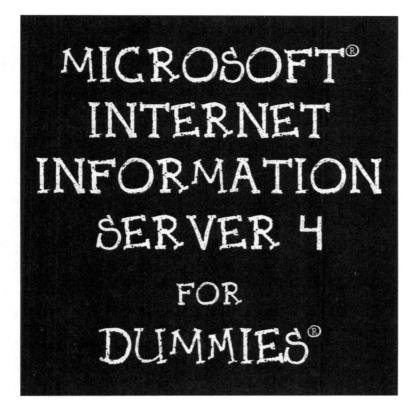

MICROSOFT® INTERNET INFORMATION SERVER 4 FOR DUMMIES®

by David Angell

IDG Books Worldwide, Inc.
An International Data Group Company

Foster City, CA ♦ Chicago, IL ♦ Indianapolis, IN ♦ New York, NY ♦ Southlake, TX

Microsoft® Internet Information Server 4 For Dummies®

Published by
IDG Books Worldwide, Inc.
An International Data Group Company
919 E. Hillsdale Blvd.
Suite 400
Foster City, CA 94404
www.idgbooks.com (IDG Books Worldwide Web site)
www.dummies.com (Dummies Press Web site)

Library of Congress Catalog Card No.: 98-84963

ISBN: 0-7645-0265-4

Printed in the United States of America

10 9 8 7 6 5 4 3 2 1

1O/RX/QU/ZY/IN

Distributed in the United States by IDG Books Worldwide, Inc.

Distributed by Macmillan Canada for Canada; by Transworld Publishers Limited in the United Kingdom; by IDG Norge Books for Norway; by IDG Sweden Books for Sweden; by Woodslane Pty. Ltd. for Australia; by Woodslane Enterprises Ltd. for New Zealand; by Longman Singapore Publishers Ltd. for Singapore, Malaysia, Thailand, and Indonesia; by Simron Pty. Ltd. for South Africa; by Toppan Company Ltd. for Japan; by Distribuidora Cuspide for Argentina; by Livraria Cultura for Brazil; by Ediciencia S.A. for Ecuador; by Addison-Wesley Publishing Company for Korea; by Ediciones ZETA S.C.R. Ltda. for Peru; by WS Computer Publishing Corporation, Inc., for the Philippines; by Unalis Corporation for Taiwan; by Contemporanea de Ediciones for Venezuela; by Computer Book & Magazine Store for Puerto Rico; by Express Computer Distributors for the Caribbean and West Indies. Authorized Sales Agent: Anthony Rudkin Associates for the Middle East and North Africa.

For general information on IDG Books Worldwide's books in the U.S., please call our Consumer Customer Service department at 800-762-2974. For reseller information, including discounts and premium sales, please call our Reseller Customer Service department at 800-434-3422.

For information on where to purchase IDG Books Worldwide's books outside the U.S., please contact our International Sales department at 650-655-3200 or fax 650-655-3295.

For information on foreign language translations, please contact our Foreign & Subsidiary Rights department at 650-655-3021 or fax 650-655-3281.

For sales inquiries and special prices for bulk quantities, please contact our Sales department at 650-655-3200 or write to the address above.

For information on using IDG Books Worldwide's books in the classroom or for ordering examination copies, please contact our Educational Sales department at 800-434-2086 or fax 817-251-8174.

For press review copies, author interviews, or other publicity information, please contact our Public Relations department at 650-655-3000 or fax 650-655-3299.

For authorization to photocopy items for corporate, personal, or educational use, please contact Copyright Clearance Center, 222 Rosewood Drive, Danvers, MA 01923, or fax 978-750-4470.

is a trademark under exclusive license to IDG Books Worldwide, Inc., from International Data Group, Inc.

About the Author

David Angell is a principle in angell.com (`www.angell.com`), a consulting and technical communications firm. He has made a career of demystifying computer technologies, authoring 20 books on a wide range of computing topics. David lives in Boston, Massachusetts, with his lovely wife Joanne and his growing intranet. You can contact David at `david@angell.com`.

ABOUT IDG BOOKS WORLDWIDE

Welcome to the world of IDG Books Worldwide.

IDG Books Worldwide, Inc., is a subsidiary of International Data Group, the world's largest publisher of computer-related information and the leading global provider of information services on information technology. IDG was founded more than 25 years ago and now employs more than 8,500 people worldwide. IDG publishes more than 275 computer publications in over 75 countries (see listing below). More than 60 million people read one or more IDG publications each month.

Launched in 1990, IDG Books Worldwide is today the #1 publisher of best-selling computer books in the United States. We are proud to have received eight awards from the Computer Press Association in recognition of editorial excellence and three from *Computer Currents'* First Annual Readers' Choice Awards. Our best-selling *...For Dummies®* series has more than 30 million copies in print with translations in 30 languages. IDG Books Worldwide, through a joint venture with IDG's Hi-Tech Beijing, became the first U.S. publisher to publish a computer book in the People's Republic of China. In record time, IDG Books Worldwide has become the first choice for millions of readers around the world who want to learn how to better manage their businesses.

Our mission is simple: Every one of our books is designed to bring extra value and skill-building instructions to the reader. Our books are written by experts who understand and care about our readers. The knowledge base of our editorial staff comes from years of experience in publishing, education, and journalism — experience we use to produce books for the '90s. In short, we care about books, so we attract the best people. We devote special attention to details such as audience, interior design, use of icons, and illustrations. And because we use an efficient process of authoring, editing, and desktop publishing our books electronically, we can spend more time ensuring superior content and spend less time on the technicalities of making books.

You can count on our commitment to deliver high-quality books at competitive prices on topics you want to read about. At IDG Books Worldwide, we continue in the IDG tradition of delivering quality for more than 25 years. You'll find no better book on a subject than one from IDG Books Worldwide.

John Kilcullen
CEO
IDG Books Worldwide, Inc.

Steven Berkowitz
President and Publisher
IDG Books Worldwide, Inc.

*Eighth Annual
Computer Press
Awards 1992*

*Ninth Annual
Computer Press
Awards 1993*

*Tenth Annual
Computer Press
Awards 1994*

*Eleventh Annual
Computer Press
Awards 1995*

IDG Books Worldwide, Inc., is a subsidiary of International Data Group, the world's largest publisher of computer-related information and the leading global provider of information services on information technology. International Data Group publishes over 275 computer publications in over 75 countries. Sixty million people read one or more International Data Group publications each month. International Data Group's publications include: **ARGENTINA:** Buyer's Guide, Computerworld Argentina, PC World Argentina; **AUSTRALIA:** Australian Macworld, Australian PC World, Australian Reseller News, Computerworld, IT Casebook, Network World, Publish, Webmaster; **AUSTRIA:** Computerwelt Osterreich, Networks Austria, PC Tip Austria; **BANGLADESH:** PC World Bangladesh; **BELARUS:** PC World Belarus; **BELGIUM:** Data News; **BRAZIL:** Annuário de Informática, Computerworld, Connections, Macworld, PC Player, PC World, Publish, Reseller News, Supergamepower; **BULGARIA:** Computerworld Bulgaria, Network World Bulgaria, PC & MacWorld Bulgaria; **CANADA:** CIO Canada, Client/Server World, ComputerWorld Canada, InfoWorld Canada, NetworkWorld Canada, WebWorld; **CHILE:** Computerworld Chile, PC World Chile; **COLOMBIA:** Computerworld Colombia, PC World Colombia; **COSTA RICA:** PC World Centro America; **THE CZECH AND SLOVAK REPUBLICS:** Computerworld Czechoslovakia, Macworld Czech Republic, PC World Czechoslovakia; **DENMARK:** Communications World Danmark, Computerworld Danmark, Macworld Danmark, PC World Danmark, Techworld Denmark; **DOMINICAN REPUBLIC:** PC World Republica Dominicana; **ECUADOR:** PC World Ecuador; **EGYPT:** Computerworld Middle East, PC World Middle East; **EL SALVADOR:** PC World Centro America; **FINLAND:** MikroPC, Tietoverkko, Tietoviikko; **FRANCE:** Distributique, Hebdo, Info PC, Le Monde Informatique, Macworld, Reseaux & Telecoms, WebMaster France; **GERMANY:** Computer Partner, Computerwoche, Computerwoche Extra, Computerwoche FOCUS, Global Online, Macwelt, PC Welt; **GREECE:** Amiga Computing, GamePro Greece, Multimedia World; **GUATEMALA:** PC World Centro America; **HONDURAS:** PC World Centro America; **HONG KONG:** Computerworld Hong Kong, PC World Hong Kong, Publish in Asia; **HUNGARY:** ABCD CD-ROM, Computerworld Szamitastechnika, Internetto online Magazine, PC World Hungary, PC-X Magazin Hungary; **ICELAND:** Tolvuheimur PC World Island; **INDIA:** Information Communications World, Information Systems Computerworld, PC World India, Publish in Asia; **INDONESIA:** InfoKomputer PC World, Komputek Computerworld, Publish in Asia; **IRELAND:** ComputerScope, PC Live!; **ISRAEL:** Macworld Israel, People & Computers/Computerworld; **ITALY:** Computerworld Italia, Macworld Italia, Networking Italia, PC World Italia; **JAPAN:** DTP World, Macworld Japan, Nikkei Personal Computing, OS/2 World Japan, SunWorld Japan, Windows NT World, Windows World Japan; **KENYA:** PC World East African; **KOREA:** Hi-Tech Information, Macworld Korea, PC World Korea; **MACEDONIA:** PC World Macedonia; **MALAYSIA:** Computerworld Malaysia, PC World Malaysia, Publish in Asia; **MALTA:** PC World Malta; **MEXICO:** Computerworld Mexico, PC World Mexico; **MYANMAR:** PC World Myanmar; **NETHERLANDS:** Computer! Totaal, LAN Internetworking Magazine, LAN World Buyers Guide, Macworld Netherlands, Net, WebWereld; **NEW ZEALAND:** Absolute Beginners Guide and Plain & Simple Series, Computer Buyer, Computer Industry Directory, Computerworld New Zealand, MTB, Network World, PC World New Zealand; **NICARAGUA:** PC World Centro America; **NORWAY:** Computerworld Norge, CW Rapport, Datamagasinet, Financial Rapport, Kursguide Norge, Macworld Norge, Multimediaworld Norge, PC World Ekspress Norge, PC World Nettverk, PC World Norge, PC World ProduktGuide Norge; **PAKISTAN:** Computerworld Pakistan; **PANAMA:** PC World Panama; **PEOPLE'S REPUBLIC OF CHINA:** China Computer Users, China Computerworld, China InfoWorld, China Telecom World Weekly, Computer & Communication, Electronic Design China, Electronics Today, Electronics Weekly, Game Software, PC World China, Popular Computer Week, Software Weekly, Software World, Telecom World; **PERU:** Computerworld Peru, PC World Profesional Peru, PC World SoHo Peru; **PHILIPPINES:** Click!, Computerworld Philippines, PC World Philippines, Publish in Asia; **POLAND:** Computerworld Poland, Computerworld Special Report Poland, Cyber, Macworld Poland, Networld Poland, PC World Komputer; **PORTUGAL:** Cerebro/PC World, Computerworld/Correio Informático, Dealer World Portugal, Mac*In/PC*In Portugal, Multimedia World; **PUERTO RICO:** PC World Puerto Rico; **ROMANIA:** Computerworld Romania, PC World Romania, Telecom Romania; **RUSSIA:** Computerworld Russia, Mir PK, Publish, Seti; **SINGAPORE:** Computerworld Singapore, PC World Singapore, Publish in Asia; **SLOVENIA:** Monitor; **SOUTH AFRICA:** Computing SA, Network World SA, Software World SA; **SPAIN:** Communicaciones World España, Computerworld España, Dealer World España, Macworld España, PC World España; **SRI LANKA:** Infolink PC World; **SWEDEN:** CAP&Design, Computer Sweden, Corporate Computing Sweden, Internetworld Sweden, it.branschen, Macworld Sweden, MaxiData Sweden, MikroDatorn, Nätverk & Kommunikation, PC World Sweden, PCaktiv, Windows World Sweden; **SWITZERLAND:** Computerworld Schweiz, Macworld Schweiz, PCtip; **TAIWAN:** Computerworld Taiwan, Macworld Taiwan, NEW ViSiON/Publish, PC World Taiwan, Windows World Taiwan; **THAILAND:** Publish in Asia, Thai Computerworld; **TURKEY:** Computerworld Turkiye, Macworld Turkiye, Network World Turkiye, PC World Turkiye; **UKRAINE:** Computerworld Kiev, Multimedia World Ukraine, PC World Ukraine; **UNITED KINGDOM:** Acorn User UK, Amiga Action UK, Amiga Computing UK, Apple Talk UK, Computing, Macworld, Parents and Computers UK, PC Advisor, PC Home, PSX Pro, The WEB; **UNITED STATES:** Cable in the Classroom, CIO Magazine, Computerworld, DOS World, Federal Computer Week, GamePro Magazine, InfoWorld, I-Way, Macworld, Network World, PC Games, PC World, Publish, Video Event, THE WEB Magazine, and WebMaster; online webzines: JavaWorld, NetscapeWorld, and SunWorld Online; **URUGUAY:** InfoWorld Uruguay; **VENEZUELA:** Computerworld Venezuela, PC World Venezuela; and **VIETNAM:** PC World Vietnam. 3/24/97

Dedication

This book is dedicated to my mother, Alberta Jane Truby, for her love, understanding, and encouragement.

Acknowledgments

Writing a book is always a rush to the finish line. Fortunately, a special group of people helped me all along the way. First, thanks to Matt Wagner at Waterside Productions for making this book deal happen. A warm thanks goes to Brent Heslop, friend and writer extraordinaire, for pitching in and accomplishing the job for both of us. I also want to thank the following folks who helped craft this book into the form you hold in your hands: Gareth Hancock and Acquistions Manager Mike Kelly, Project Editor Susan Pink, Technical Reviewer Dick Cravens, Associate Editor Suzanne Thomas, and Rich White at Best Communications.

Publisher's Acknowledgments

We're proud of this book; please register your comments through our IDG Books Worldwide Online Registration Form located at http://my2cents.dummies.com.

Some of the people who helped bring this book to market include the following:

Acquisitions, Development, and Editorial

Project Editor: Susan Pink

Acquisitions Manager: Michael Kelly

Technical Editor: Dick Craven

Editorial Manager: Mary C. Corder

Editorial Assistant: Donna Love

Production

Project Coordinator: E. Shawn Aylsworth

Layout and Graphics: Lou Boudreau, J. Tyler Connor, Angela F. Hunckler, Anna Rohrer, Brent Savage, Janet Seib, M. Anne Sipahimalani, Deirdre Smith, Kate Snell

Proofreaders: Christine Berman, Melissa D. Buddendeck, Rachel Garvey, Nancy Price, Rebecca Senninger, Janet M. Withers

Indexer: Sherry Massey

Special Help

Suzanne Thomas, Associate Editor; Christine Meloy Beck, Senior Copy Editor

General and Administrative

IDG Books Worldwide, Inc.: John Kilcullen, CEO; Steven Berkowitz, President and Publisher

IDG Books Technology Publishing: Brenda McLaughlin, Senior Vice President and Group Publisher

Dummies Technology Press and Dummies Editorial: Diane Graves Steele, Vice President and Associate Publisher; Mary Bednarek, Director of Acquisitions and Product Development; Kristin A. Cocks, Editorial Director

Dummies Trade Press: Kathleen A. Welton, Vice President and Publisher; Kevin Thornton, Acquisitions Manager

IDG Books Production for Dummies Press: Beth Jenkins Roberts, Production Director; Cindy L. Phipps, Manager of Project Coordination, Production Proofreading, and Indexing; Kathie S. Schutte, Supervisor of Page Layout; Shelley Lea, Supervisor of Graphics and Design; Debbie J. Gates, Production Systems Specialist; Robert Springer, Supervisor of Proofreading; Debbie Stailey, Special Projects Coordinator; Tony Augsburger, Supervisor of Reprints and Bluelines; Leslie Popplewell, Media Archive Coordinator

Dummies Packaging and Book Design: Patti Crane, Packaging Specialist; Kavish + Kavish, Cover Design

◆

The publisher would like to give special thanks to Patrick J. McGovern, without whom this book would not have been possible.

◆

Contents at a Glance

Cartoons at a Glance

By Rich Tennant

page 5

page 223

page 105

page 323

page 334

Fax: 978-546-7747 • E-mail: the5wave@tiac.net

Table of Contents

Introduction

*T*he rise of the World Wide Web is engendering a revolution in how organizations access and share information. A Web server can become the center of a company intranet as well as a company's public face through the Internet. The Web is changing the role of all computer-based office applications from isolated islands of content produced in proprietary formats to universal Web documents based on HTML (HyperText Markup Language). Connecting databases, word processors, spreadsheets, and presentation programs to the Web is the order of the day.

Microsoft Internet Information Server 4.0 (IIS 4) is Microsoft's state-of-the-art entry into the server side of the World Wide Web. With its easy-to-use Windows interface, IIS 4 removes any barriers to integrating the Web into an organization's operations. Internet Information Server running on Windows NT Server 4.0 creates a powerful platform designed to handle even the most demanding Web site traffic, whether you're using it as the cornerstone of an intranet or an Internet presence. IIS 4 includes not only complete Web and FTP server software but also a cornucopia of support and development tools — and best of all, IIS 4 is free.

Why This Book Is for You

Microsoft Internet Information Server 4 For Dummies shows you how to harness Internet Information Server within a real-world context. This hands-on guide goes further than other books published on the subject because I don't just show you how to work with Internet Information Server — I tell you how to use it to deliver solutions for your organization. *Microsoft Internet Information Server 4 For Dummies* is all you need to build your own full-fledged intranet or Internet Web and FTP sites.

Who You Are

Microsoft Internet Information Server 4 For Dummies gets you quickly up to speed with the workings of Internet Information Server. To get you there in the express lane, I make a few assumptions about who you are and what you already know how to do:

✔ You know your way around your computer system and the Windows NT Server operating system. This means you're comfortable with the basic workings of Windows NT from an administrator level.

✔ You've spent time surfing the Web and understand the basics of how the Internet works.

✔ You've never tried your hand at becoming a Webmaster but you want to take advantage of the benefits of running your own Web server, whether you plan to do it yourself or have others do it for you.

✔ You're familiar with Windows NT networking. You're not a guru, but you know enough to set up a bare-bones local area network and you're not afraid to open up your computer case and install a network adapter card.

✔ You've read about the many benefits of running a Web server but have been intimidated by UNIX-based solutions.

What's Inside

Internet Information Server is no small topic, so I've divided *Microsoft Internet Information Server 4 For Dummies* into four easily digestible parts.

✔ **Part I: Getting Started with Internet Information Server.** This part lays the foundation for installing IIS 4 on your Windows NT Server computer. In Chapter 1, you gain a solid understanding of what IIS 4 can do and how you can use it in your organization. In Chapter 2, you walk through preparing Windows for IIS installation, including how to get the most out of IIS. You master TCP/IP networking fundamentals in Chapters 3 and 4 so that you can create the proper habitat for running Internet Information Server as part of your intranet. Finally, in Chapter 5, you get advice on Internet connectivity and security issues involved when you link Internet Information Server to the Internet.

✔ **Part II: Taking Control of Your IIS Server.** This part begins your training in the art of becoming a Webmaster. In Chapter 6, you discover the fundamentals of working with Internet Service Manager, the control center for IIS. You also get a whirlwind tour of Web and FTP server configuration properties available to you. In Chapter 7, you start building your basic Web site management skills, and in Chapter 8, you continue with more advanced Webmaster tools to enhance your Web sites. In Chapter 9, you master setting up and running FTP (File Transfer Protocol) servers to enable fast and efficient file transfers across your intranet or the Internet. You find out in Chapter 10 how to protect your IIS servers by using a combination of IIS and Windows NT Server security features.

✔ **Part III: Beyond the Fundamentals.** Like the title says, this part guides you through IIS power tools. In Chapter 11, you find out how to host discussion newsgroups like the ones on the Internet by using Microsoft News Server to create a Usenet message-based conferencing server. In Chapter 12, you set up Microsoft Index Server so that users can search the contents of your Web and News servers. Adding to your Webmaster toolkit, in Chapter 13 you jump into using Active server pages, scripting languages, and ActiveX components to publish interactive content. You also discover, in Chapter 14, how to connect Microsoft Access and Microsoft SQL Server databases to your IIS Web sites so that you can create Web pages from database queries. This part ends with step-by-step instructions in Chapter 15 for logging the activities at your Web and FTP sites and creating graphical usage analysis reports.

✔ **Part IV: The Part of Tens.** What good is a Web site if no one visits it? Chapter 16 presents ten ways to market your Web site on the Internet. To help you in your search for new tools and other resources to keep your Web site fresh, check out Chapter 17, which includes online and offline Web site development resources and a number of third-party tools.

How to Use This Book

You don't need to start at Chapter 1 and move sequentially through the book. You can drop into any chapter to begin your journey toward IIS enlightenment. If you're new to TCP/IP networking, you may want to read the chapters on TCP/IP in Part I. If you want to cut to the chase and get started with using IIS to create your first Web site, begin with Chapter 6. To help you follow along, I use a few text conventions throughout the book:

✔ A notation such as "Choose Console⇨Open" is a condensed version of "from the Console menu, choose the Open command."

✔ Underlined letters in a menu notation indicate keyboard shortcuts. To use a keyboard shortcut, hold down the Alt key while pressing the underlined letter to open the menu. For example, to open the Console menu and choose the Open command, you press and hold down the Alt key and then press C. Release all those keys (if you want), and then press O.

✔ Internet Information Server, like most Windows programs, typically provides more than one way to accomplish tasks. For example, you can choose a menu item, or click a toolbar button, or press a keyboard shortcut, or right-click an item and then choose a command from a pop-up menu to accomplish the same task. I generally tell you the easiest way to carry out a task.

Icons Used in This Book

Icon-studded notes and sidebars highlight special information throughout this book.

This icon tells you about resources and techniques that can save you time, effort, or money.

Watch out! Rough spots along the way are marked with this icon.

This icon points you to Internet sites with additional help, free software tools, and information about related topics. Point your browser to the specified URL and shoot.

The information flagged with this icon is for those of you who want to dig a little deeper into the technical aspects of Internet Information Server and related topics.

Part I
Getting Started with Internet Information Server

The 5th Wave   By Rich Tennant

©RICHTENNANT

"It's all here, Warden. Routers, hubs, switches, all pieced together from scraps found in the machine shop. I guess the prospect of unregulated telecommunications was just too sweet to pass up."

In this part . . .

This part lays the foundation for setting up Internet Information Server on your Windows NT Server computer. It gives you a solid understanding of what IIS 4.0 can do and how you can use it in your organization. You walk through preparing Windows NT and its hardware underpinnings for installing and getting the most performance from IIS. You go on to master the fundamentals of TCP/IP networking to create the necessary habitat for running Internet Information Server as part of your intranet. Finally, you get sound advice on the connectivity and security issues involved in linking Internet Information Server to the Internet.

Chapter 1

Serving Up Internet Information Server

In This Chapter

▶ Finding out what Internet Information Server is all about

▶ Discovering what Internet Information Server means to you and your organization

▶ Identifying key features of Internet Information Server 4.0

▶ Introducing important Microsoft tools of the Web serving trade

*I*nternet Information Server (IIS) 4.0 is Microsoft's flagship entry into the server side of the World Wide Web. Internet Information Server running on Windows NT Server 4.0 creates a powerful symbiotic relationship. IIS 4.0 is designed to handle even the most demanding Web site traffic whether you're using it as the center of your intranet or for an Internet presence. IIS 4.0 not only includes Web and FTP server software but also a cornucopia of support and development tools. The first order of business is to get a grasp of what IIS 4.0 is about and what it can mean to your organization.

Internet Information Server in a Nutshell

The Internet and specifically the World Wide Web are, for any organization, the undisputed medium for communicating with the outside world. The same technologies behind the Internet and the Web are also becoming the interface for local area networks, converting them to intranets that embody the same look-and-feel as the Internet. (An *intranet* is an internal company network that uses the TCP/IP communications protocol and Web servers along with Web browsers to provide business communications.)

The World Wide Web operates as a global client/server environment, in which one computer acts as a *client* and the other acts as the *server* in any connection. The Web browser, which is the client side of the Web, has become the universal interface to the Internet and intranets. Internet Information Server (IIS) is the Web server that you can use to establish a presence for your organization on the Internet or to convert your local area network to an intranet.

Internet Information Server delivers a platform that enables you to expand your Web-serving capabilities as you add an ever-expanding range of Web-based services for Web users. At the core of Web server functions is the delivery of content to Web browsers that make requests. Requests to Web servers are made in the form of the ubiquitous URLs we all know and love. For example, entering `http://www.microsoft.com/` makes a request to the Microsoft Web server. The Web browser receives and then generates the page content, which appears in your Web browser (see Figure 1-1).

The symbiotic relationship of NT Server and IIS

It should come as no surprise that Windows NT Server and Internet Information Server are tightly integrated because both are from Microsoft. IIS is not an application that runs on top of NT; instead IIS becomes a fully integral part of NT Server. So intertwined are NT Server and IIS that you can't work with IIS without using a variety of supporting Windows NT Server tools. For

Figure 1-1:
The Web server delivers content that is then rendered in a Web browser to create the Web page.

example, directory and file security for IIS content files is handled via the New Technology File System (NTFS), which is a secure file management system incorporated into Windows NT Server 4.0.

The basic operational mechanics required to run IIS are grounded in a basic understanding of Windows NT and TCP/IP networking. Because of the tightly integrated relationship between Windows NT Server and Internet Information Server, you'll also be finding out a lot about selected Windows NT Server services in this book.

IIS: Web server and development environment

Internet Information Server is really two products in one. At the practical level, it's a complete Web server with all the bells and whistles. At the advanced programming level, IIS acts a platform for software developers to build customized Web applications.

Internet Information Server is a complete system for Web publishing on an intranet or the Internet. You can operate IIS without any programming experience. The practical operations of setting up and running servers uses the same standard Microsoft Windows NT interface of windows, dialog boxes, and graphical controls. Mastering the basics of IIS, you can create a powerful intranet or Internet presence. From this foundation, you can build customized solutions using an ever-expanding collection of Microsoft or third-party tools.

Beyond the practical operations of Internet Information Server, the second tier consists of programming environments that enable developers to create both applications to run on IIS and sophisticated Web site content. These infrastructure features are designed to provide an environment for programming a variety of custom applications to work with IIS. These features will support the addition of more sophisticated capabilities for your Web site.

What IIS Means to Your Organization

The release of Internet Information Server 4.0 removes any barriers to integrating the Web's powerful capabilities into any organization's operations. IIS is more than just a Web server — it's a way for organizations of any size to integrate their existing network resources and databases into the universal Web infrastructure. For smaller organizations running Windows 95 peer-to-peer networks, adding the dynamic duo of Windows NT Server and Internet Information Server to your existing network opens it up to the full potential of TCP/IP networking for collaboration and communications.

Breaking the UNIX barrier

The history of the Internet is synonymous with UNIX, a powerful operating system born in the days of mainframes and minicomputers. UNIX systems are designed for the demands of large-scale computing. TCP/IP (Transmission Control Protocol and Internet Protocol), the suite of networking protocols that forms the basis of the Internet, was integrated into UNIX early on. This marriage of TCP/IP and UNIX underlies the reason why UNIX systems continue to be the dominant platform for Web servers.

Although UNIX is a powerful operating system well suited for technical markets, for PC-based businesses raised on Microsoft Windows, making a switch to UNIX systems is a difficult — if not impossible — transition. Internet Information Server 4.0 running on Windows NT Server 4.0 enables these organizations to break through the UNIX barrier to operate their own powerful Web servers for intranets or the Internet.

Why Web technology is important

The rise of Web technologies is engendering a revolution in how organizations access and share information. The Web is enabling collaboration among teams of geographically dispersed individuals, and streamlining traditional, paper-based business practices. A Web server becomes a company center for information distribution and input as well as its public face via the Internet. Running a Web server is like having a giant digital canvas on which you can paint your business presence on the Internet or enable your local network to become a powerful conduit for a full range of collaboration and communication activities.

Working with Web technologies isn't just about working smarter; it's about reinventing your business operations. With the Web server as the center of this change in your business operations, the role of computer-based applications changes also. Instead of being isolated islands of content produced in proprietary formats, popular applications now generate their output as Web documents based on HTML (HyperText Markup Language). Connecting databases, word processors, spreadsheet, and presentation programs to the Web is the order of the day.

Using IIS as an intranet and Internet server offers a variety of benefits due to the efficiencies gained from the online distribution of information. Here are some of the key benefits of using a Web site for conducting business.

✔ **Communications.** Communications are being revolutionized by electronic capabilities, and technologies riding on the Web will continue this trend. New technologies and standards continue to bring new forms of communication to Web-based networks, such as digital telephony, video conferencing, and groupware applications.

- 🖛 **Cost efficiencies.** Business users are already finding significant advantages in the improved communications that an intranet and the Internet bring. For example, publishing online delivers big savings in printing and distribution costs for companies.

- 🖛 **Publishing on demand.** Traditional paper-based systems crumple against the virtually unlimited capabilities of Web publishing. The traditional paper-based mechanism for many company documents is simply outdated in the fast-paced world of today's business environment.

- 🖛 **Electronic distribution.** A Web server offers clear cost and time efficiencies to both businesses and customers in the delivery of information, files, and software.

IIS and TCP/IP networking

TCP/IP (Transmission Control Protocol/Internet Protocol) is the lingua franca of the Internet. From its Internet roots, TCP/IP is rapidly becoming the preferred protocol for company networks. According to Forrester Research, the number of companies with more than half of their network traffic on IP will grow from 36 percent in 1996 to 82 percent in 1998.

Operating Internet Information Server converts your business infrastructure over to the TCP/IP networking environment. With this conversion, the tools your network clients use to access the Internet also become the tools they use to communicate within your local network. The economics of a universal and open system for both internal networks and external networks (the Internet) are compelling for even the smallest of businesses.

IIS and Intranets

An intranet opens communications within your organization using the same set of tools used on the Internet. The Web browser becomes the interface to both your local company operations as well as the Internet. Web documents become a universal system for communications and information delivery. Any information that you want to share within your organization but don't want to publish outside your company is suitable material for your intranet site. You can create an intranet based on Internet Information Server running on an NT Server machine and Internet Explorer running on your clients.

You can set up and maintain an intranet much more easily than an Internet site because you don't have to deal with the complex connectivity and security issues inherent with making the Internet connection. Each group or individual who contributes to your intranet can maintain the content, reducing the staff needed to maintain the intranet and leveraging the resources across the company rather than concentrating demands within a single department. Because your intranet is not viewed outside your organization and because you typically have high-speed Ethernet (10 Mbps/100 Mbps) connections between your server and workstations, you can publish content that might not be appropriate on the Internet for reasons of performance or company image. Building an intranet creates the foundation for linking up your network to the Internet as well.

IIS and the Internet

As an Internet server, IIS functions as your public interface. It operates in a similar manner as it does at the center of your intranet but with the added dimensions of Internet connectivity and security issues. These added elements aren't to be taken lightly — they require scrutiny and understanding. Connecting a Windows NT-based server to the Internet requires a dedicated connection with enough bandwidth to support your anticipated traffic. And if the Windows NT Server running the IIS Web site is connected to your local network, you need to deal with protecting your private network from Internet intruders. Cost is a big factor in connecting your Web server to the Internet; the bulk of the cost is your dedicated connection to the Internet. A T1 line (1.54 Mbps) can easily run several thousand dollars a month. The good news is that more affordable, dedicated Internet connections are coming online that may enable millions of smaller businesses to establish their own presence on the Internet. (You can find out more in Chapter 5.)

A Web site on the Internet must be accessible to the Internet 24 hours a day, 7 days a week, and 365 days a year. To make your site this accessible, you need a dedicated connection to the Internet. This type of connection requires a telecommunications link, for which service is billed at a flat monthly rate rather than based on usage. Network connections are measured in terms of *bandwidth,* or the speed at which the link transmits data to the Internet. The higher the bandwidth, the more expensive the service and the more volume of users your site can handle.

The Internet Information Server Steamroller

Microsoft got Internet religion on December 7, 1995, when Bill Gates announced Microsoft's embrace of the Internet. Since then, that embrace has become a big Russian-style bear hug. Microsoft continues to aggressively attack Netscape's dominance in the Web browser marketplace by giving away Internet Explorer. Early versions of Internet Explorer were not serious contenders against Netscape, but the latest versions of Internet Explorer (4.0 and higher) are a formidable opponent.

Microsoft is giving it away

Microsoft is doing the same thing to take over the Web server market with Internet Information Server as it is doing in the Web browser market. The Microsoft strategy for capturing the Web browser market is to make Internet Explorer a good product, and then give it away. The release of Internet Information Server 4.0 represents Microsoft's all-out assault on the World Wide Web server front. Microsoft is pulling out all the stops to make Internet Information Server the leading Web server. And like Microsoft's strategy for capturing the Web browser market by giving away Internet Explorer, Microsoft is giving away Internet Information Server 4.0.

Netscape still holds the lead in the browser market, but Microsoft is closing in quickly. According to Dataquest, if Microsoft continues to gain ground at current rates, it could reach parity with Netscape Navigator as early as mid-1998. As of the third quarter of 1997, Netscape Navigator had a 58 percent share and Microsoft's Internet Explorer had a 39 percent share of the Web browser market.

Making IIS free for Windows NT Server users is part of a broader Microsoft strategy. Internet Information Server is a pure Windows NT Server 4.0 (and forthcoming Windows NT 5.0) service that works in tandem with the NT operating system. For example, Windows NT security features, such as authentication and file permissions, handle the security functions for IIS. Microsoft will make its billions selling Windows NT Server and the complete line of applications and development tools designed to create an entire Microsoft Web ecosystem.

The rise of IIS

As of November 1997, Microsoft surpassed Netscape as the leading Windows-based Web server on the World Wide Web. According to NetCraft (www.netcraft.com/survey/), a consulting firm that conducts a monthly survey of Web server software on the Internet, IIS surpassed Netscape in the percentage of servers on the Internet: 18.86 percent versus 11.11 percent. It's important to note, however, that Windows-based servers remain a distant second place (at 18 percent) to UNIX-based Web servers (at 45 percent).

Internet Information Server is not only making inroads as an Internet server platform; it's already the leading intranet server used by companies. According to a recent survey by Zona Research, 55 percent of survey respondents were using Windows NT Server as their intranet server with Internet Information Server.

IIS and the Windows NT 4.0 Option Pack

The Windows NT 4.0 Option Pack includes Internet Information Server 4.0 as well as other new and improved features for Windows NT Server 4.0. For example, the Windows NT 4.0 Option Pack includes an upgraded version of Remote Access Service to enable Internet-based virtual private networking (VPN) via the Windows NT Server connected to the Internet. *Virtual private networking* enables remote client machines to access your network using a secured, encrypted connection to create a private network that runs over the Internet. Windows NT 4.0 Option Pack also includes features that will become part of Windows NT Server 5.0, such as the Microsoft Management Console (MMC), which creates a standardized interface to network administration programs.

One big happy Microsoft BackOffice family

As Microsoft pushes its product line up the client/server food chain, it has created a new group of Microsoft products that are part of the Microsoft BackOffice family. Microsoft BackOffice gets its name from the concept that client workstations are typically on desktops in the front office, whereas the server computer and its applications are placed in the back office. Windows NT Server and Internet Information Server are members of the BackOffice family. BackOffice includes a number of products, such as Microsoft SQL Server, Microsoft Exchange Server, and Microsoft Proxy Server.

To find out more about the Microsoft BackOffice line of products, point your Web browser to www.backoffice.microsoft.com.

Meet Internet Information Server 4.0

The release of IIS 4.0 represents a crowning achievement for Microsoft in delivering a powerful Web server system. In IIS 4.0, Microsoft added a number of features to make IIS an attractive Web server option for larger organizations and Internet service providers (ISPs). Internet Information

Server 4.0 includes at least 50 new or enhanced features. These aren't
tweaks or incremental improvements. The vast majority of what's new —
especially in the areas of administration, programming, and security — is
the result of massive development. For example, IIS 4.0 supports the running
of multiple Web sites on a single Windows NT Server. Microsoft has also
expanded IIS capabilities as a Web development platform to enable programmers to develop Web server applications, with such features as Active
server pages and the Microsoft Transaction Server. This section highlights
the key features of IIS 4.0.

A snappy Internet service manager

The Internet Service Manager — the IIS control center — is now integrated
into the Microsoft Management Console (MMC). The console hosts programs called snap-ins, which administrators use to manage their networks.
MMC enables administrators to manage their network products with a single
integrated interface. IIS 4.0 is the first program to become an MMC snap-in.
Future releases of all BackOffice products, as well as third-party networking
products, will include MMC snap-ins as their administrative interface.
Figure 1-2 shows the Microsoft Management Console window with the IIS
snap-in installed.

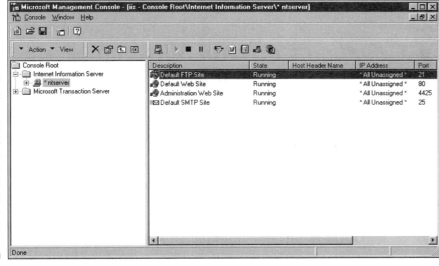

Figure 1-2:
The
Microsoft
Management
Console
houses the
IIS 4.0
Internet
Service
Manager as
a snap-in.

Running multiple Web servers in a single bound

One of the biggest improvements to IIS 4.0 is its capability to run multiple Web servers on the same Windows NT Server machine. In earlier versions of IIS, you could set up and run only one Web server with IIS. With IIS 4.0, it's possible to create an unlimited number of virtual hosts on a single IP address. And because Windows NT Server supports multiple network adapter cards, you can create a lot of Web sites assigned to each network adapter card. This enables you to create group Web sites for specific departments or groups, each with its own special configuration.

Conferencing via the Network News Server

To enhance communications, IIS 4.0 now includes the Microsoft News Server, which enables your organization to run bulletin-board messaging systems. Microsoft News Server for IIS 4.0 uses Network News Transport Protocol (NNTP) to create a conferencing system based on the Internet network news messaging system. It does not support network news feeds from the Internet. The News Server is designed to let you create a private messaging system that mimics newsgroups on the Internet. Users can use their Web browsers or newsreader programs to participate in these online forums.

Finding stuff with Microsoft Index Server 2.0

IIS 4.0 includes a new version of Microsoft Index Server, a powerful search engine integrated with Internet Information Server and Windows NT Server. After you install Index Server, it builds an index of Web server files. The index is updated automatically whenever a file on the server is added, deleted, or changed. Index Server indexes the full text and properties of documents stored on the server.

You can search the index easily from any Web browser by filling in the fields of a simple Web query form. The Web server forwards the query form to the query engine, which finds the pertinent documents and returns the results to you as a Web page. Chapter 13 explains working with Microsoft Index Server.

Better management with Site Server Express

Site Server Express 2.0, a scaled-down version of Microsoft Site Server, includes a collection of Web site management tools for large organizations and ISPs. Site Server Express has several tools you will find useful for managing your Web sites, including Content Analyst, Usage Import, Report Writer, and the Posting Acceptor.

The Content Analyst provides you with Web site visualization and link management tools to help you manage your Web site content. You can use the program to create a WebMap, which shows your entire Web site in a visual format. A WebMap includes graphical representations of the re- sources in your site, such as HTML pages, graphic images, and audio, video, and program files as well as their links. The map with its easily identifiable icons and label colors is a powerful tool that helps you quickly analyze your site's structure.

The Usage Import and Report Writer programs import server logs and enable you to generate a comprehensive suite of usage analyst reports. By choosing from the variety of summary, detail, and comprehensive analysis reports, you can provide the appropriate level of information about your site activity to those who need it. The standard reports can reveal informa- tion, such as request trends, visit trends, navigational patterns, and server load patterns.

The Posting Acceptor enables IIS to accept Web content from Microsoft Web Publishing Wizard/API (application programming interface) and Netscape Navigator 2.02 or later through any standard HTTP connection. The Microsoft Web Publishing Wizard automates the process of copying files from a computer to an Internet or intranet Web server.

Extending the IIS reach to FrontPage 98

Microsoft FrontPage 98 is the leading Web site authoring and management program and is designed to work closely with Internet Information Server 4.0. With IIS running FrontPage Server Extensions, you and others can update Web site content directly via your network or over the Internet using the FrontPage program. Developers creating custom applications can also use these server extensions.

Coming alive with Active server pages

Active server pages (ASP) is a powerful feature of IIS that allows you to create dynamic content using scripts embedded on Web pages that can be processed on the server or client side. ASP provides an easy-to-use alternative to CGI (Common Gateway Interface) and ISAPI (Internet Server Application Programming Interface) that content developers can use to combine HTML, scripts, and reusable ActiveX server components to create dynamic and powerful Web sites. *ActiveX* is a set of technologies that enable software components to interact with one another in a networked environment, regardless of the programming language in which the components were created. ActiveX was developed by Microsoft and is primarily designed for developing interactive content for the Web.

ASP is basically a script interpreter and execution environment that supports the two leading scripting languages, VBScript and JavaScript. With ASP, your scripts run on the server rather than on the client, and your Web server does all the work involved in generating the HTML pages sent to browsers. This means you don't need to worry whether a browser can process the pages; IIS does all the processing for it.

Chapter 2

Don't Stall — Install

*B*efore you install Internet Information Server 4.0, you need make sure that your Windows NT Server machine is configured for its new arrival. You need to be aware of a variety of hardware considerations, and several Windows NT Server features must be running before you actually install the Windows NT 4.0 Option Pack, which includes Internet Information Server. In this chapter, I walk you through preparing Windows NT for IIS and then explain how to install IIS.

IIS Preinstall Checklist

To properly run Internet Information Server on your Windows NT Server machine, you need to evaluate your hardware needs for running a Web server. Running a Web server demands additional hardware considerations over and above the requirements for Windows NT Server. Beyond the hardware platform issues, you also need to have the following Windows NT services and applications installed and running on your system:

✔ The Microsoft TCP/IP stack bound to at least one network adapter card

✔ A hard drive formatted as an NTFS file system; the inherent security features of NTFS make it an essential security tool for running an IIS intranet or Internet server

✔ The Windows NT Service Pack 3

✔ Microsoft Internet Explorer 4.01

For administering most system-management functions in the Windows NT environment, including installing and administering IIS, you must be an administrator with access to the Administrator Account. The Administrator Account is a special account in Windows NT that has the ultimate set of security permissions and can assign permission to any user or group. The Administrator Account is the access point for managing the entire Windows NT network. You can be either the head honcho administrator with ultimate power or a user who is part of the Administrator group with certain pre-scribed privileges.

Administrators have access to the Administrative Tools (Common) menu, which is the program group on Windows NT Server that contains utilities such as User Manager for Domains, Event Viewer, Disk Administrator, Performance Monitor, and other tools. To access this group, choose Start➪Programs➪Administrative Tools (Common).

Under the Hood of Windows NT Server

If you're already running Windows NT Server, you probably know the golden rule of NT Server-based computing: More microprocessor power, more memory, and more disk space are each a good thing. The underlying Windows NT operating system has its own minimum hardware requirements, and Internet Information Server will have additional hardware requirements. The two factors at the core of requirements for your IIS server are the number of processes the machine will be doing at one time and the number of users making requests to the server at one time. Therefore, the key factors to consider in operating your PC-based Web server are memory capacity, CPU speed, and disk capacity and speed.

Checking the list to see what's naughty and nice

The Microsoft Hardware Compatibility List (HCL) for Windows NT is the bible for determining whether a particular piece of computer hardware is compatible with Windows NT. Hardware listed in the HCL has been tested to work with Windows NT. If a product you're considering isn't on the list, be cautious. Check with the manufacturer or, better yet, get a product that is compatible with NT. In earlier versions of Windows NT, finding compatible hardware was more of a problem than it is with Windows NT 4.0. Still, incompatible hardware abounds.

You can check the latest Windows NT Hardware Compatibility List for any hardware you're thinking of buying at `www.microsoft.com/hwtest/hcl/`, which displays the Hardware Compatibility List home page shown in Figure 2-1. You can search through the HCL database by product category and company.

More processor power, more memory, Scotty!

Microsoft tells the world that Windows NT Server 4.0 will run on any processor from a 486/25 MHz on up. In the real world, operating Windows NT Server 4.0 on anything less than a Pentium 133 MHz is a joke. If you're going to be running Windows NT Server combined with Internet Information Server 4.0, you should be working with a Pentium II class processor. Given today's rapidly falling PC prices, this kind of processing power is surprisingly affordable. If a Pentium II processor isn't in the cards, at least consider a Pentium 166 MHz.

If you're using IIS for running a Web server on the Internet, the requirements for the Web server hardware are also intertwined with the capacity of the Internet connection. Chapter 5 explains Internet connectivity issues.

Figure 2-1:
The online Hardware Compatibility List lets you quickly check whether a given hardware product will work with Windows NT Server 4.0.

Memory also plays an important role in the operation of Internet Information Server. For running Internet Information Server on Windows NT Server, you should have 64MB of memory — or at least 32MB. If you anticipate a busy site, 128MB isn't unreasonable.

Finding the right mix of processor and memory components for running an IIS Web server largely depends on the number of HTML documents retrieved within a given period of time and any server application load requirements. A Web server application might be an activity such as processing forms. You need to create a matrix that looks at the combination of document-retrieval requirements and server application load requirements to figure out your processor and memory requirements. Table 2-1 shows processor and memory guidelines for handling a given volume of application processing and document retrievals. For heavy volume Web sites, you'll need to use computers that support multiple CPUs (computer processor units) or multiple computers that work in tandem. The process of connecting multiple servers together to work as one single supercomputer is called *clustering*.

Table 2-1	Processor and Memory Recommendations for Different Application Processing and Document Retrieval Rates	
Application Load	*Document Requests per Minute*	*Processor and Memory Requirements*
Low	Light (60 or less)	166 MHz Pentium with 32MB of RAM
Low	Medium (less than 600)	200 MHz Pentium with 64MB of RAM
Low	Heavy (up to 6,000)	200 MHz Pentium with 64MB of RAM up to a dual Pentium-200 machine with 128MB of RAM
Medium	Light (60 or less)	200 MHz Pentium with 64MB of RAM
Medium	Medium (less than 600)	200 MHz Pentium with 64MB of RAM up to a dual Pentium-200 machine with 128MB of RAM
Medium	Heavy (up to 6,000)	200 MHz Pentium with 64MB of RAM up to a dual Pentium-200 machine with 128MB of RAM
Heavy	Light (60 or less)	200 MHz Pentium with 64MB of RAM up to a dual Pentium-200 machine with 128MB of RAM
Heavy	Medium (less than 600)	200 MHz Pentium with 64MB of RAM, or on the upper end multiple servers
Heavy	Heavy (up to 6,000)	200 MHz Pentium with 64MB of RAM, a dual Pentium-200 machine with 12 MB of RAM, or on the upper end multiple servers

Hard drive size and speed

Hard disk storage requirements for Windows NT Server of 90MB to 120MB are a drop in the bucket compared to the requirements for running a Web site. Your NT Server with IIS will be happier and healthier using at least a 2GB hard disk. Given today's downward pricing trends for hard disks, buying a 2GB or higher disk drive won't break your piggy bank.

Hard disk size isn't the only storage consideration. If your server can't access data fast enough to handle your client requests, it slows down the entire network as your clients wait to access data. The two main hard disk technology contenders are Enhanced Integrated Drive Electronics (EIDE) and Small Computer Systems Interface (SCSI).

The Small Computer Systems Interface (SCSI) is the best solution for your primary disk subsystem. SCSI currently comes in several versions. SCSI III, which is commonly referred to as FAST SCSI or WIDE SCSI, is the latest standard. FAST SCSI extends the data transfer rate from 10MB per sec to 20MB per sec; WIDE SCSI extends the I/O interface from 8 bits to 16 bits. In a growing number of cases, vendors are offering a combination of FAST and WIDE SCSI called ULTRA WIDE SCSI, which extends the data transfer rates from 40 to 60MB per sec.

You can mix and match a SCSI system with another disk subsystem, such as Enhanced Integrated Drive Electronics (EIDE), as your secondary disk subsystem. SCSI is actually an expansion bus, not simply a disk I/O bus like IDE. You can add SCSI tape drives, SCSI scanners, SCSI printers, and any other SCSI devices to your SCSI host adapter.

Go faster with fast Ethernet cards

Windows NT works with most of today's network interface cards (NICs), which are also referred to as network adapter cards. The best network adapter cards for connecting your Windows NT-based server are fast Ethernet cards, which support up to 100 Mbps, rather than the standard 10 Mbps supported by the older network adapters. Fast Ethernet adapters let you move a lot more data across your network a lot faster, which can become an issue if your intranet has a lot of data traffic. For networks consisting of mixed technologies, you can easily get Ethernet cards that support both 10 Mbps and 100 Mbps. For example, 3Com sells such a card for a street price of around $75.

PCI (Peripheral Component Interconnect) bus-based cards are the fastest of the PC buses. Using a PCI bus for an Ethernet card improves the performance of your network over using the slower ISA (Industry Standards Association) network adapter cards. The benefit of using PCI cards goes beyond just speeding up your network. The 32-bit PCI data bus also provides a bus-mastering technique that allows processor independence. This technology reduces CPU overhead by taking control of the system bus, which improves your Windows NT Server's performance.

Use NTFS on Your NT Server

Running Internet Information Server on an NT Server machine without using NTFS (New Technology File System) simply doesn't make sense. Windows NT's NTFS provides a secure file system that lets you set security permissions for your directories and files. NTFS is one of several essential Windows NT tools that enhance the security of your Internet Information Server. If you already have an NTFS partition ready and waiting for your Internet Information Server, you can skip this section. If you don't have your hard drive formatted with NTFS, you should do so.

You can check to see how your drives are formatted by choosing Start⇨Programs⇨Administrative Tools⇨Disk Administrator. The Disk Administrator window appears and shows you the format of every drive on your system.

Installing the TCP/IP Protocol

To make your Windows NT Server ready for IIS, TCP/IP must be installed and bound to a specific network adapter card. If you did not install TCP/IP during your initial Windows NT Server installation, you can add TCP/IP by using the Network applet in the Windows NT Control Panel.

You need at least one IP address to install IIS on your system. You can use two types of IP addresses. The first type is an IP address recognized on the Internet — that is, it's registered with InterNIC and has an associated domain name. You will need to have at least one of these assigned IP addresses if you want your Web server to be recognized on the Internet. The second type of IP address is an unregistered, or private, IP address. These IP address ranges are specifically set aside for use in private intranets and are unrecognized on the Internet. You can use them to create your own intranet that is separated and unknown to the Internet. These reserved address ranges are as follows:

> 10.0.0.0 to 10.255.255.255
>
> 172.16.0.0 to 172.21.255.255
>
> 192.168.0.0 to 192.168.255.255

For example, you can create a network using 16 IP addresses, with the NT Server computer identified as 192.168.0.1 with a subnet mask of 255.255.255.0. Each additional machine on your network can be assigned IP addresses of 192.168.0.2, 192.168.0.3, and so on. If you don't have a registered TCP/IP address, you can use a private IP address to satisfy the installation of TCP/IP. You can always change your TCP/IP settings later. If you use private IP addresses, you can also make up your own private domain names. See Chapter 3 for more information on working with IP addresses and domain names.

To add TCP/IP to your Windows NT Server, do the following:

1. **In the Network dialog box, click the Protocols tab, which is shown in Figure 2-2.**

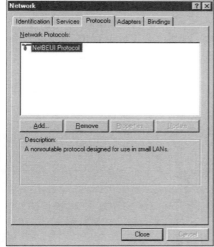

Figure 2-2:
The Protocols tab in the Network dialog box.

2. **Click the Add button.**

   The Select Network Protocol dialog box appears, as shown in Figure 2-3.

3. **In the Network Protocol list box, select TCP/IP Protocol, and then click the OK button.**

4. **When the TCP/IP Setup dialog box prompts you to use DHCP to allocate your IP address, click No (for now).**

   To find out more about DHCP, see Chapter 4.

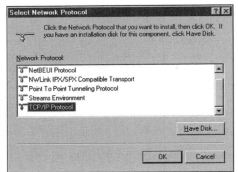

Figure 2-3: The Select Network Protocol dialog box.

5. **Respond to the prompts in the Windows NT Setup dialog box for the location of your Windows NT source file, which is usually your CD-ROM drive. Enter the drive and directory, and then click the Continue button.**

6. **In the Network dialog box, click the Close button.**

   The Microsoft TCP/IP Properties dialog box appears, as shown in Figure 2-4.

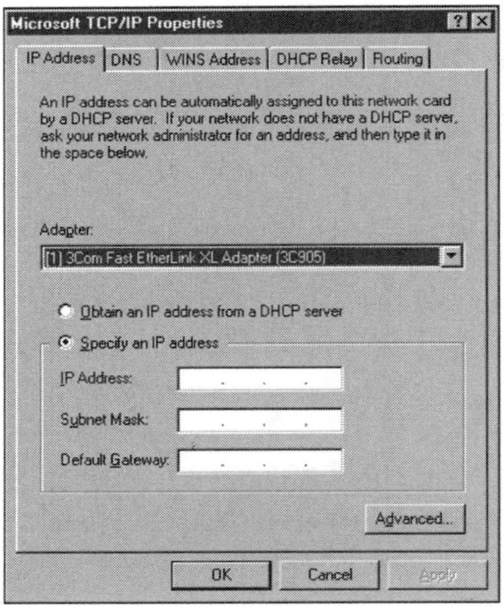

Figure 2-4: The Microsoft TCP/IP Properties dialog box.

7. **Type your IP address, subnet mask, and default gateway.**

8. **Click the DNS tab, and enter your host name (the name of your computer), your Internet domain name, and the IP addresses of your DNS servers.**

9. **Click OK.**

10. **When prompted to restart your system, click Yes if you will not be adding any additional protocols or services; otherwise, click No and continue to add your additional protocols or services.**

Adding the Windows NT Service Pack 3

Getting to the actual installation of the Windows NT Option Pack, you must first install the Windows NT Service Pack 3 on your Windows NT Server computer. You can download it (the file is around 18MB) from the Microsoft Web site or order it for $14.95 from Microsoft by calling (800) 370-8758.

If you're not sure what service pack you've got on your NT Server, you can find out by typing WINVER at the Command Prompt. You'll see a dialog box that contains version information. The service pack number, if any, is included to the right of the NT version number. Service Packs are cumulative, meaning that if you have Service Pack 3 installed, it includes all the changes from the previous two service packs.

You can get the Service Pack from the Microsoft FTP and Web sites. If the Microsoft Web site is busy, you can get the Service Pack from the FTP site by pointing your Web browser to

```
ftp://ftp.microsoft.com/bussys/winnt/winnet-public/fixes/
                   usa/nt40/ussp/i386
```

To get the Service Pack 3 from the Microsoft Web site and then install it, do the following:

1. **Point your Web browser to** http://www.microsoft.com/ msdownload/.

2. **Scroll down to Support Drivers, Patches, and Service Packs, and then select Windows NT Service Packs.**

3. **Select 4.0, and then select Service Packs.**

4. **Click Windows NT4.0 Service Pack 3 for Intel (x86) to download the file.**

   The filename is exe. Leave this filename as is.

5. **After you've downloaded the file, double-click the filename or use the Start⇨Run command.**

After you've installed the Windows NT Service Pack 3, the next step is to get and install Internet Explorer 4.01 from the Microsoft Web site.

Installing Internet Explorer 4.01

You're getting closer to installing the Windows NT 4.0 Option Pack, but before you can install it, you must install Internet Explorer 4.01 on your Windows NT Server computer. Like all the software you need for IIS, you can download Internet Explorer or order it on a CD from Microsoft. To order the Internet Explorer CD (cost is $4.95) from Microsoft, call (800) 485-2048.

You cannot install Internet Explorer 4.01 if you have not installed the Windows Service Pack 3.

To download IE 4.01 and install it, do the following:

1. **Point your Web browser to** `http://www.microsoft.com/ie/ie40/download/`.

   The Internet Explorer Page appears.

2. **Under Internet Explorer 4.0, click Internet Explorer 4.01 for Windows 95, NT 4.0, and NT Alpha.**

3. **Click the Download Now button.**

4. **Select Internet Explorer 4.01 for Windows 95 & NT 4.0 (the default) from the drop-down list, and then click Next.**

5. **Select US English (or whatever language you want), and then click Next.**

6. **Click the Install Setup Hyperlink for the Site from Which You Want to Download IE 4.01 option.**

7. **When the File Download dialog box appears, select Run This Program from Its Current Location.**

8. **In the License Agreement dialog box, click I Accept the Agreement, and then click Next.**

9. **In the Installations Options screen, choose the default Standard Installation, and then click Next.**

10. **In the Windows Desktop Update page, you can choose to update your Windows NT desktop to integrate Web functionality.**

    Use the Default setting for the desktop; you can always disable it later.

11. **In the Download Options page, select Save to Disk, and then click Next.**

12. **In the Destination Folder page, specify where you want the IE files to be downloaded to on your local machine.**

    You can use the Browse button to navigate to the directory on your system.

13. **Click the Next button.**

    The files are downloaded to your system, and a dialog box appears telling you everything is downloaded.

14. **Click OK.**

15. **Double-click ie4setup.exe, or choose Start⇨Run and enter the path where you downloaded the Internet Explorer program files.**

16. **Follow the wizard instructions.**

    If IE 4.0 is already installed on your system, an Upgrade new items dialog box appears. It recommends the default, Upgrade Only Newer Items.

17. **Click OK.**

    Your Internet Explorer is updated to 4.01.

Well, you finally made it to the point that you're ready to get the Windows NT 4.0 Option Pack.

Getting the Windows NT 4.0 Option Pack

Finally, you can actually install the Windows NT 4.0 Option Pack. As you recall, Internet Information Server 4.0 is one of several new applications and communication services for Windows NT Server bundled into the Windows NT 4.0 Option Pack. Because the Option Pack includes so many things, it's a whopping 90MB. If you're using an earlier release of Windows NT Server 4.0, you can download the Windows NT 4.0 Option Pack or buy it on CD. Newer releases of Windows NT 4.0 Server include the Option Pack. If you don't have the bandwidth capacity to download the 90MB of files in the Windows NT 4.0 Option Pack, you can get it and Internet Explorer on a CD-ROM from a Microsoft reseller for a list price of $99.95. You can search for a local Microsoft reseller at the same site you download the Windows NT 4.0 Option Pack.

Point your Web browser to `backoffice.microsoft.com/downtrial/optionpack.asp`. When the Microsoft Windows NT 4.0 Option Pack page appears, click the Find a Reseller button. Type your zip code, and click Next to see a listing of Microsoft resellers in your area.

Option Pack downloading options

There are three Windows NT 4.0 Option Pack configuration options for downloading. You can choose from Minimum, Typical, and Full download options. These three versions of the Windows NT Option Pack range in size from 26MB to 86MB.

- ✔ **The Minimum configuration** is designed to conserve bandwidth-downloading time for slower Internet connections as well as to save hard disk space. It includes the basic Internet Information Server Web server, Microsoft Transaction Server, Index Server, Microsoft FrontPage Server Extensions, and Context-sensitive help.

- ✔ **The Typical configuration** includes all the options in the Minimum installation and adds the FTP server, the HTML version of the Internet Service Manager, more extensive Web-based online documentation, and support for running Java applications.

- ✔ **The Full configuration** includes everything associated with the Windows NT Service Pack. It includes all the things included in the Typical option along with SMTP Service, NNTP Service, Certificate Server, Microsoft Site Server Express, Microsoft Script debugger, Windows Scripting Host, Microsoft Remote Access Services, Microsoft Clustering, and complete documentation.

I strongly recommend that you get the Full version of the Windows NT 4.0 Option Pack because it includes a number of things you'll want to use with IIS 4.0. If your Internet connection is too slow to download the 86MB size of the Full installation option, you'll probably need to purchase the CD-ROM.

Downloading the Windows NT 4.0 Option Pack

The first step in the Microsoft download gauntlet is filling out forms. To download the Windows NT 4.0 Option Pack from the Microsoft Web site, you'll first need to fill out three pages of online forms. After you complete the forms, you can return to the site without filling out the forms.

To download the Windows NT 4.0 Option Pack from the Microsoft Web site, do the following:

1. **Point your Web browser to** `http://backoffice.microsoft.com/downtrial/optionpack.asp`.

   The Download and Trial Center page appears for the Microsoft Windows NT 4.0 Option Pack.

2. **Click the Download button to display a form page that you need to complete.**

   An asterisk next to a field means it's a required entry.

3. **Complete the first page, and then click Next.**

   The Security Alert box appears, warning you of risks associated with Internet communications. Click Yes each time this box appears, which is after every Next button and after the Finish button.

4. **Complete the next form, and then click Next.**

5. **Fill out the final page of information, and then click Finish.**

6. **In the Download Options, click Option 1, which is for Windows 95 and Windows NT machines.**

7. **Choose the Windows platform you're using for the Download wizard.**

   This is the Windows operating system you're using to download IIS 4.0, which doesn't have to be Windows NT Server 4.0.

   • If you're using Windows 95 to download IIS.40, choose IIS/PWS 4.0 Download Wizard for Windows 95.

   • If you're using Windows NT Server 4.0 to download IIS 4.0, choose IIS/PWS 4.0 Download Wizard for NT Server 4.0

8. **Click Next.**

9. **Choose the language you want (the default is US English), and then click Next.**

10. **Click the Download from This Site button for the download site you want to use.**

11. **Select Windows NT Option Pack Download Wizard for Windows 95 (NT) (download.exe).**

12. **In the File Download dialog box, select Run This Program from Its Current Location, and click OK.**

    The download.exe file is downloaded to a temporary folder on your system.

13. **In the Security Warning dialog box, click the Yes button.**

    For more information on using VeriSign digital certificates security to authenticate this download, click More Info.

14. **In the license dialog box, click Yes to accept the Microsoft License Agreement for the Windows NT 4.0 Option Pack.**

15. **In the Download Options dialog box, choose Download Only, and then click Next.**

    You can choose Install if you're downloading the NT Option Pack directly onto your NT Server, but I recommend that you don't choose the Install option.

16. **Choose your language (the default is US English) and x86: NT Server, and then click Next.**

    The x86 stands for Intel processors.

17. **Choose Full Installation to get all the programs included with the Windows NT 4.0 Option Pack, and then click Next.**

    Although you could choose Minimum Installation or Typical Installation, in most cases you'll want all the programs available on your system.

18. **Specify the directory you want to save the files in, and then click Next.**

19. **In the Download location page, choose the download location, and then click Next.**

20. **In the Security Warning dialog box, click Yes.**

    The files are downloaded to the directory you specify.

Installing the Windows NT Option Pack

Well, you've finally made it to actually installing the Windows NT 4.0 Option Pack. With the NT Service Pack 3 and Internet Explorer 4.01 installed on your system, you're ready to install the Windows NT 4.0 Option Pack.

Installing the Option Pack

The Windows NT 4.0 Option Pack setup program offers three types of setup options that are common for most Windows programs: Minimum, Typical, and Custom. The Typical installation option is the best starting point; you can add additional components as you build up your IIS skills. The Custom option offers a choice of all components included with IIS.

Before you can install the Windows NT 4.0 Option Pack, you must have the Windows NT Service Pack 3 and Internet Explorer 4.01 installed on the Windows NT Server that you plan to install Internet Information Server 4.0 on.

To install the Windows NT 4.0 Option Pack, do the following:

1. **Double-click setup.exe. You can also choose Start⇨Run, type the path for the IIS directory, and then type** setup.exe.

   The Microsoft Windows NT 4.0 Option Pack Setup wizard appears.

   After you start the installation process, don't cancel. Canceling setup may leave files on your drive that the uninstall process can't remove. If you decide you don't want IIS on your computer, finish the setup process before attempting to remove IIS. I explain how to remove IIS in the next section.

2. **Click Next; when the End User License Agreement page appears, click Accept.**

3. **Click the Typical Installation option.**

   The next screen shows the default directories that IIS will create for the Web and FTP servers as well as the program files.

4. **Click Next to use the default directories for the WWW, FTP, and Application installation paths.**

5. **Click Next again to use the default path for your Mailroot directory.**

   The Setup program begins installing IIS onto your system. A progress indicator appears to display the status of the installation.

6. **When the final page of the Setup wizard appears, click Finish.**

   Setup finalizes the installation.

7. **After the installation is complete, click Yes to restart Windows NT Server.**

Uninstalling the Option Pack

If, for any reason, you want or need to uninstall Windows NT 4.0 Option Pack, you must rerun the Setup program. You can access the Setup program in several ways. The easiest method is to do the following:

1. **Choose Start⇨Programs⇨Windows NT 4.0 Option Pack⇨Windows NT 4.0 Option Pack Setup.**

   The Microsoft Windows NT 4.0 Option Pack Setup wizard appears.

2. **Click Next.**

3. **Do one of the following:**

   - To remove the entire Windows NT 4.0 Option Pack, click the Remove All button.

   - To remove selected components, click the Add/Remove button. A listing of the Windows NT 4.0 Option Pack appears, as shown in Figure 2-5. Click to clear the check mark for features you want to uninstall, and then click Next to proceed through the uninstallation process. If the Show Subcomponents button is activated, subcomponents exist under the selected component. Clicking the Show Subcomponents button displays them for the selected component.

Figure 2-5:
The
Windows
NT 4.0
Option Pack
list of
available
and
installed
components.

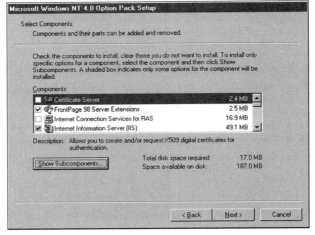

Adding Option Pack programs

To get things off to a smooth start, you installed the Windows NT 4.0 Option Pack using the Typical installation option. As you progress through working with IIS 4.0, you'll undoubtedly be adding other programs. You can easily add and remove any Windows NT 4.0 Option Pack component at any time by doing the following:

1. **Choose Start⇨Programs⇨Windows NT 4.0 Option Pack⇨Windows NT 4.0 Option Pack Setup.**

   The Microsoft Windows NT 4.0 Option Pack Setup wizard appears.

2. **Click the Add/Remove button.**

3. **Select check boxes for optional items you want to install and clear check boxes on any items you want to uninstall.**

4. **Follow the onscreen directions to complete the setup process.**

Checking Out Internet Information Server

After you install the Windows NT 4.0 Option Pack, you can quickly check to see whether your Web site is running. To do so, follow these steps:

1. **Choose Start⇨Programs⇨Windows NT 4.0 Option Pack⇨Microsoft Internet Information Server⇨Internet Service Manager.**

   The Microsoft Management Console window appears with a Tip of the Day dialog box.

2. **Click Close.**

   The dialog box is removed, leaving the Microsoft Management Console window. Microsoft Management Console (MMC) is a new Windows NT feature. And part of MMC is Internet Service Manager (ISM) in IIS 4.0. Internet Service Manager is the heart and soul of IIS administration.

3. **To check the status of your IIS servers in the MMC window, click the expand icon (plus sign) to the left of the Internet Information Server folder in the left pane.**

   A computer icon labeled with the name of your NT server appears.

4. **Click the computer name to display the default IIS services running on your NT Server machine.**

   As you can see in the right pane of the MMC window shown in Figure 2-6, the Default FTP Site, Default Web Site, Administration Web Site, and the Default SMTP Site all display *Running* in the State column.

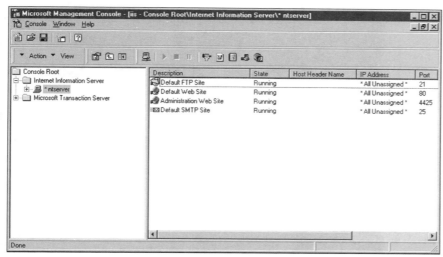

Figure 2-6: The IIS servers running on your NT machine after you installed IIS.

Testing Your Web Site from a Network Client

The Internet Information Server is installed as a Web server that you can immediately access by any client on your local network. You can test your installation of the default Web server by using Internet Explorer or Netscape Navigator on any Windows client on your network. Your Windows client must have the Microsoft TCP/IP protocol installed and configured with the necessary TCP/IP address settings. The only other thing you need to know is the IP address you're using for the Windows NT Server that IIS is running on. Here's how to check out the default Web site's home page:

1. **Start a Web browser on any Windows client computer on your network.**

2. **Enter the IP address of the NT Server machine running IIS.**

   For example, you might enter http://199.232.255.114.

3. **Press Enter.**

   Internet Information Server displays the default Web site home page (default.asp), as shown in Figure 2-7. The Web page default.asp refers to the fact that the home page is a Microsoft Active server page, which enables HTML pages running on IIS to include interactive features.

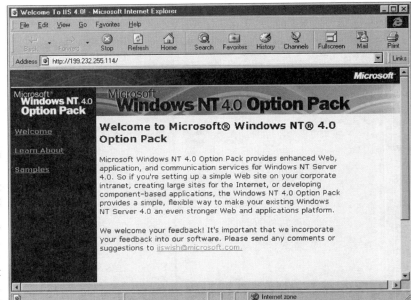

Figure 2-7: The default Internet Information Server home page appearing in Internet Explorer.

You can also check out the FTP site running on your NT Server by using your Web browser. Enter **ftp://199.232.255.114** and a blank page appears. When the FTP directory contains files, the page is no longer blank; instead, it displays a listing of files as hyperlinks.

Installing IIS Is Just the Beginning

Setting up the environment for installing IIS is the starting point for creating either an intranet or an Internet presence with IIS. After you've installed Internet Information Server 4.0, you can then proceed to build a fully functioning TCP/IP networking environment for your intranet. See Chapters 3 and 4 for details on working with any TCP/IP network — intranet or Internet. Or perhaps you want to add Internet connectivity to your network. Chapter 5 tells you more about connecting your network to the Internet.

Chapter 3

Using TCP/IP for Fun and Profit

• •

In This Chapter

▶ Understanding TCP/IP networking fundamentals

▶ Working with IP addresses

▶ Translating domain names to IP addresses

▶ Assigning multiple IP addresses to a single computer or a single network card

• •

TCP/IP, the suite of networking protocols behind the Internet, is invading every facet of today's computing and networking environment. TCP/IP provides the networking foundation for operating Internet Information Server, whether you're building an intranet or establishing a presence on the Internet. This chapter explains the fundamentals of TCP/IP networking.

TCP/IP Fundamentals

TCP/IP (Transmission Control Protocol/Internet Protocol) rules as the networking protocol of choice for both the Internet and local area networks. It defines how communication between computers takes place as well as defines the basis for a variety of network services including the World Wide Web. A *protocol* is a set of rules used to allow interoperability among different systems. The explosive popularity of TCP/IP as the networking protocol for the Internet has spilled over to local area networks and is transforming them into intranets. An *intranet* uses the same Web technologies used on the Internet to create a friendly Web-based interface to a company's resources. At the heart of an intranet is the Web server.

According to Forrester Research, the number of companies with more than half of their network traffic on IP will grow from 36 percent in 1996 to 82 percent in 1998. TCP/IP is an open networking protocol that is rapidly replacing proprietary network operating systems. Microsoft saw the writing on the wall and added TCP/IP functionality to Windows 95 and Windows NT to enable both the seamless integration of local area networks with the Internet as well as the easy building of intranets.

Why use TCP/IP?

TCP/IP is popular because it's a robust collection of protocols based on an elegant and efficient architecture. It was developed with each component, or layer, performing unique and vital functions. In fact, TCP/IP software is often called a TCP/IP stack because it's constructed in layers. Understanding the TCP/IP architecture helps you understand why it's worth making the effort to use TCP/IP in the first place:

- ✔ TCP/IP is a routable protocol, which means it can send datagrams over a specified route, thus reducing traffic on other parts of the network. A *datagram* is a unit, or packet, of data along with delivery information, such as a destination address.

- ✔ TCP/IP was designed as a system that can continue to operate even if parts of the network crash or disappear. This also enables new networks to be connected without disrupting existing services.

- ✔ TCP/IP can handle high error rates and still provide reliable end-to-end service by using switching to retransmit missing or damaged packets.

- ✔ TCP/IP is an open system that isn't tied to any single proprietary system controlled by a single company. Independence from a particular vendor or type of network is at the center of the TCP/IP architecture.

- ✔ TCP/IP is an efficient protocol in that it has a low data overhead from the networking protocol itself. This means faster transmissions and more efficient service.

- ✔ TCP/IP can send data between different computer systems running completely different operating systems, from small PCs all the way up to mainframes.

- ✔ TCP/IP is separated from the underlying hardware and will run over Ethernet and telecommunications links for wide area networking.

- ✔ TCP/IP uses a common addressing scheme. Therefore, any system can address any other system, even in a network as large as the Internet.

The five layers of TCP/IP

TCP/IP takes a layered protocol approach, which means each protocol is independent of the others. TCP/IP loosely follows the Open Systems Interconnection (OSI) model, which defines the layers and protocols that networks must contain to control interactions between computers. The OSI model defines the framework for implementing protocols in seven layers: application, presentation, session, transport, network, data link, and physical. When information passes from computer to computer through a protocol, control of the data passes from one layer to the next, starting at the application layer and proceeding through to the physical layer. It then proceeds to the bottom layer of the next system and up the hierarchy in that second system.

The TCP/IP protocol consists of five layers that perform the functions of the OSI model's seven layers. The five layers of TCP/IP are described in Table 3-1.

Table 3-1	The Five Layers of TCP/IP
Layer	*What It Is*
Application	The highest layer. Supports the protocols that form the basis of TCP/IP applications, such as HTTP for the Web and FTP for file transfers.
Transport	Adds transport data via TCP and other protocols to the packet and passes it to the Internet layer.
Internet	Adds IP information to the packet before passing it to the network.
Network Interface	Interfaces with the physical layer, which is the hardware and network medium.
Physical	Defines the mechanism for communicating with the transmission medium and the interface hardware.

How TCP and IP work together

TCP/IP is actually a combination of two key protocols. Transmission Control Protocol (TCP) is the transmission layer of the protocol and serves to ensure reliable, verifiable data exchange between hosts on the network. A *host* is any computer connected to a network. TCP breaks data into pieces, wrapping each piece with the information needed to route it to its destination and reassembling the pieces at the receiving end of the communications link. The wrapped and bundled pieces are called *datagrams*. TCP puts a header on the datagram that provides the information needed to get the data to its destination. When the header is in the datagram, TCP passes the datagram to IP to be routed to its destination.

The network layer portion of TCP/IP is the Internet Protocol (IP). IP actually moves the data from point A to point B via a process called *routing*. IP is referred to as *connectionless*, which means it does not swap control information (handshaking information) before establishing an end-to-end connection and starting a transmission. The Internet Protocol relies on TCP to determine whether the data arrived successfully at its destination and to retransmit the data if it did not. IP's only job is to route the data to its destination. IP inserts its own header in the datagram when it's received from TCP.

Routing in packet-based networking

TCP/IP is based on a technology known as *packet-based networking.* In a packet (datagram) network, data travels across a network in small, independent units that can be routed over different network paths to reach the ultimate destination. As information is broken down into datagrams, it is transmitted over the network. Each station that encounters a packet examines the header to determine whether the packet is intended for that station. If not, the packet is passed on in a direction closer to the ultimate destination. Eventually, the packets arrive at the intended destination and are reassembled in the order originally intended. The benefit of the packet-switched network is that packets in a message do not have to travel to the destination along the same route.

In fact, packets can travel many different routes but end up at the same destination. This independent routing of packets over a network allows data to be transmitted even if parts of the network are disrupted. *Routing* is the process of getting your data from point A to point B through a network. The IP portion of the TCP/IP protocol inserts its header in the datagram, but before the datagram can begin its journey, IP determines whether it knows the destination. If it knows it, IP sends the datagram on its way. If it doesn't know and can't find out, IP sends the datagram to the host's gateway.

Packets allow information in all sizes to be broken down and mixed with other information to keep traffic moving smoothly. The use of packets relieves congestion and helps smooth the information transfer. Sending packets along differing routes provides the following advantages:

 ✔ **Enables a more even use of the network.** If you try to cram all the message packets along a given route when other routes are available, you are not using resources wisely.

 ✔ **Provides alternate routes for data to travel.** This means it's harder to break down the entire network, even if one segment is destroyed. Packet traffic is simply rerouted around the affected area.

 ✔ **Allows easier error correction.** If a packet error is detected at the receiving end, only that packet, not the entire message, must be re-sent. This approach saves both time and network resources.

Gateways to the TCP/IP universe

Each host (computer or other network device) on a TCP/IP network has a *gateway,* an off-ramp for datagrams not destined for the local network. Each gateway has a defined set of routing tables that tells the gateway the route to specific destinations. Because gateways don't know the location of every IP address, they have their own gateways that act just like any TCP/IP host. In the event the first gateway doesn't know the way to the destination, it forwards the datagram to its gateway. This forwarding, or routing, continues until the datagram reaches its destination. The entire path to the destination is known as the *route*. Datagrams intended for the same destination may actually take different routes to get there because many variables determine the ultimate route.

A *gateway* is a functional device that enables the routing of datagrams. This gateway typically takes form as a device called a *router*. The router is at the core of IP networking. A router allows data to be routed to different networks based on packet address and protocol information associated with the data.

Routers route data by looking at your data packet addressing and protocol. Routers read the data passing through them and make decisions on where the data is sent to, or not sent to. This decision-making functionality, called *filtering*, allows the router to monitor and selectively choose packets as they enter or leave it. With filtering, a router can protect your network from unwanted intrusion and prevent selected local network traffic from leaving your local network. This is a powerful feature for managing incoming and outgoing data for your site.

Ports and sockets

On a TCP/IP network, data travels from a port on the sending computer to a port on the receiving computer. A *port* is an address that identifies the application associated with the data. Ports are typically transparent to network users because many ports are universally assigned to specific TCP/IP services. For example, Web servers normally run on port 80, and FTP servers run on port 21. This means when users connect to a Web server, their Web browsers automatically connect to port 80. If a Web server is using a different port number, a user who doesn't know the unique TCP/IP port can't access it. The URL for this nonstandard Web site would be something like `http://www.angell.com:8001`, where 8001 is the port number. Typically, port numbers above 255 are reserved for private use of the local machine, and numbers below 255 are defined as defaults for a variety of universal TCP/IP applications and services.

Each communication circuit into and out of the TCP/IP layer is uniquely identified by a combination of two numbers, which together are called a *socket*. The socket, whether on the sending or receiving machine, is composed of the IP address of that machine and the port number used by the TCP software. A request for service from a Web browser, for example, has at least the IP address of the server system and the port number 80. Because the IP address is unique across a network and the port numbers will be unique to the individual machine, the socket numbers will also be unique across the entire network.

Creating Identity with IP Addresses

Within any networking protocol, there must be a way to identify individual computers or other networked devices. TCP/IP is no exception and includes an addressing scheme that pervades the Internet and intranets. It's helpful to think of Internet Protocol (IP) addresses as the unique telephone numbers for specific computers or other network devices on any TCP/IP network.

An IP address is a software-based numeric identifier assigned to each machine on an IP network. The IP address is a unique 32-bit number written as a series of four numbers separated by periods, for example, 199.232.255.114. Each of the four numbers in this IP address — 199, 232, 255, and 114 — is called an *octet* and represents one byte of the full 32-bit address. No octet can have a value above 255. This means that the lowest possible IP address is 0.0.0.0 and the highest is 255.255.255.255.

One part of an IP address is designated as the network address, and the other part is a node address (the specific device), giving the IP address a layered, hierarchical structure. The network address uniquely identifies each network. Every machine on the same network shares that network address as part of its IP address. For example, in the address 199.232.255.114, the 199.232 part is the network address. The node address is assigned to each machine on a network. This part of the address must be unique because it identifies a particular machine. This number is also referred to as a *host address.* In the sample address 199.232.255.114, the 255 part is the node, or host, address.

IP addresses have class and no class

Traditionally, IP addresses were assigned to networks based on three classifications based on size: Class A, Class B, and Class C. This breakdown of IP addresses was simply a way of allocating addresses among the different networks that access the Internet:

- ✔ **Class A** addresses are provided for very large networks. Only 126 Class A addresses are possible in the world, and each Class A network can have in excess of 16 million computers in its individual networks.

- ✔ Each **Class B** network can have up to approximately 65,000 workstations on the network. There can be approximately 16,000 Class B networks in the world.

- ✔ Each **Class C** network can have up to 256 workstations. Several million Class C networks are possible.

Until 1994, Class C addresses were the smallest block of IP addresses that could be assigned by the InterNIC. (InterNIC is the organization responsible for domain name registration and IP registration for the Internet.) Many smaller companies that need IP addresses don't need a Class C network with 256 IP addresses. Likewise, some companies need more than a Class C but less than a Class B, and so on. In response to the limitations of A, B, and C classes of IP addresses, InterNIC implemented Classless Internet Domain Routing (CIDR, which is pronounced "cider"). CIDR networks are described as slash x networks, where *x* represents the number of bits in the IP address range that the InterNIC controls. Table 3-2 lists a sampling of slash x network configurations that support a specific number of IP addresses.

Table 3-2	Common Slash x Network Configurations	
Network Type	*Subnet*	*Number of IP Addresses*
Slash 27	255.255.255.224	32
Slash 28	255.255.255.240	16
Slash 29	255.255.255.248	8
Slash 30	255.255.255.252	4

Subnet subdivision

TCP/IP enables the subdivision of IP networks into smaller, logical groups of networks called *subnets.* This is achieved by using the host portion of an IP address to create something called a *subnet address,* or *subnet mask.* This IP address allows the workstation to identify the network of which it is a part. You can think of a subnet as a workgroup within a larger domain or network, or as all of the computers physically connected to a particular network. In reality, the subnet mask is used to mask out the parts of the IP address that are not necessary for the network your group belongs to.

If you have an intranet with a single subnet, all the devices in your network can transmit data directly to each other without any routing. If you have a larger organization or are connecting geographically dispersed computers (via the Internet), you'll be using subnets to divide your network into smaller groupings with routers.

Unassigned IP addresses

With the proliferation of TCP/IP as the networking protocol of choice for any network, organizations needed IP addresses that they could use for their private networks. The Internet Engineering Task Force (IETF), the group responsible for implementing and maintaining Internet standards, set aside a Class A, B, and C series of IP addresses that can be used exclusively for intranets. These "private" IP addresses can never be assigned on the Internet and will not route through the Internet. Therefore, any organization of any size can use these IP addresses for its intranet. The address ranges reserved as private IP addresses are as follows:

10.0.0.0 – 10.255.255.255

172.16.0.0 – 172.31.255.255

192.168.0.0 – 192.168.255.255

For building your own intranet, this means you don't have to rent IP addresses from an Internet service provider to set up a TCP/IP network.

Static IP addressing

The use of static IP addresses means that a fixed IP address is assigned to a specific computer or other device on your network. This fixed IP address can be a registered address recognized on the Internet or an unassigned IP address. The IP address remains associated with the specific device until an administrator changes it.

Using static IP addressing on a network requires enough IP addresses for each device on the network. In addition, administering static IP addresses requires the assignment and tracking of IP addresses for each computer on the network. As a network administrator, you must configure each client computer and other device with its own IP address and other information, such as the subnet mask. For smaller networks that don't change very often, this isn't a problem. For larger networks, however, this task can be time-consuming for network administrators.

Dynamic IP addressing with DHCP

Dynamic IP addressing uses a server to temporarily assign IP addresses to clients on an as-needed basis. A Dynamic Host Configuration Protocol (DHCP) server temporarily leases an IP address (from its pool of currently available addresses) to a client whenever the client logs on to the network. The address is leased for a set amount of time. When the client logs off, the address is released again and can be reassigned to a new client. The DHCP server also assigns subnet mask and default gateway IP addresses with the client IP address. The IP addresses in the DHCP server pool can be either assigned or unassigned IP addresses.

The DHCP protocol effectively removes the requirement that individual workstations must have static IP addresses. Instead, a network can designate a DHCP server that automatically manages the assignment of IP addresses and routing information to network nodes as they sign in. The server then manages the IP address table, making sure that only one address is assigned to each active workstation. The IP address is leased to the workstation, meaning that it is provided for only a limited time. From a user's perspective, these negotiation and assignment procedures are transparent.

Windows NT Server 4.0 includes the Microsoft DHCP Server, which allows you to use dynamic IP addressing on your network. Windows NT Workstation 4.0 and Windows 95 include DHCP client support as part of the Microsoft TCP/IP stack. In addition, many routers now include built-in DHCP servers to enable dynamic IP addressing. (For more on working with the Microsoft DHCP server in Windows NT Server 4.0, see Chapter 4.)

Translating IP addresses with NAT

Network Address Translation (NAT) is an Internet standard that allows your local network to use unregistered IP addresses that are not recognized on the Internet while making the Internet connection with an IP address recognized on the Internet. NAT works with DHCP to provide a dynamic LAN-to-Internet access capability that doesn't require a static IP address assigned to every PC on the LAN. Routers that support both DHCP and NAT let you assign private IP addresses to your internal users; when they want to connect to the outside Internet, the NAT feature creates a temporary connection between the private IP address and the Internet-routable IP address.

As a result, smaller organizations can realize significant cost savings because only a single-user Internet access account is required for connecting an entire LAN to the Internet. For example, many ISDN routers include these features. NAT also provides increased security because the IP addresses used on the intranet are unrecognizable on the Internet.

Name Resolution Basics

If IP addresses are the equivalent of telephone numbers on the Internet, domain names are equivalent to the name of the person or organization that the telephone number is assigned to. As people move around, their telephone numbers change but not their names. *Domain names* identify the organization or computer network to which the user belongs. You know these domain names as URLs for Web sites, such as www.angell.com, which is text interface to an IP address, which might be 199.232.255.114.

When you provide an address for most Internet operations, such as pointing your Web browser to a Web site or sending e-mail, you can use either the IP address or the domain name method. Most organizations use domain names as their form of addressing because they are easier to read and understand. The process of converting domain names to machine-readable IP addresses is called *name resolution*. During the resolution process, the domain name is translated automatically into an IP address by a computer called a DNS (Domain Name System) server.

Domains and subdomains

Domain names are based on a hierarchical structure, with each level denoted with a period. Each period within the domain name identifies another sublevel of the overall organization through which the message must pass to arrive at the ultimate destination. The order of levels in a domain always proceeds from the most specific to most general when viewed from left to right. Longer domain names simply mean that more organizational levels are necessary to uniquely identify a host system.

No common way exists to decode the meaning of different levels within a name. The person setting up the address defines the nomenclature used in the address. It is not unusual for different domain levels in a name to represent different levels in an organization. For instance, one domain level may refer to an overall organization, while the name to the left of it refers to a department or building. The level to the left of that may represent a specific network within the department or building, and still another level may identify a workgroup within the network. Only the structure and imagination of the individuals assigning the names limit the complexity of a domain address.

A *host name* is an assigned identifier called an *alias* that is used to designate a specific TCP/IP host machine. A host name is typically the name of the device that has a specific IP address and on the Internet is part of what is known as a *fully qualified domain name* (FQDN). A fully qualified domain name consists of the host name and the domain name. For example, in the fully qualified domain name www.angell.com, the host name is www, and the domain name is angell.com.

Each host belongs to a domain, and each domain is classified further into domain types. The format of a host name with a domain name is

> HostName.DomainName.TopLevelDomain

For example, sales.angell.com is an example of a domain name for a host computer called sales. The domain name is angell, and the top-level domain is .com. Top-level domains are explained in the next section.

A computer connected to any TCP/IP network will refer to a Domain Name System server to resolve names listed in the hierarchy. The Domain Name System provides a centralized online database for resolving domain names to their corresponding IP addresses.

Domain names can be further subdivided into *subdomains*. These are arbitrary names assigned by a network administrator to further differentiate a domain name. Think of them as network nicknames. The format of a host name with both subdomain and domain names is

HostName.SubdomainName.DomainName.TopLevelDomain

Both the domain and subdomain names serve as additional descriptors for a machine, for example, `david.sales.angell.com`.

Top-level domain names

At the end of all Internet addresses is a three-letter domain level such as com or edu, which is referred to as a *top-level domain*. These top-level domains provide an indication of the organization that owns the address, and they always appear at the end of the domain name. The purpose of the top-level domain is to provide another level of distinction for a full domain address. Within the United States, you'll find seven different organizational domains, as shown in Table 3-3.

Table 3-3	Organizational Domains in the United States
Organizational Domain	*Entity*
.com	For-profit commercial organizations
.edu	Educational institutions
.gov	Nonmilitary government organizations
.int	International (NATO) institutions
.mil	Military installations
.net	Network resources
.org	Nonprofit groups

Some domain names don't include organizational domains, but instead rely on geographic domains, such as .au for Australia, .uk for United Kingdom, or .jp for Japan. This is particularly true with domain names outside the United States. Geographic domains indicate the country in which the name originates. In almost all instances, the geographic domains are based on the two-letter country codes specified by the International Standards Organization, a standards body.

A new generation of top-level domains

Like so many other areas of the Internet, the pool of available domain names ending with the traditional three-letter top-level domain name is dwindling rapidly. As a result, a new crop of top-level domain names is available for use on the Internet. The International Ad Hoc Committee (IAHC), which is comprised of Internet standard-setting bodies and legal and communications experts, is implementing seven new top-level domain names. Table 3-4 describes and lists these new top-level domain names. The IAHC plans to establish as many as 28 competing registration firms to handle the Internet registration of these new domain names.

Table 3-4	The Seven New IAHC Top-Level Domain Names
Top-Level Domain Name	*What It Is*
.arts	Cultural or entertainment organization
.firm	General category for a business or other organization
.info	Entity that provides free informational services
.nom	Individual's personal Web site
.rec	Recreational-activity site
.store	Business offering goods or services for sale at its Web site
.web	Organization that specializes in Web-related activities

Getting your domain name

Domain names are chosen by the organization requesting the name and are then registered with the InterNIC. The InterNIC is the shortened name for the Internet Network Information Center. The registration of domain names on the Internet is handled by registration services, which are managed by Network Solutions Inc., or NSI.

Typically, your Internet service provider will register your domain name with InterNIC as part of establishing your Internet service. Registering a domain name will cost you $100 for the first two years and $50 a year thereafter. You can file for your own domain name, but you'll need to know the host names and IP addresses of the primary and secondary domain name servers for the domain to be registered, as well as the administrative, technical, and billing contact information. Registrations performed over the InterNIC Web interface are usually completed in a few hours. The billing for your domain name may take awhile. What takes time in the domain name registration process is the propagation of new domain information to all the DNS servers on the Internet.

Names are registered on a first-come, first-served basis. Registering a domain name implies no legal ownership of the name. For example, you may be able to register a domain name that is the name of another company, but that company can send its lawyers after you for using its trade name.

Having your own domain name also allows you to move Internet access providers without any disruption of your Internet addresses. Because you, not your ISP, own your domain name, you can move it as needed. In most cases, your domain name is the same as your name or a business name so you can capitalize on any name recognition associated with your name. Remember, your business e-mail addresses as well as any Web site URLs are tied to your domain name.

Domain names are not case sensitive, so it doesn't matter whether letters are uppercase or lowercase. No spaces are allowed in a domain name, but you can use the underscore (_) to indicate a space. You can use a combination of the letters *A* through *Z*, the digits 0 through 9, and the hyphen. You cannot use the period (.), at sign (@), percent sign (%), or exclamation point (!) as part of your domain name. DNS servers and other network systems use these characters to construct e-mail addresses.

After you have decided on your domain name(s), you should check to see whether they are available. Because of the immense popularity of the Internet, finding a domain name that isn't already in use is becoming harder. You should do your own checking of domain names before you decide on a domain name and submit it to your ISP. The best way to check out the availability of a domain name is to use your Web browser and point it to `http://www.rs.internic.net`, which takes you to the InterNIC Web site. Here you can get all the information you need about how to register your domain name. You can even register a domain name online at this site if you know all the ISP server information.

At the InterNIC site, you can search the domain name database to see whether someone else already registered the name you want. In the text field, simply type in the name you're interested in, including the organization name, and press Enter. If the name is available, the database tells you that no match was found. If the name is registered, the public information about the domain name holder, including the name and address of the holder and contact information, as well as IP addresses connected with the domain name, is displayed.

Setting Up a Multihomed Host

A *multihomed host* is a computer that has been configured with multiple IP addresses for a single network interface card. A multihomed host can also be a computer that contains multiple network interface cards and is attached to several physically separate networks. For example, one network card can be bound to the TCP/IP protocol, and another network card can be bound to NetBEUI, the Microsoft networking protocol. For now, I focus on the multiple IP addresses for a single network adapter card, which lets you create multiple Web sites with unique domain names.

One of the big improvements in Internet Information Server 4.0 is its capability to support multiple Web servers running on the same Windows NT Server, which are called virtual Web servers. *Virtual Web servers* allow one physical Web server to act as if it were several Web servers. Without the virtual Web server capability, a single Web server that houses several Web sites would have to use URLs that all include the Web server's domain name. Using multihomed hosts enables the same Web server to host multiple Web sites, each with its own domain name, such as www.angell.com and www.bookware.com.

Windows NT Server allows you to assign multiple IP addresses to a single network adapter. Using Windows NT Server's advanced IP addressing feature, you can add multiple IP addresses to a network adapter card. After you add the IP addresses to the specified network adapter card, you can host multiple Web sites, each with its own IP address and domain name. You can also add multiple network adapter cards, each of which can have multiple IP addresses assigned to support a number of Web servers. You use the IIS Internet Service Manager and DNS to configure the IP address and domain names.

To set up multiple IP addresses for a single network adapter card in Windows NT Server, do the following:

1. **Double-click the Network applet icon in the Control Panel to display the Network dialog box.**

2. **Click the Protocol tab, and then double-click the TCP/IP Protocol entry.**

   The Microsoft TCP/IP Properties dialog box appears.

3. **Click the Advanced button.**

   The Advanced IP Addressing dialog box appears, as shown in Figure 3-1.

4. **Click the Add button.**

   The TCP/IP Address dialog box appears, as shown in Figure 3-2.

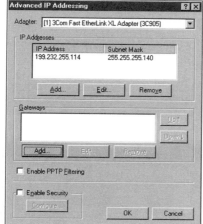

Figure 3-1:
The
Advanced IP
Addressing
dialog box.

Figure 3-2:
The TCP/IP
Address
dialog box.

5. **Enter the IP address and Subnet Mask IP address, and then click Add.**

6. **Click OK three times to return to the desktop, and then reboot Windows NT Server.**

Armed with TCP/IP fundamentals, you're ready to transform your local network into an intranet. At the center of your intranet will be Internet Information Server acting as a conduit for information and communications. Chapter 4 explains using several Windows NT Server tools that let you construct an intranet.

Chapter 4

Building a TCP/IP Habitat for IIS

In This Chapter

▶ Setting up the Microsoft DNS server

▶ Working with the Microsoft WINS server

▶ Using dynamic IP addressing with the Microsoft DHCP server

▶ Configuring Windows clients for TCP/IP networking

*R*oll up your sleeves, because it's time to build your TCP/IP intranet habitat for running Internet Information Server. Using Windows NT Server TCP/IP and name resolution tools, you can create a sophisticated TCP/IP network to access your Web servers using friendly domain names. At the same time, you'll be constructing the TCP/IP foundation for connecting your network and Internet Information Server to the Internet. This chapter explains how to use three Windows NT Server tools — the Microsoft DNS, DHCP, and WINS servers — to construct your intranet and shows you how to configure Windows-based clients for TCP/IP networking.

NT Server Tools of the TCP/IP Trade

Internet Information Server rests on top of TCP/IP networking whether you're using it as a Web server for your intranet or as a server on the Internet. Windows NT Server includes three tools for creating TCP/IP networks: DNS (Domain Name System) server, WINS (Windows Internet Naming Services), and DHCP (Dynamic Host Configuration Protocol) server. These TCP/IP name resolution and IP address management tools can work together or in various combinations. For example, using Microsoft DNS server, you can give your Web server a domain name such as sales.angell.com. This means a client on your intranet can access a Web server devoted to the sales group by entering the URL sales.angell.com.

If you installed Internet Information Server on your Windows NT Server without activating any name resolution services, the only way to connect to the Web site is by entering the IP address in the URL field. You can add DHCP service with DNS to create dynamic IP address assignments combined with easy-to-remember domain names for your Web and FTP servers. Both Windows NT Workstation and Windows 95 support DNS, WINS, and DHCP services on the client side as part of their TCP/IP configurations.

Microsoft DNS server

A Domain Name System (DNS) server is an essential part of any TCP/IP network because it enables your network to use domain names instead of IP addresses for accessing an IIS server. This means network clients using Internet Explorer or Netscape Navigator can access your intranet Web sites using the same domain name addressing used on the Internet. The Microsoft DNS server translates host names and domain names to IP addresses, which are defined using the DNS Manager.

DNS utilizes a static list of computer host names to IP addresses that is organized into tables. These tables are comprised of records, and each record contains a host name, a record type, and an IP address. Several types of records are used by DNS. For example, the address record, commonly known as the *A record,* maps a host name to an IP address. The CNAME record, which is commonly known as the *alias record,* allows hosts to have more than one name. When all these records are in a file, they're called a *DNS table.* A DNS server also includes an MX record. The purpose of the MX record is to identify the SMTP (Simple Mail Transfer Protocol) host in each domain. This is the host used to handle any e-mail addresses containing the specified domain name, plus outbound messages from those hosts addressed to other domains.

In the hierarchy of the domain name service, when a DNS server cannot resolve a name locally, it refers the name query to another DNS server higher up the chain in an effort to resolve the name. This is also the way the domain name system works on your intranet using the Microsoft DNS server. If a name resolution request isn't found on your intranet DNS server, it is bounced to the next DNS server you specify, such as the DNS servers used by your Internet service provider.

Microsoft WINS server

Windows NT can use TCP/IP as a networking protocol by encapsulating NetBIOS information as TCP/IP datagrams. NetBIOS (Network Basic Input/Output System) is a session-layer network protocol that enables lower-level networking services. Because much of NT networking still relies on NetBIOS names for networking, Microsoft developed WINS (Windows Internet Naming Service) to provide NetBIOS to TCP/IP name resolution. WINS is a NetBIOS name server that enables NetBIOS names to be resolved to IP addresses. Each time you access a network resource on a Windows NT network using TCP/IP, your system needs to know the host name or IP address. If WINS is installed, you can continue using the NetBIOS name you previously used to access resources because WINS provides the cross-reference from name to address for you.

NetBIOS on the Microsoft implementation of TCP/IP is essential because if the TCP/IP didn't have a NetBIOS component, PC-based workstations using Windows clients couldn't talk to the NT Server. Microsoft calls this service NetBIOS on TCP/IP or NBT. With the WINS server running, Web browsers can access a Web server using the NetBIOS name. For example, if the NT Server machine name running the Web server is named `ntserver`, the URL is `//ntserver/`.

Unlike DNS, the WINS server maintains the database of computer names and IP addresses dynamically. However, Microsoft DNS integrates with WINS service to provide dynamic DNS. Microsoft developed a new DNS record that allows the DNS server to work in perfect harmony with a WINS server. The Microsoft DNS server software lets you use WINS to avoid having to build complex DNS tables to establish and configure name resolution on your server; Microsoft DNS relies entirely on WINS to tell it the addresses it needs to resolve. And because WINS builds its tables automatically, you don't have to edit the DNS tables when addresses change; WINS takes care of this for you.

The DNS and WINS combination are not ISP friendly. You'll find that most Internet service providers (ISPs) don't know how to deal with or support DNS and WINS together. So you should get used to using a DNS server if you plan to connect to the Internet.

Utilizing WINS, machines automatically register their NetBIOS computer names and IP addresses every time they start up. When a workstation running TCP/IP is booted and attached to the network, it uses the WINS address settings in the TCP/IP configuration to communicate with the WINS server. The workstation gives the WINS server various information about itself, such as the NetBIOS host name, the actual user name logged on to the workstation, and the workstation's IP address. WINS stores this information for use on the network and periodically refreshes it to maintain accuracy.

You can use both WINS and DNS on your network, or you can use one without the other. Your choice is determined by whether your network is connected to the Internet and whether your host addresses are dynamically assigned. When you are connected to the Internet, you must use DNS to resolve host names and addresses because TCP/IP depends on DNS service for address resolution.

Microsoft's next release of Windows NT Server, version 5.0, will include a dynamic DNS server for Windows-based clients. This new dynamic DNS server will replace WINS.

Microsoft DHCP server

Dynamic Host Configuration Protocol (DHCP) provides dynamic IP address assignments to your network clients rather than manually configuring each client with a static IP address and other TCP/IP information. DHCP can make your life easier when you're administering your network. Instead of running around to every workstation and server and resetting the IP address to a new address, you simply reset the IP address pool on the DHCP server. You can use the Microsoft DHCP server to automatically assign either Internet registered or private unregistered IP addresses.

When DHCP service is used, pools of IP addresses are assigned for distribution to client computers on an as-needed basis. The address pools are centralized on the DHCP server, allowing all IP addresses on your network to be administered from a single server. As a client starts up and accesses the network for the first time, the client is automatically assigned an IP address, subnet mask, default gateway, and WINS server IP address (if a WINS server is being used). After the session ends, the IP address is returned to the pool of available IP addresses. DHCP utilizes a time-based mechanism called a *lease,* which can specify time limits on the use of an IP address.

If you're using a router that includes DHCP service built in, you need to decide which DHCP service you want to use: the service associated with the router or the DHCP service that comes with Windows NT Server. If you want to use an ISDN router that has built-in DHCP serving capabilities with Windows NT Server on your network, don't use the Microsoft DHCP server. Use the DHCP server functionality of the router instead.

Setting Up the Microsoft DNS Server

The Microsoft DNS server uses a graphical manager to ease the task of building tables of records for IP address to domain name resolutions. After you install the Microsoft DNS server on your Windows NT Server system, you configure it for the domain names you want to use for your Web servers. This section explains how to set up the Microsoft DNS server on Windows NT Server.

Installing DNS server

The Microsoft DNS server isn't installed as part of the default Windows NT Server installation. You install the DNS server service through the Network applet in the Windows NT Control Panel. To install the Microsoft DNS server service, you must be a member of the Administrators group on the Windows NT Server computer on which you want to install the service. Also, make sure you have the Windows NT Server distribution CD handy because you'll need it to install Microsoft DNS server.

To install the Microsoft DNS server, do the following:

1. **Launch the Control Panel Network applet to display the Network dialog box.**

2. **Click the Services tab to display the Services page, and then click the Add button.**

   The Select Network Service dialog box appears.

3. **Select Microsoft DNS Server, and then click OK.**

4. **When prompted, enter the path to the Windows NT Server distribution files, and then click the Continue button.**

   The DNS server files are copied to your computer.

5. **Click the Close button to close the Network Control Panel.**

6. **Restart your system when prompted.**

Setting up a DNS server

After you install the Microsoft DNS server, you're ready to configure it for your network. Choose Start⇨Programs⇨Administrative Tools⇨DNS Manager to display the Domain Name Service Manager window. The first time you launch the DNS Manager, it shows the address of the local machine. Double-clicking on the IP address entry in the left pane displays the Server Statistics in the right pane, as shown in Figure 4-1.

The first step in getting your DNS service up and running is to create a DNS server in the Domain Name Service Manager window. You can create multiple DNS servers, but for small intranets you need to create only a single DNS server.

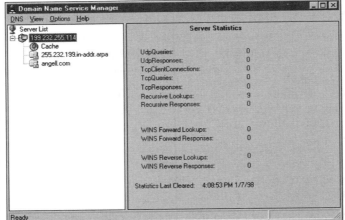

Figure 4-1:
The Domain
Name
Service
Manager
window.

To create a new DNS server, do the following:

1. **In the Domain Name Service Manager window, choose DNS⇨ New Server.**

   The Add DNS Server dialog box appears.

2. **Enter the IP address or the fully qualified domain name of your NT server, and then click OK.**

   Your new DNS server appears under the Server List in the left pane of the DNS Manager window.

Creating a DNS zone

After installing the DNS service and creating a DNS server, you need to create a DNS zone. A *zone* is the administrative unit in the domain name system that acts as a subdivision or subtree of the domain name system. For example, you could configure your system so that the domain angell.com, the subdomain sales.angell.com, and the subdomain admin.angell.com are all part of a single administrative zone configured by one organization. In this case, angell.com is the administrative zone name.

To create a DNS server zone, do the following:

1. **Select the DNS server you just created, and then choose DNS⇨ New Zone.**

   The Create New Zone window appears.

2. **Choose _P_rimary, and then click the Next button.**

   The Primary option defines the specified DNS server as the master copy of the domain name database. This database contains the records for all hosts in the zone as well as records for all the subdomains. The Secondary option defines the specified DNS server as a holder of a copy of the record database for the domain and subdomains. When changes are made to the domain, they are made to the primary DNS server, and the updated database is replicated to all secondary DNS servers.

3. **In the Zone Name box, type your zone name, such as** `angell.com`.

   When you tab to the Zone File box, a filename is automatically entered. For example, entering `angell.com` in the Zone Name box and pressing the Tab key displays `angell.com.dns` in the Zone File box. This is the file that stores the DNS database for the zone you just created.

   Note that the zone file is stored in `\system32\dns\`_filename_, where _filename_ is the filename you entered in the Zone File box.

4. **Click Next, and then click Finish.**

By default, two records are created in the domain: an NS entry and an SOA entry. The NS record specifies the selected machine as a name server in the domain, and the SOA record is known as the Start of Authority. Every domain must contain an SOA, which details the name server that is the best source of authoritative information for the zone as well as the e-mail address of a contact responsible for the domain.

Creating a reverse DNS lookup file

The _reverse lookup file_ is used for reverse lookups of a particular DNS host name when supplied with an IP number instead of a domain name. The reverse lookup file allows a user to provide an IP address and request a matching host name. If the zone you created is at IP address 199.232.255.114, for example, you need to create another zone for reverse lookups. It must be named using the reverse numbering of the IP address in quads. The reverse DNS lookup for the IP address of 199.232.255.114 would become 255.232.199 with the 114 dropped.

To create a reverse lookup zone, do the following:

1. **In the Domain Name Service Manager window, click the DNS server you created.**

2. **Choose _D_NS⇨New _Z_one.**

   The Creating New Zone dialog box appears.

3. **In the Zone Type group, click the option for Primary, and then click the Next button.**

4. **In the Zone Name box, enter your reverse IP address.**

   For example, using the IP address of 199.232.255.114, you would enter the following:

   ```
   255.232.199.in-addr.arpa
   ```

Regardless of the IP address you use, you must add `in-addr.arpa` to the end. Make sure you use a hyphen, not a period, between *in* and *addr*.

5. **Press the Tab key.**

   The DNS Manager creates the zone file automatically, which appears in the Zone File box.

6. **Click Next, and then click Finish.**

   The entry you typed in Step 4 appears as a new zone in your DNS Server zone list (the left pane of the DNS Manager window).

Adding hosts to a domain

After you create a DNS server, a domain zone (such as `angell.com`), and a reverse lookup DNS database file, you're ready to populate your domain zone with hosts. Adding hosts lets you create specific DNS names for your Web servers. For example, to create a URL address for a Web server, you create a record for sales. After you create the record under the `angell.com` zone, intranet users can enter the URL `http://sales.angell.com` in their Web browsers to access the specified Web server. Here is how to add a host to your DNS server:

1. **In the Domain Name Service Manager window, click the domain where you want the host to reside.**

   For example, if `angell.com` is the domain, select it in the Server List (the left pane of the window).

2. **Choose DNS⇨New Host.**

   The New Host dialog box appears, as shown in Figure 4-2.

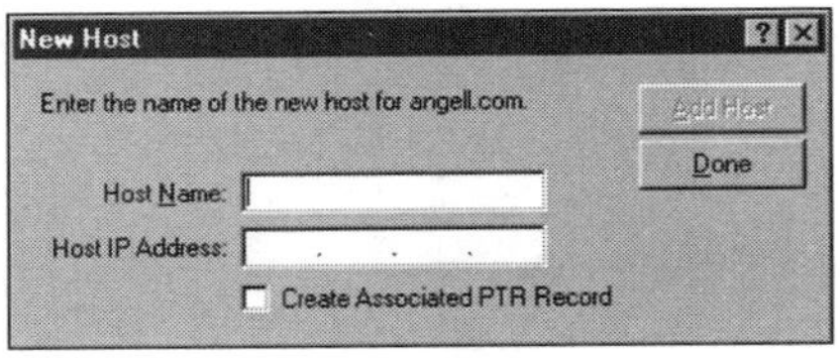

Figure 4-2:
The New
Host dialog
box.

New Host	? X
Enter the name of the new host for angell.com.	Add Host
	Done
Host Name:	
Host IP Address: . . .	
☐ Create Associated PTR Record	

3. **Enter the host name and IP address.**

   For example, if you wanted to designate the Web server at IP address 199.232.255.114 as `sales.angell.com`, you would enter *sales* in the Host Name box and 199.232.255.114 in the Host IP Address box.

4. **Click the Create Associated PTR Record check box.**

5. **Click the Add Host button.**

   You can add additional host entries by repeating Steps 3 through 5.

6. **When you have finished entering hosts, click the Done button.**

Creating subdomains

The DNS is a hierarchical naming system, so you can divide your DNS network into various sublevels or subdomains. For example, you may want to create Web sites for specific groups in your organization, each with their own unique URL. To create a subdomain, do the following:

1. **In the Domain Name Service Manager window, click the zone where you want to create a subdomain.**

   The available zones are listed in the Server List under the DNS server you created.

2. **Choose DNS⇨New Domain.**

   The New Domain dialog box appears.

3. **Enter the name for the subdomain, and then click OK.**

   For example, with the domain name `angell.com`, entering *sales* creates a new subdomain address of `sales.angell.com`.

Enabling WINS resolution

You can enable DNS to check your WINS server (if it's installed). By doing so, you provide an effective means for the DNS service to resolve dynamically assigned IP addresses, because the WINS server understands dynamic addressing but the DNS server does not. The DNS server will attempt to use WINS for resolution only if it cannot find a matching host name.

When the DNS is asked to resolve a DNS name and it can't find an entry for the name anywhere in the DNS database, the DNS service takes the leftmost part of the host name (the characters up to the first period) and passes this to the WINS server for resolution. If the WINS server has a matching NetBIOS name in its database, it returns the corresponding IP address to the DNS service, which returns it to the client. The client can then connect to the resource.

You should have the WINS server installed and know the IP address you plan to use for it before enabling WINS resolution. See "Working with WINS" later in this chapter.

To enable WINS resolution for a zone, do the following:

1. **In the Domain Name Service Manager window, click the zone for which you want to enable WINS resolution.**

2. **Choose DNS⇨Properties.**

3. **Click the WINS Resolution tab.**

4. **Select the Use WINS Resolution option.**

5. **Enter the WINS server IP address in the order it should be queried.**

6. **Click OK.**

   The Zone Properties dialog box closes. A WINS server record appears in the zone information list for each WINS server you configured.

Working with WINS

The Windows Internet Name Service (WINS) provides NetBIOS name resolution for computers using the TCP/IP protocol on your network. The WINS server makes your job as a network administrator easier by automating the process of mapping computer names to IP addresses for NetBIOS name resolution on a TCP/IP-based network. Using WINS with the DNS service enables you to use dynamic IP addressing on your intranet.

Installing WINS

The Microsoft WINS server isn't installed as part of the default Windows NT Server installation. You install the WINS server through the Network applet in the Windows NT Control Panel. To install the WINS server, you must be a member of the Administrators group on the Windows NT Server computer on which you want to install the service. Also, make sure you have the Windows NT Server distribution CD handy because you'll need it to install the WINS server.

To install WINS, do the following:

1. **Launch the Control Panel Network applet.**

   The Network dialog box appears.

2. **Click the Services tab.**

3. **Click the Add button.**

    The Select Network Service dialog box appears.

4. **Select the Windows Internet Name Service, and then click the OK button.**

5. **When prompted, enter the path to the distribution files, and then click the Continue button.**

    The WINS files are copied to your computer.

6. **Click the Close button to close the Network Control Panel.**

7. **When prompted, restart your system.**

Setting up your WINS server

Setting up the Microsoft WINS server is considerably easier than setting up the DNS Server because WINS operates by automatically tracking clients as they connect or disconnect to your Windows NT Server.

Choose Start⇨Programs⇨Administrative Tools⇨WINS Manager to display the WINS Manager window, which is shown in Figure 4-3. The IP address of your Windows NT Server machine appears in the WINS Servers list on the left pane of the WINS Manager window. The right pane displays statistics on the status of your WINS server activities.

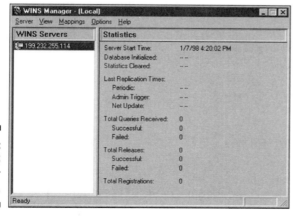

Figure 4-3:
The WINS
Manager
window.

The first thing you may need to do on your WINS server is to inform it of the machines on your subnet that have static IP addresses. If you're using DHCP to assign IP addresses, you don't need to use this feature unless you have some machines on your network that are assigned static IP addresses. To inform the WINS server of any static IP addresses on your system, do the following:

1. In the WINS Manager window, choose Mappings⇨Static Mappings.

The Static Mappings dialog box appears, as shown in Figure 4-4.

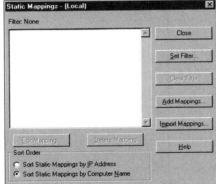

Figure 4-4:
The Static
Mappings
dialog box.

2. Click the Add Mappings button.

The Add Static Mappings dialog box appears, as shown in Figure 4-5.

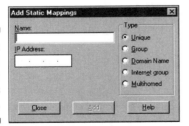

Figure 4-5:
The Add
Static
Mappings
dialog box.

3. In the Name box, type the host name of the computer on your network.

4. In the IP Address box, type the IP address of the computer.

5. Click OK.

The entry appears in the Static Mappings dialog box list.

If you make a mistake when entering a name and an address for a mapping in the Add Static Mappings dialog box, return to the Static Mappings dialog box and click the Edit Mapping button.

Changing WINS Manager displays

You can change the display of information in the WINS Manager window and other settings by choosing Options⇨Preferences, which displays the Preferences dialog box, as shown in Figure 4-6. Using settings in the Preferences dialog box, you can specify how you want addresses to appear in the WINS Manager. The default setting is by IP addresses, but you can choose from several options, such as by computer name and IP address or just by computer name. You can specify also how frequently the server statistics are updated in the WINS Manager window. The default is 60 seconds.

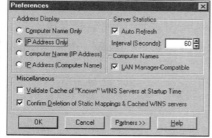

Figure 4-6:
The WINS
Manager
Preferences
dialog box.

Dynamic IP Addressing with the Microsoft DHCP Server

When you use the Microsoft DHCP (Dynamic Host Configuration Protocol) server, you place all your IP addresses into a centralized DHCP server running on your Windows NT server. This approach to managing IP addresses means that configuring your Windows clients becomes easier. Instead of configuring each client with static IP addresses, the DHCP server handles them automatically whenever a client starts up. The DHCP server also assigns DNS server, gateway, and subnet mask IP addresses.

Before you install the DHCP server on your NT server, make sure you don't already have a DHCP server running on your network. If you're using a router with a built-in DHCP server and NAT, use it instead of the Microsoft DHCP server because the Microsoft DHCP server doesn't include NAT.

Installing the DHCP server

The DHCP server service is installed through the Network applet in the Windows NT Server's Control Panel Network. To install the DHCP server, you must be a member of the Administrators group on the Windows NT Server computer on which you want to install the service. Also, make sure you have the Windows NT Server distribution CD handy, because you'll need it to install the DHCP server.

To install the DHCP service on Windows NT Server, do the following:

1. **Launch the Network applet in the Control Panel.**

   The Network dialog box appears.

2. **Click the Services tab.**

3. **Click the Add button.**

   The Select Network Service dialog box appears.

4. **Select the Microsoft DHCP Server, and then click the OK button.**

5. **When prompted, enter the path to the distribution files, and then click the Continue button.**

   The DHCP Server files are copied to your computer.

6. **Click the Close button.**

7. **When prompted, restart your system.**

Creating a DHCP server scope

The DHCP Manager is your interface for managing the DHCP service. Choose Start⇨Programs⇨Administrative Tools⇨DHCP Manager to display the DHCP Manager window, as shown in Figure 4-7.

Before you can use the DHCP server to assign IP addresses and relevant configuration options to your network clients, you have to create a DHCP scope. A *scope* is at the heart of your DHCP service. It is based on an IP address range or subnet. A scope can include only one subnet; within that subnet you can define the IP range to be used as the basis for your DHCP clients, exclude any IP addresses, and perform other DHCP management tasks. When you run the DHCP Manager for the first time, no scopes are defined for it.

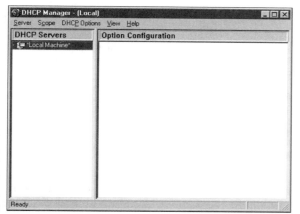

Figure 4-7:
The DHCP
Manager
window.

To add a DHCP server to your DHCP Manager and create a scope, do the
following:

1. **In the DHCP Manager window, choose Server⇨Add.**

    The Add DHCP Server to Server List dialog box appears.

2. **In the DHCP Server box, type the IP address of the DHCP server, and
   then click OK.**

    The IP address appears in the DHCP server window.

3. **In the DHCP server window, select the IP address in the DHCP server
   window where you want to create a new scope.**

4. **Choose Scope⇨Create.**

    The Create Scope dialog box appears, as shown in Figure 4-8.

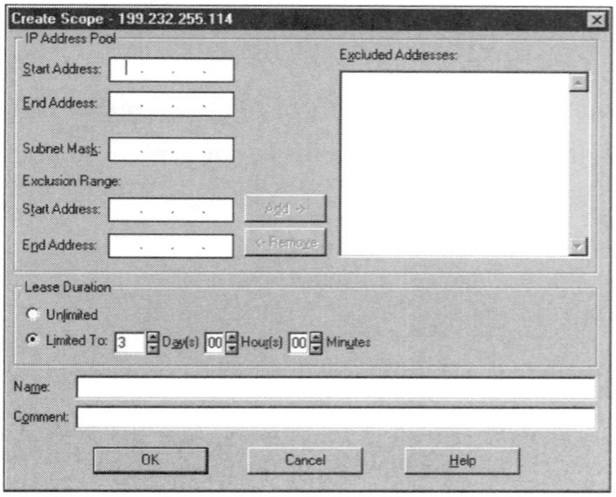

Figure 4-8:
The Create
Scope
dialog box.

5. **In the Start Address box, type the beginning IP address of your subnet.**

   Enter the full range of your IP addresses for your subnet. After you've entered the range, you can exclude any static IP address assignments using the Exclusion Range box.

6. **In the End Address box, type the last IP address of your subnet.**

7. **In the Subnet Mask box, type the subnet mask to be assigned to your DHCP clients.**

8. **Exclude IP addresses as necessary.**

   If your scope includes statically assigned IP addresses, for example, the static IP address of the DHCP server machine or the machine running IIS 4.0 needs to be on a machine with a static IP address. To exclude addresses, do the following:

   • To exclude a single IP address, type the IP address in the Start Address box and then click Add. The IP address appears in the Excluded Addresses list.

   • To enter more than one consecutive IP address to be excluded, type the beginning IP address in the Start Address box, type the last IP address in the End Address box, and then click the Add button. The IP address range appears in the Excluded Addresses list.

   • To modify or remove an address range, select it in the Excluded Addresses box, and then click the Remove button. This step places the address range in the Exclusion Range box, where you can modify it and later return it to the Excluded Addresses box.

9. **In the Lease Duration group, click the Limited To option to specify the lease parameters.**

   Don't assign the Unlimited lease type unless you are absolutely sure that no computer will ever be upgraded, replaced, or moved. If you choose an unlimited lease, you can't automatically recover IP addresses that have been assigned to a DHCP client.

10. **In the Name box, type a name (up to 120 characters) for the scope.**

    This name, along with the scope address, appears in the DHCP server window. You can enter an optional description for the scope in the Comment box.

11. **Click OK.**

    A message box appears, informing you that the scope hasn't been activated.

12. **Click Yes to activate the scope.**

At this point, you've created your scope and specified the IP addresses you will and won't use with your DHCP server. Before you activate the DHCP server, you need to configure the scope, as described in the next section. After the scope is configured, you can activate your DHCP server by choosing Scope⇨Activate.

Configuring a DHCP scope for WINS

If you are planning to use DHCP to configure your WINS clients automatically, you need to modify the properties of your scope. This involves setting the WINS server IP address and the node type to be used. A *node type* specifies the mechanism the TCP/IP protocol uses to resolve NetBIOS name requests and to convert a NetBIOS name to an IP address. These two settings are assigned as options 44 and 46 in the DHCP server. Option 44 specifies the WINS server IP addresses to be assigned to the WINS client, and option 46 specifies the TCP/IP node type to be used.

DHCP uses several types of nodes, including the following:

- **B-node resolves names using broadcast messages.** This node works best in a small network with a single subnet. A good reason to use B-node is that computers located on the same subnet can find each other even if the WINS server or DNS server is down or otherwise unavailable. Using the B-node can essentially eliminate the need to maintain a WINS database, and for small networks very little bandwidth is used. On large networks, B-node can create huge volumes of traffic that can slow down the network.

- **P-node resolves names with a name server (WINS or DNS) using point-to-point communications.** In point-to-point communications, linkages are from one IP address to another IP address. P-node requires the updating of LMHOSTS files.

- **M-node uses B-node first (broadcasts) to resolve the name and then P-node (name queries) if the broadcast fails to resolve a name.**

- **H-node uses P-node (name queries) first to resolve the name and then B-node (broadcasts) if the name service is unavailable or if the name is not registered in the WINS server's database.**

  This node type is the most efficient to use and practically guarantees that the resource will be found, even if the LMHOST file or WINS database does not contain the requested resource's IP address. H-node is the default node type when configuring TCP/IP manually, unless the WINS IP address box is left empty.

To modify a scope in the DHCP server, do the following:

1. **In the DHCP server window that contains the scope you want to modify, select the DHCP server and then select the scope.**

2. **To set the properties for the selected scope, choose DHCP Options⇨Scope.**

   The DHCP Options: Scope dialog box appears, as shown in Figure 4-9.

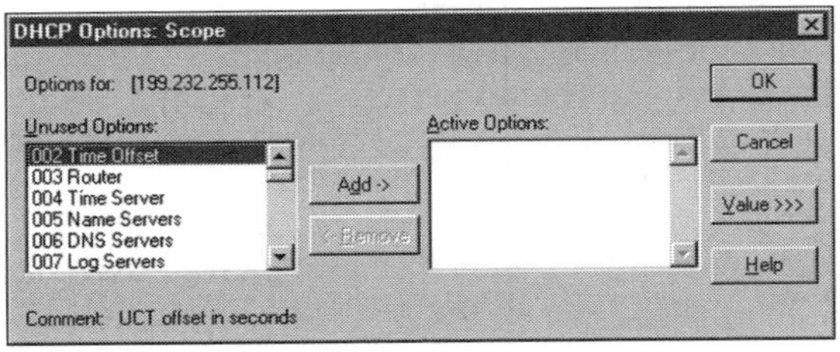

Figure 4-9: The DHCP Options: Scope dialog box.

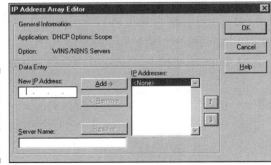

3. **In the Unused Options list, select 044 WINS/NBNS Servers, and then click Add.**

   A dialog box appears, telling you to set the P-node, M-node, or H-node values.

4. **Click OK.**

   The 044 WINS/NBNS Servers option appears in the Active Options list.

5. **In the Active Options list, select 044 WINS/NBNS Servers, and then click the Value button.**

   The IP Address Array Editor appears, as shown in Figure 4-10.

6. **In the New IP Address box, type the IP address of your WINS server, click Add, and then click OK.**

Figure 4-10: The IP Address Array Editor.

Adding the IP address of your WINS server allows the DHCP server to send the WINS server information automatically to every client that requests an IP address. This saves you from having to enter an IP address for the WINS server in every client machine with TCP/IP properties. For each client, however, you need to activate the Use DHCP for WINS Resolution setting in the WINS Configuration tab.

7. **In the Unused Options list, select 046 WINS/NBT Node Type, and then click Add.**

   046 WINS/NBT Node Type option appears in the Active Options list.

8. **In the Active Options list, select the 046 WINS/NBT Node Type option, and then click the Value button.**

   An expanded DHCP Options dialog box appears, as shown in Figure 4-11.

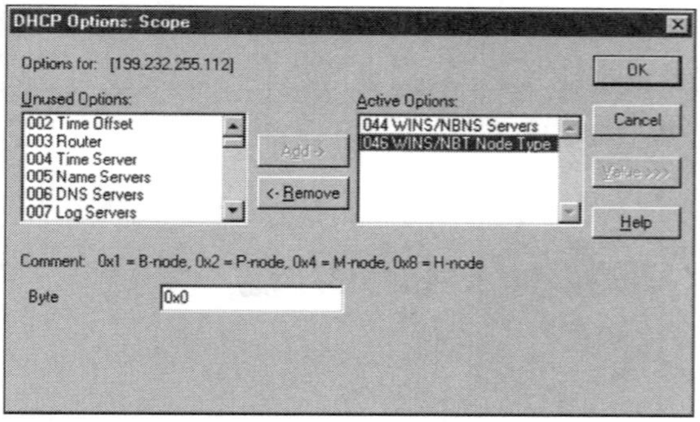

Figure 4-11: The expanded DHCP Options dialog box allows you to specify the node type you want to use with DHCP.

9. **Enter the node option you want to use.**

   The values for each node appear above the Byte box. For example, you might enter 0x1 for the B-node option.

10. **Click OK.**

    The settings you established in the DHCP Options dialog box appear in the Option Configuration pane in the DHCP Manager window.

Deleting a scope

Before you delete a scope, deactivate it from the DHCP Manager window by choosing Scope⇨Deactivate. After the scope lease time has expired and you are sure that no DHCP clients are using a lease from the scope, you can delete it. To delete a scope, follow these steps:

1. **In the DHCP window that contains the scope you want to delete, select the DHCP server.**

   If you are deleting a scope on the computer running the DHCP server service, this entry will be Local Machine; otherwise, it will be an IP address.

   After the DHCP server has been connected, the scopes for the server will be listed.

2. **Select the scope you want to delete.**

3. **Choose S̲cope⇨D̲elete.**

   A message warns you that clients may still have active leases.

4. **Click OK to delete the scope.**

If you delete a scope with active clients, you can force the client to discontinue using this current lease by issuing the IPCONFIG/RENEW command at the command prompt for a Windows NT machine. For a computer running Windows 95, you can use the WINIPCFG program by clicking the Release button. See the next section, "Configuring Windows Clients for Your Intranet" for more information.

Configuring Windows Clients for Your Intranet

At this point, you're probably suffering from an overload of setting up DNS, WINS, and DHCP servers. Now it's time to complete the construction of your intranet by bringing your Windows-based clients into the network fold. This section explains how to set up your intranet to work with DNS, WINS, and DHCP servers from the client side.

When you installed Internet Information Server 4.0 on Windows NT Server 4.0, the Setup program automatically created a special user account named *IUSR-computername,* where *computername* is the name of your NT Server machine. This default IIS user account enables clients to anonymously log on to any IIS server. As such, to make your IIS servers available to clients on your network, you don't have to create any user accounts using the User Manager for Domains program in Windows NT Server. As you find out in Chapter 10, you can create private Web servers using Windows NT Server and IIS security features.

Configuring Windows clients for DNS and static IP addresses

For your Windows clients to access your Web server using DNS with static IP addresses, each client's TCP/IP stack must be running and configured to access the DNS server. After the Windows client is configured, you can connect to the IIS Web server by opening Internet Explorer and then typing the DNS name in the URL field for your Web server (for example, http://sales.angell.com/).

Setting up a Windows 95 client

To set up DNS with static IP addresses in Windows 95, do the following.

1. **In the Windows 95 Control Panel, double-click the Network applet icon.**

    The Network dialog box appears.

2. **Select your TCP/IP component for the computer's Ethernet adapter, and then click the Properties button.**

    The TCP/IP Properties dialog box appears.

3. **Click the IP Address tab.**

4. **Select the Specify an IP Address setting.**

5. **Type the IP address and subnet mask IP address in their respective boxes.**

6. **Click the DNS Configuration tab.**

7. **Select the Enable DNS option.**

8. **In the Host box, type a host name for the client PC; in the Domain box, type the domain name you created in the DNS server.**

    For example, the host machine might be named david and the domain might be angell.com.

9. **In the DNS Server Search Order group, type the IP address of your DNS server, and then click the Add button.**

If you have Internet DNS server IP addresses associated with your Internet access service and you're using a router to connect to the Internet, make sure the DNS server IP address for the Windows NT server's DNS server appears at the top of the list. This ensures that a client browser request looks at the local DNS server first before going to the Internet service provider's DNS server, which activates the router to connect to your ISP. This can save you telephone company charges for each connection.

10. **Click OK twice to exit the TCP/IP Properties and Network dialog boxes.**

11. **Restart Windows 95.**

12. **If prompted, insert your distribution disk or CD.**

Setting up a Windows NT Workstation client

Setting up a Windows NT Workstation 4.0 client is similar to setting up a Windows 95 client. To set up a Windows NT Workstation client for DNS, do the following:

1. **In the Control Panel, double-click the Network icon.**

   The Network dialog box appears.

2. **Click the Protocols tab.**

3. **Select the TCP/IP Protocol option, and then click Properties.**

   The Microsoft TCP/IP Properties dialog box appears.

4. **Click the IP Address tab.**

5. **Select the Specify an IP Address option.**

6. **Type the IP address and subnet mask IP address in their respective boxes.**

7. **Click the DNS tab.**

8. **In the Host Name box, type the host name of the client; in the Domain box, type the domain name.**

9. **In the DNS Service Search Order group, click the Add button.**

   The TCP/IP DNS Service dialog box appears.

If you have Internet DNS server IP addresses associated with your Internet access service and you're using a router to connect to the Internet, make sure the DNS server IP address for the Windows NT server's DNS server appears at the top of the list. This ensures that a client browser request looks at the local DNS server first before going to the Internet service provider's DNS server, which activates the router to connect to your ISP. This can save you telephone company charges for each connection.

10. **Type the IP address of your NT server running the DNS server, and then click the Add button.**

11. **Click OK twice to exit the Microsoft TCP/IP Properties and Network dialog boxes.**

12. **Restart Windows NT Workstation.**

13. **If prompted, insert your distribution disk or CD.**

Configuring WINS clients

WINS clients are Windows 95 and Windows NT Workstations. To configure the clients to recognize the WINS servers, you use the Network applet in the Control Panel. After the Windows client is configured, you can connect to the IIS Web server by opening Internet Explorer and then typing the NetBIOS name of the NT Server machine in the URL field for your Web server (for example, http://ntserver/).

Setting up a Windows 95 client for WINS

To configure Windows 95 clients for WINS, do the following:

1. **Choose Start⇨Settings⇨Control Panel, and then double-click the Network applet.**

2. **In the network components list, select the network adapter with the TCP/IP binding, and then click the Properties button.**

    The TCP/IP Properties dialog box appears.

3. **Click the WINS Configuration tab.**

4. **Select the Enable WINS Resolution option.**

    The settings in the WINS Configuration tab become active.

5. **In the Primary WINS Server box, type the IP address of the machine running your WINS server (your NT Server machine).**

6. **Click OK twice to exit the Network applet.**

7. **Restart Windows 95.**

Setting up a Windows NT Workstation client for WINS

Setting a Windows NT Workstation 4.0 client is similar to setting up a Windows 95 client. To configure an NT Workstation 4.0 client for WINS, do the following:

1. **Choose Start⇨Settings⇨Control Panel, and then double-click the Network applet.**

    The Network dialog box appears.

2. **Click the Protocols tab.**

3. **Select the TCP/IP option, and then click the Properties button.**

4. **Click the WINS Address tab.**

    If necessary, select the adapter card if you're using more than one card.

5. **In the Primary WINS Server box, type the IP address of the WINS server.**

6. **Click OK twice.**

7. **Restart Windows NT.**

Configuring Windows clients for DHCP and dynamic IP addressing

For your Windows clients to dynamically get their IP addresses and other information, you must set up each client to receive IP addresses dynamically. In Windows 95 and Windows NT Workstation, this involves using the Network applet in the Control Panel. After you configure your Windows clients for DHCP, whenever you boot up the client machine, it will lease the IP address information it needs to work on your intranet.

Setting up a Windows 95 client for DHCP

The default TCP/IP setting for Windows 95 is with DHCP enabled. If you need to set up Windows 95 clients for DHCP, however, do the following:

1. **Choose Start⇨Settings⇨Control Panel, and then double-click the Network applet.**

2. **In the network components list, select the network adapter with the TCP/IP binding, and then click the Properties button.**

    The TCP/IP Properties dialog box appears.

3. **Click the IP Address tab.**

4. **Select the Obtain an IP Address Automatically option.**

5. **Click OK twice to exit the Network applet.**

6. **Restart Windows.**

Setting up a Windows NT client for DHCP

Like Windows 95, the Windows NT Workstation default TCP/IP setting is with DHCP enabled. If you need to configure NT Workstation 4.0 clients for DHCP, however, do the following:

1. **Choose Start⇨Settings⇨Control Panel, and then double-click the Network applet.**

    The Network dialog box appears.

2. **Click the Protocols tab.**

3. **Select the TCP/IP option, and then click the Properties button.**

4. **Click the IP Address tab.**

    If necessary, select the adapter card if you're using more than one card.

5. **Select the Obtain an IP Address from a DHCP Server option.**

6. **Click OK twice to exit the Network applet.**

7. **Restart Windows NT.**

Checking assigned TCP/IP settings for a DHCP client

After you've set up your DHCP server and configured your clients, you can check to see the assigned IP addresses and other information that the DHCP server sent to a Windows client. Windows 95 clients use the Winipcfg program, which is a friendly GUI program that lets you view information about your TCP/IP and network adapter card settings.

To run Winipcfg, do the following:

1. **Choose Start⇨Run.**

2. **Type** winipcfg.exe.

3. **Click OK.**

   The IP Configuration window appears, as shown in Figure 4-12. You can use the IP Configuration to release TCP/IP settings assigned to a Windows 95 client.

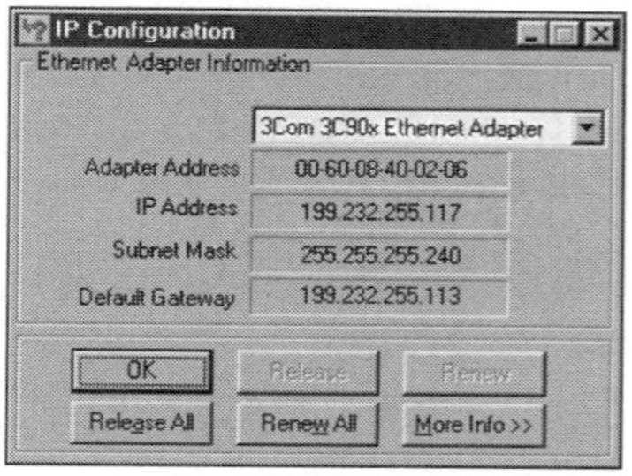

Figure 4-12:
The IP Configuration window displays useful information about your TCP/IP and Ethernet card settings.

For Windows NT clients, the ipconfig.exe program (a command-line program) is used to handle these functions. Entering **ipconfig/all** lists all the IP address attributes. Simply typing **ipconfig** displays only the IP address, subnet mask, and default gateway.

Chapter 5

Making All the Right Internet Connections

*U*sing Internet Information Server to establish a presence on the Internet for your organization takes you into the complex, murky, and expensive world of Internet connectivity. Adding to the Internet connectivity issues is the complexity of the added security requirements for protecting your local network from Internet intruders. This chapter provides an overview of the connectivity and security issues involved in connecting your Internet Information Server to the Internet.

Web Serving on the Internet

Getting an Internet connection involves two parts. The first is the actual data communications link, and the second is the Internet service provider (ISP) connection to the Internet. In most cases, these two parts are intertwined, and you order and set them up through the Internet service provider. Your local telephone company is usually the supplier of the communications link. For running a Web server, you need a dedicated connection that stays connected to your Internet provider 24 hours a day, 7 days a week. Dedicated service is commonly referred to as 24x7 service.

Essentially, you can connect your Windows NT Server running Internet Information Server to the Internet in two ways. The first method is to place your NT Server machine at an ISP site, which in turn connects directly to the ISP's high-speed Internet hookup. The second method is to get a dedicated telecommunications link that connects to your NT Server located at your premises.

Down on the Web farm

Placing your Windows NT Server machine at an Internet service provider's site, which in turn is directly connected to the ISP's high-speed Internet connection, is referred to as *co-location service*. The ISP site for this service is often referred to as a *Web server farm* because your NT Server machine is placed on racks or cages with other Web servers sharing the Internet connection. This service enables your Web site to piggyback the ISP's high-speed infrastructure. You access the machine located at the ISP via a secured Internet connection to manage your Web server.

Although using a co-location service may be less expensive than getting your own dedicated connection, it's not cheap and can quickly become a lot more expensive. For example, many co-location services charge you based on the amount of traffic your Web site is generating. If your site becomes popular, you could face charges that can easily exceed the cost of installing your own dedicated connection. Do some comparative calculations to determine what the service will end up costing you compared to using your own dedicated connection.

Bringing the Internet connection to your doorstep

Connecting your Windows NT Server to the Internet via a dedicated communications link to an Internet service provider offers the most control over your Web server activities. Your communications link to the ISP can be one of many different technologies, but it's important that the connection capacity matches your anticipated Web site traffic.

Most dedicated connections are digital communications technologies, which means they exchange information in binary form rather than in analog signals used for modem communications. Digital communications not only support high-speed data transmissions but are also a more reliable medium. Most digital communications lines use standard twisted-pair telephone company wiring used by voice communications. The difference is in the devices placed at each end of the lines, which condition the lines to push more data through the copper wiring. Your Internet connection links to your Windows NT Server machine via a router connected to your network.

The term *bandwidth* refers to the amount of information that can be transmitted and received in a given interval of time. A link to the Internet that has a higher bandwidth allows more information to be communicated in a shorter time to more people. Bandwidth is measured in bits per second (bps), kilobits per second (Kbps), or megabits per second (Mbps). One Kbps is equivalent to 1,024 bps, and 1 Mbps is equal to 1,024 Kbps.

Two major cost categories are associated with connecting your Internet Information Server to the Internet from your premises. The first involves the one-time setup charges from both the telephone company and ISP. These setup charges typically include the cost of a router device placed at your site. This setup charge can easily run into a few thousand dollars, depending on the connection type you're installing. The next cost category associated with a dedicated connection is the monthly charges for the use of the telecommunications line as well as the ISP's Internet connectivity services. These monthly charges can add up to anywhere between a few hundred dollars to a few thousand dollars a month, again depending on the capacity of your communications link.

Which way should you go?

The dedicated connection is the way your organization will want to go in the long run. As the Internet plays an increasingly important role in your organization, control over the entire process of running an Internet presence becomes an essential business requirement. If the dedicated connection option is simply too expensive for your organization at this stage, consider using a Web server co-location service to get started. The key element in using either of these two options is that you control your Internet presence.

Although the cost of dedicated connections to the Internet is still high, changes are happening in the telecommunications industry that promise to make dedicated connections more affordable, enabling smaller organizations to establish their own Internet presence. One of the most promising of these changes is Digital Subscriber Line (DSL) service from the telephone companies. I explain DSL in more detail later in this chapter.

Telcos Are between You and the Net

The conduit for connecting two or more physically isolated networks is a wide area network (WAN). This is where the telephone companies come into play. To communicate between dispersed networks, you need a data communications link that enables networking protocols, such as TCP/IP, to work with each other over long distances. The role of the wide area network is that of a background conduit for connecting client and server computers and networks not in the same location. This is the basis of the Internet and internetworking.

The integration of all telephone company networks forms the basis of the global, public wide area network. The same telephone companies that handle voice traffic also control data communications. In the United States, the telephone system is made up of telephone companies that act as common carriers for all kinds of communications. As part of connecting your Web server to the Internet, you need to enter the world of telecommunications to understand the lingo of Internet connectivity. This section provides an overview of the telecommunications industry.

LECs, IECs, and CLECs

Telecommunications services are broken down into two distinct groups of providers. *Local exchange carriers (LECs)* consist of independent telephone companies (ITCs), such as GTE and the Regional Bell Operating Companies (RBOCs), such as Ameritech, Bell Atlantic, Bell South, Pacific Bell, Southwestern Bell, and US West. LECs operate as monopolies within their respective service areas.

What is important about LECs is that they control the physical telephone line connections to every telecommunications user in the United States. This is called the *last mile* in the telecommunications network. The last mile represents the link between homes and businesses within a given geographical area that is serviced by a telephone company switching facility called a *central office,* or simply *CO.* The lines between these central offices and customer sites are called *local loops.* Thousands of these facilities are scattered across the United States. Just about everyone lives within a few miles of a CO.

An *interexchange carrier* (IEC) is a long-distance telecommunications carrier, such as AT&T, MCI, and US Sprint. These telephone companies use local exchange carrier switches as the gateway for calls into their long-distance telecommunications network. They lack a direct connection to most homes and businesses, so they must rely on the LECs to deliver their services.

A *Competitive Local Exchange Carrier* (CLEC) is a new player in the telecommunications industry. A CLEC is a company or Internet service provider that buys telecommunications services at discount from the incumbent LEC to resell to customers. The Telecommunications Act of 1996 allowed CLECs as a way to try to bring competition into local telephone service.

Telco monopolies and the high cost of bandwidth

The U.S. Congress passed the Telecommunications Act of 1996 in an attempt to open up the telecommunications industry at the local level to more competition. For a consumer of telecommunication services, the theoretical benefits of competition are better service at lower prices. In reality, the results of the Telecommunications Act are disappointing. The RBOCs continue to maintain their stranglehold on local telephone service. Although the FCC (Federal Communications Commission) regulates interstate and foreign telecommunications, it lacks authority in intrastate telecommunications, which is where the LECs operate.

At the state level, regulatory functions for the telecommunications industry are performed by public agencies, which are usually referred to as *public utilities commissions (PUCs)*. These government agencies are chartered to look after the public interest against the backdrop of a telecommunications monopoly. Unfortunately, most agencies are telephone company friendly or rely on telephone company data to justify their rates.

The RBOCs file tariffs in every state in which they offer service. Thus, the same service typically is priced differently across states. Prices are referred to as *tariffs* in the telecommunications industry, which is a published price that sets the allowed rate for telecommunications services. Each state has its own published tariffs for services. The RBOCs thrive on the fragmented state-by-state approach to tariffs because it allows them to extract more profits by being able to charge different rates.

As a result of the monopoly power of the telephone companies, the cost of dedicated connections to the Internet are considerably more expensive than if telecommunications services operated in a competitive marketplace. The only other serious contender for providing bandwidth in a capacity usable by Web servers is the cable television industry. Unfortunately, the cable industry doesn't appear to be interested in selling bandwidth for Web serving, and the shared architecture it uses doesn't fit well as a Web server connection. The one benefit of cable service may be its influence on the prices charged by telephone companies for high-speed connections. Cable modem service is generally priced aggressively compared to the prices charged by the telephone companies for comparable bandwidth capacity.

The Bandwidth Buffet

The telephone companies offer a number of data communications technologies. The leading bandwidth technologies available for dedicated connections are analog modem, ISDN, Frame Relay, Fractional T1, T1, and the new kid on the block, xDSL. This section explains the different dedicated bandwidth options available for connecting your Web server to an Internet service provider.

Although the telephone companies are the primary purveyors of the actual telecommunication links, in many cases your Internet service provider manages the setup of your telecommunications link as part of a total Internet connectivity solution.

Bandwidth bandits

No, "bandwidth bandits" doesn't refer to the telephone companies. These bandits come from a variety of factors that affect the true throughput of any connection. *Throughput* is the overall measure of a communications link's performance in terms of its real-world speed, not the theoretically possible maximum speed. Factors affecting throughput include distance, switching components (routers, network traffic), and electrical interference. As a result of these bandwidth bandits, your data communications speeds fluctuate and never reach the theoretical values touted by the sellers of bandwidth. Additionally, Internet data traffic conditions affect the performance of a data communications link as well as the communications link used by the client.

Bandwidth scalability

You will undoubtedly need to increase the capacity for your Web site as it becomes more popular with both visitors and people within your organization. Over time, you'll need to consider upgrading your communications link. Selecting a communications technology today that doesn't provide for a smooth upgrade can become expensive when it's time to upgrade your service. Frame Relay, Fractional T1, and DSL are *scalable,* which means you can upgrade within the technology.

Dedicated analog modem service

Using a dedicated analog modem and voice grade line provides a limited connection for your Web server. Analog transmission methods have inherent reliability problems that require error-correction and detection mechanisms and data retransmissions, which reduce the data-carrying capacity of the connection.

Even with the new 56K modems, the analog modem as the basis for a dedicated Web server isn't a realistic option. The 56K modems operate differently from earlier modems in that they deliver data at different rates for downstream and upstream. 56K modems deliver a maximum of around 53 Kbps downstream, that is, from the Internet to your Web server, but only 28.8 or 33.6 Kbps upstream. Because the majority of data traffic is going upstream from your Web server to the user, your server is denied the faster speed. The major advantage to using an analog modem over a dedicated voice grade telephone line is the cost. You can get a dedicated analog connection to the Internet for under $100 in many areas.

One new development in modem-based Internet connectivity is the combining of analog modem connections. The idea behind this technology is to combine two or more modem connections to create a single, larger bandwidth connection. This process is referred to as *bonding* and is based on the Multilink PPP protocol, which turns two or more modem connections into one IP session. Two 28.8 modem calls become one 57.6 Kbps pipe. This dual-modem service is new and is not widely available yet.

ISDN service

Integrated Service Digital Network (ISDN) is a digital service that delivers data communications at speeds of up to 128 Kbps without compression. It's delivered to homes and businesses using existing twisted-pair telephone wires used for voice communications. ISDN has slowly gained ground in the United States and is now widely available in many metropolitan areas. The biggest drawback to dedicated ISDN service is the cost for this low-end connection, which typically runs in the $300 to $500 per month range .

Frame relay service

Frame relay is a packet-oriented data communications link widely deployed by local and long-distance telephone companies. Most telephone companies offer point-to-point frame relay services as a way to set up virtual wide area connections for geographically dispersed sites. With the advent of the Internet, frame relay is becoming a popular option for dedicated connections. Frame relay bandwidth can be packaged in increments from 56 Kbps up to 1.54 Mbps. Connections into a frame relay network require a router and a line from the customer site to the carrier's point of entry. After an initial startup cost of $1,000 to $2,500, a connection will cost around $100 to $200 a month and up, depending on your bandwidth.

T1 and fractional T1 service

A T1 is a point-to-point, dedicated communications link that provides a total bandwidth of 1.544 Mbps. A fractional T1 is just what its name implies, a part of a full T1 line. A full T1 line provides 24 channels of 64 Kbps. You can contract for one or more of these channels in 64 Kbps increments. Fractional T1 lines are typically made up into packages of 384 Kbps (6 channels), 512 Kbps (8 channels), and 768 Kbps (12 channels). One of the big benefits of using fractional T1 lines is their inherent capacity for a smooth upgrading to more bandwidth capacity. T1 lines are the bread and butter of dedicated telecommunications links for the telephone companies. A T1 connection costs $1,500 to $2,500 a month along with startup and equipment costs. A fractional T1 line service is priced accordingly but with an added-on premium. A T3 line, which is equivalent to 28 T1 lines, is also available, although it's used primarily by large organizations and Internet service providers.

xDSL service

Originally, Digital Subscriber Line (DSL) technologies were designed for use as a data communications technology for delivering video-on-demand (VOD). The telephone companies envisioned entering the cable TV market with this technology. The Internet bushwhacked the VOD dream, and the telephone companies are now positioning DSL as an Internet connection technology. Telephone companies move very slowly, but DSL started being deployed in 1998 and is being positioned as a competitive technology to high-speed Internet access services being deployed by the cable companies.

Digital Subscriber Line service is an always-on service, which makes it ideal for connecting Web servers to the Internet. It can be packaged in a variety of increments ranging from 128 Kbps up to 6 Mbps. DSL technology offers the potential to dramatically lower the cost of dedicated connections for Web service because it costs the telephone companies less than other digital communication technologies, such as ISDN. Installing DSL services bypasses the existing telephone-switching infrastructure, so telephone companies can quickly add support for DSL services without costly changes to the telephone system.

Digital Subscriber Line refers not to the line, but to the modem technologies that convert a standard POTS (plain old telephone service) line into a high-speed digital pipeline. Telephone companies and Internet service providers operating as CLECs (Competitive Local Exchange Carriers) use the existing infrastructure of copper wiring, of which there is an estimated 600 million lines in the United States. Nothing in telecommunications is ever straightforward, however, and an assortment of technical issues make xDSL more complex that just plugging in two DSL modems at each end of a telephone line.

The DSL family

The *x* in xDSL is a placeholder for the several members that make up the Digital Subscriber Line family. These members include ADSL, HDSL, IDSL, RADSL, SDSL, and VDSL. Table 5-1 describes the capacities of each technology.

Table 5-1	The xDSL Family
DSL Type	*What It Does*
ADSL (Asynchronous Digital Subscriber Line)	Supports 32 Kbps to 9 Mbps downstream, and 32 Kbps to 1.088 Mbps upstream
HDSL (High data-rate Digital Subscriber Line)	Supports symmetrical service at 1.54 Mbps to 2.048 Mbps
IDSL (ISDN Digital Subscriber Line)	Supports symmetrical 128 Kbps service
RADSL (Rate-Adaptive Digital Subscriber Line)	A rate-adaptive variation of ADSL, which means the data rates can be packaged in increments
SDSL (Symmetrical Digital Subscriber Line)	Supports symmetrical service at 160 Kbps to 2.048 Mbps
VDSL (Very high-rate Digital Subscriber Line)	Supports up to 51 Mbps

Pacific Bell's FastTrak DSL

Pacific Bell began rolling out DSL service in California in 1998 by introducing two RADSL packages called FastTrak DSL. Pacific Bell is offering two packages for business and residential customers:

- ✔ **A 384 Kbps service in both directions.** For business service, the cost is $125 for installation and $135 a month. For residential service, the cost is $125 for installation and $80 a month.

- ✔ **A 1.5 Mbps downstream and 384 Kbps upstream service.** For business service, the cost is $125 for installation and $250 a month. For residential service, the cost is $125 for installation and $150 a month.

The installation charges don't include the cost of the DSL hardware, which Pacific Bell offers at $435 to $660, depending on the installation package. You also need to add the cost of your ISP connection, which is around $80 a month for 384/384 service or $150 for 1.54 Mbps/384 Kbps service.

Cable modem service

The cable companies are rolling out cable modem service in selected areas. Although cable is a great buy for end users, the industry simply doesn't appear to want to make it available for customers wanting Web sites. Many cable operators contractually forbid using cable modem service to operate any kind of server. MediaOne, for example, offers an impressive 1.54 Mbps/ 300 Kbps service for a mere $39.95, but you are not allowed to run a Web server on it. MediaOne thwarts using its service for operating your own Web server by not allowing you to use your own domain name — an essential part of your Web site identity on the Internet. The other negative aspect about cable service is that it's a shared connection. The cable system uses neighborhood networks that service between 500 and 2,500 homes. If traffic is heavy within the neighborhood network, the whole system slows down.

Estimating Your Bandwidth Requirements

Although more bandwidth is always better, you need to plan wisely because bandwidth is expensive. You need to make some calculations on what kind of traffic you anticipate for your Web site. Choosing the right connection is, at best, making an educated guess. Capacity planning is one of the most important and the most difficult tasks you undertake in setting up your Internet site. Ironically, it's possible that the worst thing that can happen when you debut your Web presence is that it becomes too popular. If users are unable to access your site for long periods of time because it's busy, they're likely to quit trying.

A number of factors come into play when trying to evaluate your bandwidth needs. Figuring out the average size of your content files, the amount of time files of that size take to send, and the number of simultaneous users you want to support can help you arrive at some kind of estimate. Bandwidth capacity also has a direct influence on what features your Web site can offer in terms of content. For example, lots of graphics and multimedia features mean more demand on your telecommunications link.

Another important factor in bandwidth capacity is the Web server's intended audience. If the majority of your audience will be small businesses or individuals who are likely to be connecting to your site over dial-up connections, their access speeds will depend on their own lines and modems as well as yours. If your audience will be companies or individuals in companies that have high-speed access to the Net, or you anticipate that your Web site will have a tremendous amount of traffic from the outset, you'll need a more powerful connection.

Calculating page sizes

The first step in calculating the bandwidth requirements for your Web server is to estimate the average file size of your Web site. An average Web text page is about 500 words, or about 7K, but as soon as you add a graphic or two, the size increases rapidly. A number somewhere between 30K and 50K is a reasonable starting point. You can use this number if you have not yet designed any of your Web pages.

You can estimate the average file size of your Web site also by multiplying 8 bits for each character in a document. A full page of text has 80 characters per line times 66 lines, which equals 42,240 bits per page. For every 8 bits of data transferred, add 4 bits of overhead. Multiply 42,240 bits per page times 1.5 bits used to transfer 1 bit of data, and you get 63,360 bits per page transferred.

This calculation assumes a solid text page with no graphics, most typically seen when converting text documents to HTML format. The typical home page is generally much less text intensive and probably closer to 24,000 bits per page, including overhead. Also, the typical home page may also contain one or more graphics files, each requiring a connection between the client and the server.

Calculating bandwidth

To calculate bandwidth based on a given average file size, you convert the number of bytes in your default-sized file into bits by multiplying the number of bytes by 12 (8 bits in a byte plus 4 control bits), and then express the results in terms of seconds. If your data is recorded in bytes per hour, multiply the number of hours by 3,600, which is the number of seconds in one hour. For example, if your plans call for 500,000,000 bytes to be transferred over a 12-hour period, the equation becomes

$$500,000,000 \text{ bits} \times 12 \div (12 \text{ hours} \times 3,600 \text{ seconds})$$

which becomes

$$6,000,000,000 \text{ bits} \div (43,200 \text{ seconds} \times 1,024 \text{ bits})$$

which finally calculates a bandwidth of

135.6 Kbps

Estimating hit rates

Another important calculation for estimating your bandwidth capacity needs is to estimate the number of times a day you think your site will be visited, or hit. This is difficult to estimate, but you can make some sensible assumptions. You will probably see a large number of hits as people discover your new site. As time and promotion goes on, you will see an increase. At some point, you'll see the hit rate level off. To get an idea of the traffic that all this involves, you can use the hit rate you expect along with the average size of your Web pages with this formula:

(Expected number of hits per day ÷ Number of seconds in 24 hours) × (Document size in $K \times 12$)

which leads to the following formula:

(Expected number of hits per day ÷ 86,400) × (Document size in $K \times 12$).

For example, if you expect your Web server to attract 2,000 connections in an average day, and your default page size is 70K, the formula becomes:

$(2000 \div 86,400) \times (70 \times 1,024 \times 12)$

which generates the following result:

19.9 Kbps

Number of simultaneous users

A big question — and perhaps the most important to estimate — is how many simultaneous users your Web server will be. Although the capabilities of your computer hardware platform play a role in determining the number of simultaneous users your Web site can support, the capacity of your Internet connection is usually the bottleneck. The more successful your Web site, the more demand there will be for connections. Table 5-2 shows the range of users that can be supported for various connection capacities.

Table 5-2	Number of Simultaneous Users Supported by a Given Connection Capacity	
Connection Bandwidth	*Maximum Number of Users*
28.8 Kbps	1 to 3
56 Kbps/64 Kbps	10 to 20
128 Kbps	10 to 50
1.54 Mbps	100 to 500

To calculate the number of simultaneous users that a given data communications capacity can support, you can do the following calculation:

1. **Assuming that you want to stay within the five-second transmission time for a page of text, and assuming a text file size of 63,360 bits transmitted for the user to receive the page, divide the 63,360 bits by 5 seconds = 12,672 bits per second per user.**

2. **Divide the connection speed by the bits per second per user.**

   For instance, for a T1 line, divide 1,540,000 bps by 12,672 bps per user = 121 simultaneous users on a T1 connection.

Where the WAN Meets the LAN

Routers are at the heart of most digital connections to the Internet. You connect a router to your LAN network via a standard 10BaseT Ethernet connection. The digital communications link from the telephone company connects to the router. Connecting the router to your LAN makes the router the gateway for your entire network. (A *gateway* is a functional device that enables two or more networks to communicate as a single entity.) The router is a separate network device that has its own IP address, which is your gateway IP address.

Defining gateways in Windows NT

You can define the default gateway for your TCP/IP network in the Microsoft TCP/IP Properties dialog box. You use the Default Gateway setting only if you're using static IP addressing on your system. Dynamic IP addressing automatically provides the Default Gateway IP address to clients on the network. You enter the IP address of your network gateway in the TCP/IP Properties dialog box (in the Network applet). You can also specify additional gateways for each specified network interface card by clicking the Advanced button in the Microsoft TCP/IP Properties dialog box. If you're running the Microsoft DHCP server on your Windows NT server or through a router, the default gateway is automatically sent to your client machines when they boot up.

The router's job

Routers form the basis of the Internet. The router's job is to receive packets, look at the whole address stored in the packet, and then forward the packets to another computer if the router recognizes the address. This decision-making functionality, which is called *filtering*, makes it possible for the router to monitor and selectively choose packets as they enter or leave the router. This filtering is also at the heart of protecting your local network from unwanted intrusion, and prevents selected local network traffic from leaving your LAN through the router.

Routers contain special tables that inform them of the addresses of all networks connected to them. The Internet is defined as all the addresses stored in all the router tables of all routers on the Internet. Routers are organized hierarchically in layers. If a router cannot route a packet to the networks it knows about, it merely passes off the packet to a router at a higher level in the hierarchy. This process continues until the packet finds its destination.

This gateway function is built into network routers that connect networks to other networks via communication links or WANs. The fundamentals of internetworking devices are similar regardless of the type of telecommunications link you're using to connect to the Internet.

Most router vendors now offer affordable and relatively easy-to-use routers designed for smaller organizations. ISDN spawned the first generation of these new low-cost routers for smaller organizations to connect their Microsoft Windows networks to the Internet. Comparable routers are now available for most other digital communication technologies, such as Frame Relay and DSL (Digital Subscriber Line). Router vendors include Cisco (www.cisco.com), Ascend (www.ascend.com), Netopia (www.netopia.com), Bay Networks (www.baynetworks.com), and 3Com (www.3com.com).

Microsoft's RRAS service

Microsoft's Routing and Remote Access Service (RRAS) software provides routing capabilities that enable you to use your Windows NT Server as a router. RRAS provides small office sites with routing and remote access, as well as Virtual Private Network (VPN) all in one package, which is free for the downloading from the Microsoft Web site (www.microsoft.com).

RRAS is a software solution that must be used with third-party adapter cards. You can use RRAS with most industry-standard PC hardware and LAN-to-WAN cards. For example, using a Diamond Multimedia NetCommander ISDN adapter as the device, you can run the card as a router for connecting your LAN to the Internet via ISDN. This solution can save hundreds of dollars — due to an adapter card costing under $200 versus a $700 router. Routing becomes a functions of Windows NT software, not router firmware.

Routing and Remote Access Service features include the following:

- A unified service for routing and remote access that's integrated with the operating system
- A full set of routing protocols for IP and APIs for third-party routing protocols
- An easy, intuitive graphical user interface
- Demand-dial routing
- PPTP (Point-to-Point Tunneling Protocol) server-to-server for secure Virtual Private Networks
- RADIUS (Remote Authentication Dial-In User Service) client support

Before you install RRAS, you need to install all the hardware on the computer you will be using as a router. This hardware includes modems, ISDN devices, or other remote access devices for remote access connectivity, as well as network adapters for network connectivity.

Microsoft Internet Connection Service

The Windows NT 4.0 Option Pack includes an upgrade to the Windows NT Remote Access Service (RAS) called Internet Connection Service (ICS). RAS is a Windows NT Server feature that lets mobile or remote users connect to the NT Server network via a dial-up connection. ICS extends RAS services to access to an NT Server network via the Virtual Private Network (VPN). VPN is a technology that creates a private tunnel between two computers over the Internet. This tunnel carries encrypted data over the unsecured Internet that only the two computers using the VPN technology can decipher.

Your organization can use VPN to replace standard dial-up lines for users to connect to your intranet. Instead of having a user dial in to a dedicated line at the office, you set up VPN on the Windows NT Server and the client computer. The user accesses the Internet via any Internet service provider and uses the VPN tunnel to access the Windows NT Server connected to the Internet. This configuration lets you provide network services over the VPN tunnel without incurring the costs for traditional dial-up telephone lines and modems. The downside of VPN is its reliance on the Internet as the transport vehicle for your data, which means your VPN traffic must vie with your general Internet traffic for the bandwidth.

Making the ISP Connection

Shopping for the right Internet service provider is important and is well worth the time it takes to research your options. Connecting to an ISP that provides poor service and having to change to another ISP is a time-consuming and expensive proposition, so be sure that you evaluate and understand all the steps along the way.

Internet service providers are at the center of your Internet connection. The ISP typically acts as your interface for the entire process of getting your Internet connection up and running. The local telephone company, however, installs and maintains the communications link. An ISP is really the retailer of bandwidth from large wholesalers, which are the telephone companies.

Your bandwidth capacity to the ISP and, in turn, to the Internet is only as good as the ISP's connection to the Internet. ISPs are in the business of leveraging bandwidth by sharing it among multiple users. In heavy traffic conditions, you may get less bandwidth than you're paying for — a common problem. If possible, go with an Internet provider that has a direct connection to the Internet, not one that connects to another wholesale Internet service provider. The more layers between your Web server and the Internet, the more likely you'll be shortchanged in bandwidth delivery. Providers that connect to the Internet backbone have direct access. If your provider leases a connection from one of the direct access providers, your connection may or may not be slow, depending on the connection; but the farther away you are from the backbone, the slower your connection is likely to be.

Finding an Internet service provider

Currently, approximately 2,500 ISPs are in the United States. Internet access is available from national, regional, and local Internet service providers. In many cases, you may prefer regional or local ISPs to the larger national providers, but it depends on your location and the level of competition in your area. Regional and local ISPs are more likely to offer better services and rates than those of the nationals, although you can always find exceptions.

Internet.com's "The List" provides the most comprehensive database of ISPs at `thelist.internet.com`. You can search by area code or country code as well as for national ISPs in the United States and Canada. You can also find ISPs in the Yellow Pages under Computers and Networking, and perhaps in the business section of your local newspaper.

Measuring ISP performance and reliability

Bandwidth by itself is not the only determining factor in choosing a connection. An Internet service provider's performance is also important. If an ISP's network is being slowed down by large amounts of packet loss or long delivery times, called latency, you are not getting the delivery rate you're paying for. The service provider's own network can create a bottleneck that can hamper your connection, regardless of the bandwidth between the ISP and your premises.

Latency and packet loss can also have a dramatic impact on your Internet connection. Network *packet loss* happens when a packet doesn't make it to its destination within a reasonable amount of time and must be re-sent. *Latency* is the time it takes to get data from one point to another. Latency affects Web users in terms of the amount of time it takes for a user to get the request from the browser to the server, followed by the time it takes to get the data from the server back to the browser. *Throughput,* the total amount of data that gets from one point to another in a certain period of time, is connected to both packet loss and latency.

Another important point about your Internet connection is that it works consistently. All networks fail at some time, but the important factor is how quickly the ISP corrects the problem and restores your service. Some ISPs offer service guarantees; others offer rebates for downtime.

Pinging an ISP

A simple way to evaluate an ISP is to ping its host machines and look at the statistics returned. You use the `ping` command at the Windows NT command prompt to check the IP address of the ISP's gateway. A ping returns important statistics that will help you evaluate the ISP's performance, including minimum, average, and maximum latencies and the percentage of lost packets. Good latency times for a local ISP are 45ms (milliseconds) for a 56 Kbps connection and 7ms for a 1.54 Mbps connection. An acceptable packet loss range is 1 to 4 percent. Use `ping` over a period of time to develop a chart of statistics that will give you a reasonable profile of what kind of service you can expect from the ISP.

Using Net.Medic

Net.Medic from VitalSigns Software (www.vitalsigns.com) lets you monitor behind the scenes of your Internet connection. With Net.Medic, you can monitor and diagnose the cause of slow response times from Web sites, whether the cause is at the client level, the ISP, the Internet backbone, or the Web server. Figure 5-1 shows the Net.Medic window display.

Figure 5-1:
The Net.Medic window provides a real-time, visual readout of the status of your Internet connection.

Net.Medic animates your end-to-end connection, showing you exactly what is occurring across the Internet, including traffic jams and bottlenecks. It tells you whether the network is congested or the connection is slow by using green, yellow, and red indicators to highlight the responsiveness of each component. Net.Medic monitors and reports your ISP's performance, including the average connect rates and other data about the service levels you actually experience.

Net.Medic Pro lets you simulate a user's experience connecting to your Web server. This gives you additional insight into your Internet-based server activities as well as the ability to prevent problems before they occur. You can use Net.Medic on your intranet as well. Net.Medic lists for $49.95, and Net.Medic Pro lists for $499.95.

Know the ISP's upgrade options

In most cases, you'll want to upgrade your connection as the popularity of your Web site grows. The cost is usually incremental when you upgrade within the same type of bandwidth technology, such as from a 384 Kbps Fractional T1 to a 784 Kbps Fractional T1. Upgrading gets expensive when you change from one technology to another. You need to figure out your upgrade plan and how an ISP handles upgrades before you commit to your dedicated connection. Also keep in mind that changes in your Internet connection can take time — from a few days to months.

Internet Security Issues

Connecting your Web server to the Internet opens up the issue of protection for your Web server and your local network from outside intruders. Security starts with planning the Web server's placement within the context of your organization's existing network. Connecting your Web server to your local network and the Internet requires more sophisticated security solutions. To prevent an external user from accessing unauthorized areas on your network or to prevent your internal network clients from accessing external resources, you must enter the realm of firewalls, proxy agents, and other alternatives. In many cases, you share your Web server's Internet connection with clients on your network. This section presents an overview of the security issues and options you need to address as part of connecting your Windows NT Server running IIS to the Internet.

Using a standalone Web server

For security at the simplest level, yet offering the best protection for your internal network, you can build a standalone Web server. This means using a dedicated Windows NT Server machine running IIS that isn't connected to your internal network. The dedicated connection to the Internet from your ISP connects exclusively to that PC. This can be a reasonable option for small businesses because it protects the internal network from exposure to the Internet and allocates the full resources of the PC and the Internet connection to serving Internet users. Setting up your NT Server as a standalone Internet server guarantees that the worst an intruder can do is to damage the particular server because there is no physical connection between the networks. The Web server running on this isolated PC can be managed from that particular machine or by a remote connection via the Internet. Internet Information Server provides tools for remote management. The downside is that you deny bandwidth access to your internal network users, and you add more complexity to managing the Web site from other PCs in your organization.

Using the two-protocol solution

A step above the standalone system approach is using the two-network-card solution, or dual-homed solution. One network card is bound to TCP/IP and a specific IP address for communicating with a router that connects to the Internet. The other network card installed on the Windows NT Server machine handles internal network traffic based on a different network protocol, such as the Microsoft NetBEUI protocol. This approach separates one network from another by preventing the mixing of packets. In this way, the two networks operate separately on the Windows NT machine. This enables your local network to have access to the NT machine and IIS, but prevents clients from having access to the Internet via TCP/IP.

As you can find out later in this chapter, a variation of this two-network-card solution uses a special piece of software called a proxy server, which allows both networks to use TCP/IP.

Types of Internet threats

The Internet is a double-edged sword. On the one side, its open TCP/IP protocols and networking environment facilitate information sharing, improve connectivity, and provide greater access to the underlying network. On the other side, the same open protocols and networking systems that make the Internet popular also increase the threat of malicious attacks. Connecting your local network to the Internet via TCP/IP can open the doors to a variety of attacks from outsiders to gain access to your private resources or to create havoc in your local network or Internet connection.

Following are the three common forms of security attacks to networks:

- **Denial of service attack.** This form of attack is usually achieved by flooding target victims with enough volume that they cannot use the service in question. Flooding an e-mail box is a common use of this threat. However, any type of service for which users rely on timely access is potentially vulnerable to this type of attack.

- **Network packet sniffing.** Programs called *packet sniffers* capture packets from the local area network and display them in a readable manner. The source and destination users of this information probably never even know that the information has been tapped.

- **IP spoofing.** An *IP spoof* is when an attacker uses a unique Internet address of an unsuspecting target user. The key issue in an IP spoof attack is that the IP address of a particular machine on the Internet or within an intranet is controlled and managed entirely by the owner or administrator of that machine and not an intruder.

Firewalls

A *firewall* is an intermediary computer running special software or a standalone device (such as a router) that stands between the Internet and your network. A firewall imposes a specifically configured gateway between the outside world and your local network. It protects your network by keeping unauthorized individuals from directly accessing machines on your private network.

A firewall can lessen the risk associated with an Internet connection to your network, but it can never remove all risks.

A firewall's primary purpose is to control access, which it does by using identification information associated with TCP/IP packets to make a decision about whether to pass the data on to the local network or deny access. This decision is based on a set of rules that describe which packets or sessions are allowed.

Firewalls differ in their architecture and features. The two primary types of firewall architectures are packet filter firewalls and proxy firewalls. Hybrid firewalls incorporate some mix of both architectures.

At a minimum, all firewalls use the five pieces of information found in the IP packet to make decisions, as described in Table 5-3. These basic components are the protocol, destination IP address, destination IP port, source IP address, and source IP port. By using the destination and source IP addresses and IP port information contained with the packet, a firewall can either accept or reject the packet. It can also accept or reject packets based on the protocol contained within the packet. The firewall can log this activity to determine who may be attempting to access the network and issue an alarm to the administrator to help detect suspicious activity as it is occurring.

Table 5-3	Basic Components Used by a Firewall in an Internet Environment
Component	*What It Is or Does*
Protocol	Transmission Control Protocol (TCP) or User Datagram Protocol (UDP)
Destination IP address	Identifies the location of the computer receiving the data transmission
Destination IP port	Identifies the application on the computer receiving the data transmission
Source IP address	Identifies the location of the computer initiating the data transmission
Source IP port	Identifies the application on the computer initiating the data transmission

Packet filter firewalls

A *packet filter firewall,* also known as a *screened-host gateway,* offers basic network access control based on protocol information in the IP packet. When the IP packet arrives at the firewall, this information is compared to a collection of filtering rules. These rules specify the conditions under which packets should be passed through or denied access. Most packet filter firewalls are incorporated into routers because packet filtering to restrict access is a logical extension of the router's functionality. As far as the outside world is concerned, the only accessible machine on the inner network is the specified host machine. Packet filtering firewalls are generally considered less secure than application-level gateways.

Proxy firewalls

Proxy firewalls, which are also referred to as *application* or *session-level firewalls,* go beyond the basic packet-filtering mechanism. They utilize a network session as their key means to accept or reject network requests. Sessions are represented by a set of IP packets that have the same address information. A given network application may spawn several sessions to perform its service. For example, Web browsers such as Internet Explorer will generate multiple sessions as they request files from various parts of the Internet. Session-aware firewalls provide better security than just plain packet-filtering firewalls.

A proxy firewall stops all network sessions, and then creates a new separate session to the desired destination as authorized. It shuttles information from the original connection to the second connection. Proxy firewalls are implemented as software gateways on a host platform, which can be a computer or a router. A proxy server does not allow any packets to pass directly between two networks. Instead, the proxy server requires that the original connection be made to a special-purpose application — referred to as the *proxy* — on the firewall. The proxy application determines whether to actually establish a connection to the requested destination host on behalf of the originating host.

In essence, the proxy server masquerades as the destination computer to the network client and as the network client to the destination computer. To gain access to your internal network, external users have to know the IP address of the client computer, the IP address of the proxy server, and the IP port that the proxy server is monitoring. They will also have to be on the allowed access list (usually based on the external client's IP address). If any of these items are unknown, the external user cannot connect to the client on the other side of the proxy server.

The proxy server relies on a *dual-homed gateway,* a computer with two separate network interface cards. One interface is connected to the local network and the other is connected to the outside world. No direct traffic exists between the two networks, so to provide access to the Internet from the internal network, programs known as proxies run on the gateway machine. A proxy's job is to accept requests from a machine on the internal network, screen them for acceptability according to specified rules, then forward them to a remote host on the Internet. Firewalls based on the dual-homed gateway are usually the most restrictive. Outgoing calls are restricted to the number of services for which the proxy software is available, and all network-aware programs on the internal network have to be modified to work with the proxies.

Microsoft Proxy Server

Microsoft Proxy Server 2.0 is a full-featured firewall product that delivers controlled Internet access and Web usage monitoring. Microsoft Proxy Server creates faster and more efficient Web access for your network clients and protects your network against outside threats from the Internet. As a BackOffice family member, it's designed specifically for Windows NT Server. Microsoft Proxy Server 2.0 lists for $995, but you can download a free evaluation copy from the Microsoft Web site at www.backoffice.microsoft.com/downtrial/.

Proxy Server also includes a Web cache server. *Caching* improves the performance your network clients see by cutting down on the number of requests the client needs to generate for servers on the Internet. Cached information is stored on the Proxy Server machine and is typically updated every few hours or days. Caching is only as good as the delays in information your company will accept.

One of the nicest features of the Proxy Server is network separation and address translation. Using two network interfaces, namely any combination of network interface cards, modems, or ISDN adapter cards, you can truly separate your internal network from the Internet. The Proxy Server's Web Watcher Proxy sets itself up on your Windows NT Server and broadcasts only one registered IP address to the Internet. When the Proxy Server receives an internal request (a client on the network trying to access a Web page), it hides the client's unregistered IP address and presents the request using the one fully qualified address. This means you can set up an unregistered TCP/IP network to access the Internet through one valid IP address.

Proxy Server 2.0 delivers firewall-class security via its packet-filtering capability. Besides being resistant to common attacks such as IP spoofing, Proxy Server provides packet filtering and access control to block users behind the proxy from accessing certain sites and resources. This feature lets an administrator reject specific packet types at the IP level before they reach higher-level application layer services.

Enabling packet filtering causes Proxy Server to drop all packets sent to a destination, except those that match a list of predefined packet filters. You can create a filter for the packet types you want the Proxy Server to accept, or use one of Microsoft's default packet filters. Microsoft has defined a set of default packet filters, which are reasonable configurations. Proxy Server 2.0 can alert you to suspicious activity at the packet level. For example, if the proxy server rejects more than 20 packets in one second (the default), you're alerted that your network may be under attack.

Proxy Server includes a new feature called *dynamic packet filtering*. As you might recall, a packet filter does its job based on a TCP service and a port number. For example, a Web server typically uses port 80. A packet filter must always be listening at port 80 for any traffic bound for the Web server. This means the system has a port that is always open, which an intruder could exploit. In dynamic packet filtering, the proxy listens to port 80 but the port is not truly open. When a request is made at port 80 for an HTML document, the proxy opens the port to allow the packet through. As soon as the conversation is over, the proxy closes the port and the system is locked down again.

For more information on the Microsoft Proxy Server, point your Web browser to `www.microsoft.com/proxy/`.

Part II
Taking Control of Your IIS Server

The 5th Wave   By Rich Tennant

"Hurry, Stuart!! Hurry!! The screen's starting to flicker out!!"

In this part . . .

This part begins your Webmaster training starting with the fundamentals of working with the Internet Service Manager snap-in, which is part of Microsoft Management Console. You then take a whirlwind tour of all the Web and FTP server configuration properties available to you. Building on your Web site administration skills, you continue working with more Web site management tools. You then go on to master setting up and running FTP (File Transfer Protocol) servers for fast and efficient file transfers across your intranet or the Internet. This part ends with detailed coverage on how to enhance your Web and FTP servers with a variety of security protections using a combination of IIS and Windows NT Server security features.

Chapter 6

Internet Service Manager Fundamentals

· ·

· ·

The first step to mastering Internet Information Server is to become acquainted with Internet Service Manager — the control center for managing all your IIS servers. Getting to Internet Service Manager in IIS 4 requires navigating through a new Windows NT tool called Microsoft Management Console. This chapter explains the fundamentals of working with both Microsoft Management Console and Internet Service Manager, followed by a whirlwind tour of Web and FTP server configuration properties.

Taking Control of Microsoft Management Console

Microsoft Management Console (MMC) is part of the Windows NT 4.0 Option Pack and was automatically added to Windows NT Server when you installed IIS. MMC provides a framework in which programs called snap-ins operate using a standardized interface. MMC has no management control of any applications; it's simply a container for organizing and integrating multiple applications.

Microsoft is making MMC the new interface for the administration of all Microsoft BackOffice and third-party applications in Windows NT 4.0, as well as in the forthcoming Windows NT 5.0. Internet Information Server 4.0 is the first application to use the MMC interface. Figure 6-1 shows the Microsoft Management Console window with the Internet Information Server and Microsoft Transaction Server snap-ins. The Microsoft Transaction Server snap-in is part of Internet Information Server.

The Microsoft Management Console window borrows heavily from the Windows NT Explorer interface. Like other Windows applications, the application window is the parent window, and the document window is a child window. With an application in the MMC, the two panes of a console document include objects from the specific snap-in. An MMC snap-in can be a standalone application or an extension snap-in that works only with another snap-in. A snap-in adds its own collection of context menu items, property pages, toolbars, and wizards.

Using MMC, you can create custom documents with any collection of objects you want to use for specific operations. You can create and save document windows as MSC files, which you can then open as needed and even send to other users for their own use. MSC (Management Saved Console) files contain the settings and components for a specific document. You can create documents that include a collection of objects for handling one specific task or an entire series of operations.

Figure 6-1:
The
Microsoft
Management
Console
window
showing the
Internet
Information
Server and
Microsoft
Transaction
Server
snap-ins.

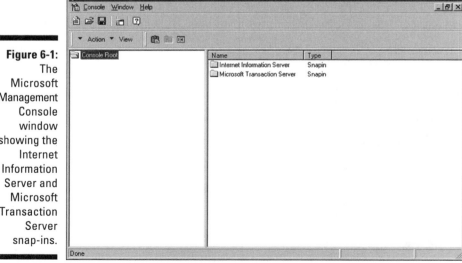

Looking around the MMC windows

Like other Windows programs, the MMC window includes a parent window for the application and a document window. Clicking on the Restore button for the document window shows the document window for the default IIS setup, as shown in Figure 6-2.

The MMC parent window contains the master menus and toolbars. The console document has two items on the left toolbar named Action and View. These drop-down menus include some standard MMC menu items as well as menu items provided by the snap-in. MMC has a few standard elements: creating new windows, opening and saving consoles, creating new consoles, and managing snap-ins. All other management operations are a function of the snap-in. The document toolbar for the IIS snap-in includes its own collection of command buttons.

You can look at the folders and files in the results pane in four standard views, by clicking the View menu. The default view is the Detail view, which provides the most information. You can click the Show/Hide Scope button to hide the scope pane, as shown in Figure 6-3. Clicking the Show/Hide Scope button again returns the document window to the original scope and results pane view.

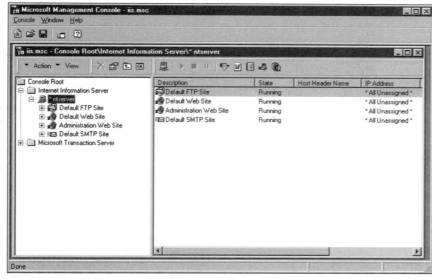

Figure 6-2:
The
Microsoft
Management
Console
parent
window and
child
document
window.

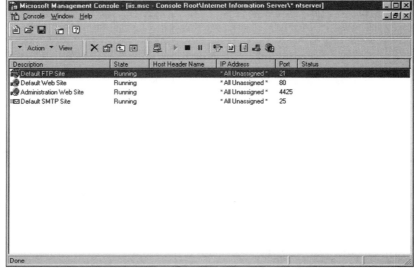

Figure 6-3:
The IIS
document
window
with the
scope pane
hidden.

Left pane, right pane

Like the Windows NT Explorer window, the MMC window includes a left and right pane arrangement. The left pane is called the *scope pane,* and the right pane is the *results pane*. The scope pane is a tree-structured name space, which you can expand and contract; the results of these actions appear in the results pane. When you select a snap-in object in the scope pane, a toolbar appears for the specific snap-in.

You can change how you view folders and files in the scope pane of the MCC window. The scope pane contains the folder view, and the results pane displays the contents of each folder. The listing of folders and subfolders can be expanded wherever you see a plus sign (+) next to the resource in the left pane. You can contract the list whenever you see a minus sign (–) next to a resource. You can choose from the standard large icon, small icon, list, and detail views by using the View menu on the MCC toolbar.

Clicking the + sign next to the name of your Windows NT Server computer (under the Internet Information Server folder) in the scope pane displays in the results pane all the servers running on the Windows NT Server machine. Clicking the + sign next to an object displays all the folders under that object. Double-clicking any folder in the scope pane displays the folder's contents in the results pane.

The IIS document window

Internet Information Server comes with its own default MMC document file, which appears whenever you open the Internet Service Manager. The default MMC document for Internet Information Server is iis.msc. The filename extension .msc means the file is an MMC document file. This document is your main interface to working with IIS. When you're comfortable with working with IIS, you can use the MMC to create documents that enable you to create different interfaces to IIS for performing specific functions.

Any time you make any changes to the iis.msc document, such as adding a new Web or FTP site, MMC prompts you to save your changes. Click Yes to save your changes. You can also save your changes periodically by clicking the Save button on the MMC toolbar.

You don't really need to master MMC beyond the default iis.msc document to work with Internet Information fundamentals. When you're more comfortable working with IIS, however, you'll probably want to spend time mastering the MMC.

Getting Started with Internet Service Manager

Internet Service Manager is where it all happens. It's where you manage, create, and remove Web, FTP, and other IIS servers. To start Internet Service Manager, choose Start⇨Programs⇨Windows NT 4.0⇨Option Pack⇨ Microsoft Internet Information Server⇨Internet Service Manager. The Microsoft Management Console window appears with the IIS snap-in.

The first time you open the MMC window, a Tip of the Day dialog box appears that includes a series of tips about Microsoft Management Console. If you want to keep the Tip box display for subsequent MMC startups, click the Close button after reading the tip. If you don't want the Tip of the Day popping up every time you execute MMC, click the Show Tips on Startup check box to remove the tip from subsequent MMC startups. You can always return to the Tip of the Day dialog box by choosing Help⇨Tip of the Day.

To display the IIS servers running on your Windows NT Server, do the following:

1. **In the scope pane, double-click the Console Root folder.**

    The Internet Information Server and the Microsoft Transaction Server snap-ins appear.

2. In the scope pane, double-click the Internet Information Server folder.

The console displays a computer icon with the name of your NT server computer.

3. Click the computer name.

The results pane displays all IIS servers installed on your NT server computer. A group of servers appears in the results pane. Figure 6-4 shows the default IIS servers running as a result of using the typical installation option.

The servers that appear in the results pane after selecting Internet Information Server include the following:

✔ **The Default Web Site** is the Web server you can use to build your first Web site. The Default Web Site is a fully operational Web site that allows anonymous access via TCP port 80.

✔ **The Administration Web Site** enables remote administration of your Web server via a Web browser.

✔ **The Default FTP Site** is a fully operational FTP (File Transfer Protocol) server using anonymous access TCP port 21.

✔ **The Default SMTP Site** supports the universal SMTP (Simple Mail Transport Protocol) for the Internet. This server can only forward mail from a Web site to a full-fledged e-mail server, such as Microsoft Exchange. The SMTP server forwards messages generated by users sending e-mail via the IIS Web server using the HTML `mailto` command.

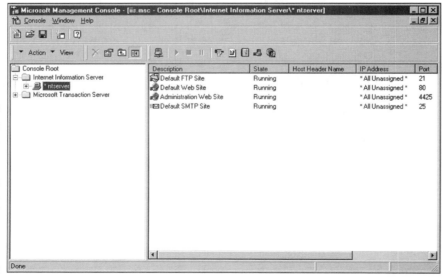

Figure 6-4:
The typical installation of IIS activates four servers that appear in the results pane.

Besides listing the IIS servers, the results pane also displays additional information about each server. Table 6-1 describes the six column headers that appear in the results pane.

Table 6-1	The Six Columns in the Results Pane
Column Header	*What It Does*
Description	Lists the name of every IIS server currently installed.
State	Displays the status of all installed servers. The default status is Running, which means the server is active. If you stop or pause a server, the State column displays Stopped or Paused, respectively.
Host Header Name	Provides a listing of any assigned host header names. A host header name is a way to use multiple domain names on one IP address. Initially, no host header names are assigned.
IP Address	Displays the entry All Unassigned, which means that no specific IP address has been assigned to the particular server. Any site using the All Unassigned IP address setting will respond to any unassigned IP address available on the NT Server.
Port	Displays the assigned port numbers for each server. Notice that the default port for the FTP server is 21, and the default port for the Web server is 80. Both these ports are the standard ports of entry for anonymous access to both sites.
Status	Displays information on activities affecting the specific server.

Starting, stopping, and pausing a server

Your IIS Web and FTP sites start automatically whenever you start up the Windows NT Server computer. You can stop a site from running or pause it while you make changes. To stop, pause, or restart a Web or FTP site, you can use two methods. The easiest method is to right-click the server in the results pane, and then choose Stop, Pause, or Start from the pop-up menu. The status of your sites appears in the State column in the results pane of Internet Service Manager.

The other method for stopping, pausing, or restarting a site is to use the Stop, Pause, or Start buttons, respectively, on the Internet Service Manager toolbar. Select the Web or FTP site in the results pane, and then click the Stop or Pause button. To start the Web site again, simply select it and click the Start button.

Express service to the Explorers

Many of the activities you'll be working with in managing your Web and FTP sites involve firing up Windows NT Explorer for folder and file management and Internet Explorer for browsing site content. For example, whenever you want to create a new site or virtual directory, you need to first create the directory you plan to use. Creating new directories is the province of Windows NT Explorer. Internet Service Manager makes opening these applications from inside the MCC window a breeze.

Right-clicking any server or folder in the results pane and then choosing Open or Explore displays the Windows NT Explorer window with the directory contents. For example, right-clicking the Default FTP Site and then choosing Open displays the Windows NT Explorer with the home directory `\Inetpub\ftproot` as the current directory. Within the Windows NT Explorer window, you can then create directories or navigate to any other directory on your local computer or network.

You can quickly check out any HTML file from the results pane by right-clicking the file and then choosing Browse from the pop-up menu. Internet Explorer appears with the contents of the HTML file.

Levels of IIS Properties

Properties are another term for settings that affect the operation of an object. Within the Internet Information Server constellation is a hierarchy of three levels of properties. These properties are inherited from the top to the bottom level, but each of the bottom two levels has veto power over the top-level properties. This enables a wide range of configuration options for your IIS servers.

Properties that define the settings for all servers are called *master properties.* These properties let you set the default settings for any Web or FTP sites you create. The Default Web Site and the Default FTP Site are based on the default configuration of the master properties. Master properties are the starting point for configuring a specific Web or FTP server.

In addition to the master properties that affect all Web or FTP servers, each server has its own properties. Each Web and FTP server includes a dialog box that contains the same properties included in the master properties dialog box for the respective server type (Web or FTP). Setting properties at the server level overrides the default settings that were used to create the site. The server-level properties, in turn, affect all folders and files associated with the specific Web or FTP server. Using folder and file properties, you can customize folders and files in a Web or FTP site.

Master of the properties

The IIS master properties are the default settings that appear whenever you create new Web and FTP sites. In other words, these properties are inherited from the master properties to the individual server properties. Settings on the higher global level are automatically passed on (that is, inherited) by the lower levels, but you can still edit these settings individually at the lower level by changing the specific server's properties. After a property is changed at the individual server level, the master defaults will not automatically override the individual settings. Instead, you'll receive a warning message asking you whether you want to change the individual site settings to match the new defaults.

Right-clicking your Windows NT Server computer in the scope pane and choosing Properties from the pop-up menu displays the *computername* Properties dialog box shown in Figure 6-5, where *computername* is the name of your NT Server computer.

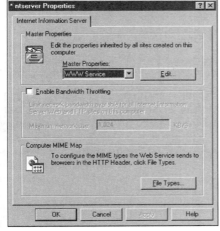

Figure 6-5:
The
computer-
name
Properties
dialog box.

Choosing WWW Service in the Master Properties list and then clicking the Edit button displays the WWW Service Master Properties dialog box shown in Figure 6-6. Most properties listed in the WWW Service Master Properties dialog box are the same settings that appear in the Default Web Site Properties dialog box (which is shown later in Figure 6-8).

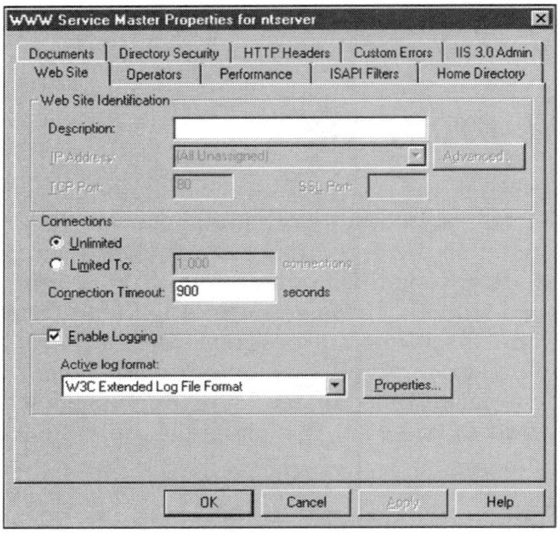

Figure 6-6:
The WWW
Service
Master
Properties
dialog box.

Choosing FTP Service in the Master Properties list and then clicking the Edit button displays the FTP Service Master Properties dialog box shown in Figure 6-7. As is the case with the WWW Service Master Properties dialog box, the settings are similar to the ones in the Default FTP Site Properties dialog box.

Server properties

Each server listed in Internet Service Manager has its own properties dialog box. To view the properties for a specific server in the results pane of the Internet Service Manager console, you can do one of the following:

- ✓ Right-click the site in the results pane, and then choose Properties from the shortcut menu.

- ✓ Click the site in the results pane, and then click the Properties button.

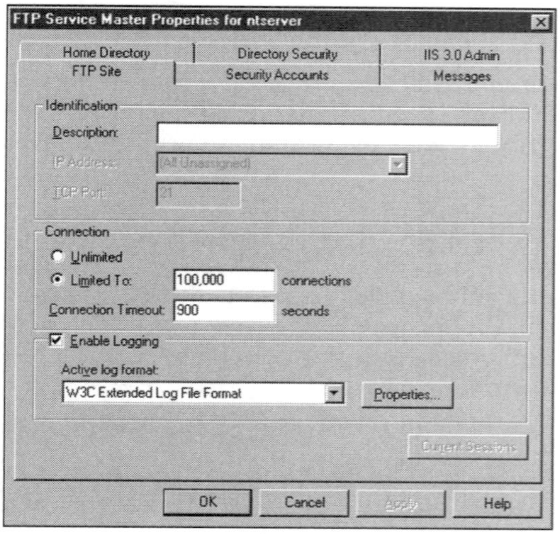

Figure 6-7:
The FTP
Service
Master
Properties
dialog box.

For example, you can display the properties of the Default Web Site by right-clicking it and then choosing Properties from the pop-up menu. The Default Web Site Properties dialog box appears, as shown in Figure 6-8. These properties enable you to customize the initial default settings of the specific Web server.

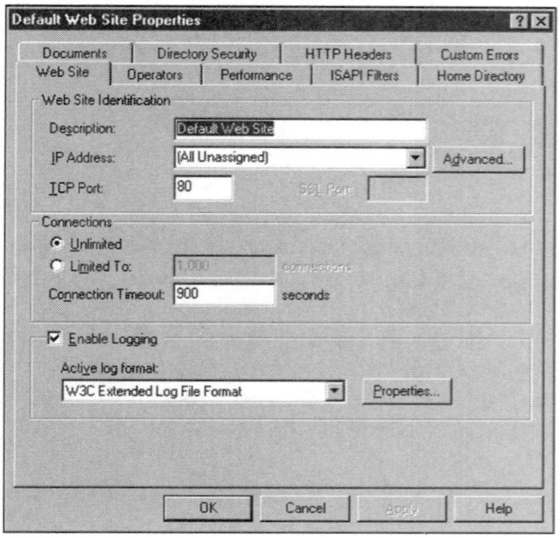

Figure 6-8:
The Default
Web Site
Properties
dialog box.

Folder and file properties

At the bottom of the properties hierarchy are the folder and file properties. These properties are for the specific folder or files within a Web or FTP site. Folder and file properties include a subset of the properties available to the entire site.

Right-clicking a file in the results pane and then choosing Properties in the pop-up menu displays the Properties dialog box for that specific file. For example, clicking the default.asp file in the Default Web Site root directory displays the default.asp Properties dialog box shown in Figure 6-9. File properties dialog boxes include four property pages: File, File Security, HTTP Headers, and Custom Errors.

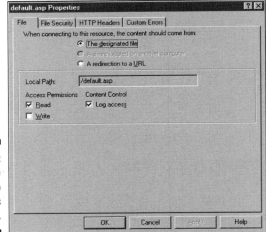

Figure 6-9:
The
default.asp
Properties
dialog box.

Right-clicking a folder in the results pane and then choosing Properties in the pop-up menu displays the Properties dialog box for the specific folder. For example, clicking the images folder in the Default Web Site root directory displays the images Properties dialog box shown in Figure 6-10. The folder properties dialog box includes five property pages: Directory, Documents, Directory Security, HTTP Headers, and Custom Errors.

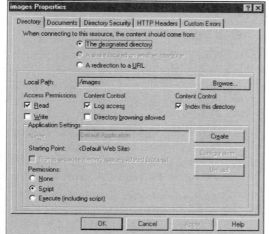

Figure 6-10:
The images
Properties
dialog box.

Touring the Web Server Properties

Each Web server has a number of properties you can use to manage it and improve its performance. The Default Web Site already running on your system is a good place to start your tour of the Web site properties. In the results pane, right-click Default Web Site, and then choose Properties from the pop-up menu.

The first thing you'll notice about the Default Web Site dialog box is the nine property sheets, each with its own tab. Table 6-2 briefly describes the primary purposes of each property sheet. The following sections go into more detail about the controls contained in these property pages to give you an overview of the organization of Web site properties. Don't worry about understanding every detail here; just relax and get oriented.

Table 6-2 The Property Pages in the Web Properties Dialog Box

Property Page	What It Does
Web Site	Sets the identification parameters for your Web site and manages connections and Web site logging.
Operators	Designates the Windows NT User Accounts for which you want to allow special Web site management privileges.
Performance	Improves the performance of the Web server by managing memory and bandwidth use.

(continued)

Table 6-2 *(continued)*

Property Page	What It Does
ISAPI Filters	Configures ISAPI (Internet Server Application Program Interface) filters. ISAPI is an application program interface for Windows NT that resides on a server computer for initiating software services executed from the Web server.
Home Directory	Changes the home directory for your Web site or modifies the properties (permissions and applications) of your home directory. The home directory is the central location for the files published in your Web site.
Documents	Defines the default document and document footers. A default document is your home page. A footer is a short addition to every Web page sent out by the server, such as a company logo.
Directory Security	Configures authentication schemes for user access to the Web server.
HTTP Headers	Defines content expiration parameters, custom HTTP headers, content ratings, and MIME (Multipurpose Internet Mail Extension) mappings.
Custom Errors	Creates custom error messages sent by the Web server to Web browsers.

Web Site

On the Web Site property sheet, rearing its head in Figure 6-11, you set the identification parameters for your Web site as well as manage connections and Web site logging. Table 6-3 describes the settings in the Web Site property sheet.

Table 6-3   Settings in the Web Site Property Sheet

Control	What It Does
Description	Names your Web site. This name appears in the Internet Service Manager. You can type any name you want for the server name because it has nothing to do with domain names used to access your Web server.

Control	What It Does
IP Address	Responds to all IP addresses assigned to this computer and not assigned to other sites, if you do not assign a specific IP address. For an address to appear in this box, it must have already been defined in the Windows NT Server's Network applet in the Control panel.
Advanced	Lets you add additional identities to your Web site using a unique combination of IP Address, TCP Port, and Host Header Name. A unique Web site can share two of these three characteristics.
TCP Port	Determines the port on which the service is running. The default is port 80. You can change the port to any unique TCP port number; however, clients must know in advance to request that port number, or their requests fail to connect to your server. A port number is required and cannot be left blank.
SSL Port	Determines the port used by Secure Sockets Layer (SSL) transmission. SSL is a protocol that supplies secure data communications through data encryption. This option is not available unless you already have a server certificate installed. The default is port 443.
Unlimited	Allows an unlimited number of connections to occur simultaneously.
Limited To	Limits the maximum number of simultaneous connections to the site. In the dialog box, type the maximum number of connections permitted.
Connection Timeout	Sets the length of time in seconds before the server disconnects an inactive user. This ensures that all connections are closed if the HTTP protocol fails to close a connection.
Enable Logging	Enables logging of your Web site activities to record details about user activity. You can create logs in your choice of format. The logs can tell you which users accessed your Web sites and what information they accessed. After you enable logging, you select a logging format in the Active log format list. The default logging file format is W3C Extended Log File Format.
Properties	Configures properties for the log format selected in the Enable Logging setting.

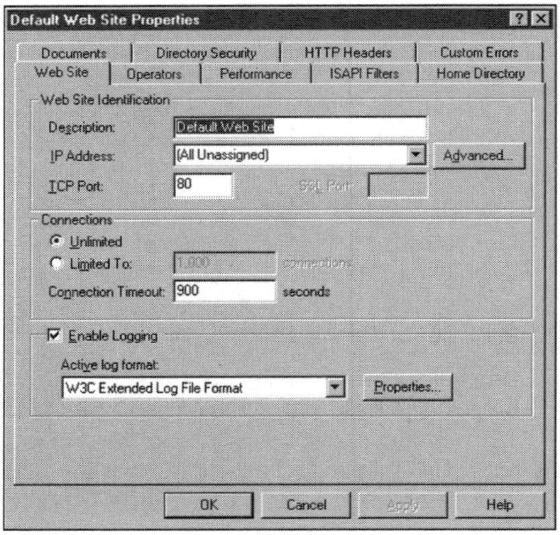

Figure 6-11:
The Web
Site
property
sheet.

Operators

The Operators property sheet, proudly shown in Figure 6-12, enables you to designate the Windows NT User Accounts for which you want to have administrative privileges for managing the specific Web site. To add a Windows NT User Account to the current list of accounts that have Web site administrative privileges, click the Add button. You can then choose your Web site operators from the Windows NT Server's User Manager for Domains listing. Clicking the Remove button removes the selected operator. Web site administrator accounts need not necessarily be members of a Windows NT Administrators group. However, a Web site operator can carry out only a limited number of administrative functions.

Performance

The Performance property sheet, displayed for your viewing pleasure in Figure 6-13, lets you set properties that affect memory and bandwidth use for your Web site. Table 6-4 describes the settings in the Performance sheet.

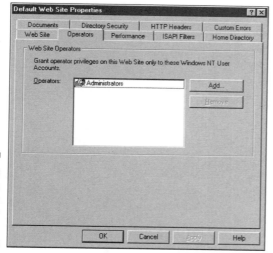

Figure 6-12:
The
Operators
property
sheet.

Table 6-4	Settings in the Performance Property Sheet
Control	***What It Does***
Performance Tuning	Defines the number of daily connections (hits) you anticipate for the Web site. If the number is set slightly higher than the actual number of connections, the connections are made more quickly and server performance is improved. If the number is much greater than the actual connection attempts, you waste server memory and reduce overall server performance.
Enable Bandwidth Throttling	Limits the bandwidth used by this Web site. This setting comes into play if you're sharing the Web server connection with other important network traffic.
Connection Configuration	HTTP Keep-Alives Enabled allows a client to maintain an open connection with the Web server, rather than reopening the client connection with each new request. Keep-Alives are enabled by default.

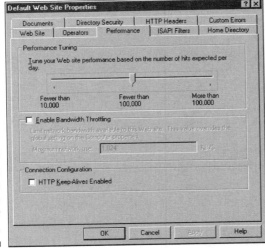

ISAPI filters

The ISAPI Filters property sheet, clearly displayed in Figure 6-14, lets you specify ISAPI (Internet Server Application Program Interface) filters, which are programs that respond to events during the processing of an HTTP request. Web browsers can use ISAPI to run remote applications that users activate by requesting a URL mapped to a filter. The table lists the status of each filter (loaded, unloaded, or disabled), the name of the filter, and the priority rating of the filter (high, medium, or low) set inside the DILL. The Add, Remove, and Edit buttons are used to modify filter mappings, and the Enable and Disable buttons (this is actually one button that changes names) are used to modify the status of filters.

Home directory

The Home Directory property sheet, which makes its debut in Figure 6-15, lets you change the home directory for your Web site or modify the properties of your home directory. The *home directory* is the central location for the files published in your Web site. A default home directory, called Wwwroot, is created for the Default Web Site when you installed IIS.

The following describes the key settings in the Home Directory sheet:

> ✔ The When Connecting to This Resource, the Content Should Come From option lets you specify the location of your content files for this particular Web site, which can be on the local computer, a shared directory on another computer on your local network, or a redirection to a specified URL.

✔ The Access Permissions properties appear when you are working with a local directory or a network share. Use these check boxes to determine the type of access allowed to a directory based on Windows NT File System permissions. <u>R</u>ead and <u>W</u>rite are the two settings.

✔ The Content Control properties appear when you are working with a local directory or a network share. These properties are Log Acces<u>s</u>, Directory <u>B</u>rowsing Allowed, <u>I</u>ndex This Directory, and <u>F</u>rontPage Web. Table 6-5 briefly describes these settings.

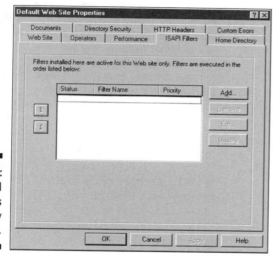

Figure 6-14:
The ISAPI
Filters
property
sheet.

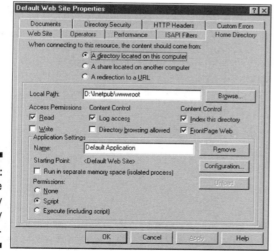

Figure 6-15:
The Home
Directory
property
sheet.

Table 6-5	Content Control Settings
Control	*What It Does*
Log Access	Records visits to this directory in a log file. Visits are recorded only if logging is enabled for this Web site. Logging is enabled by default. To turn logging off, select the Web site, click the Properties button on the toolbar, select the Web Site property sheet, and then clear the Enable Logging check box.
Directory browsing allowed	Shows the user a hypertext listing of the files and subdirectories in this virtual directory so that the user can navigate through the directory structure. A hypertext directory listing is generated automatically and sent to the user when a browser request does not include a specific filename and when no default document is in the specified directory. Because directory browsing reveals your Web site's structure to a user, you should generally leave this option disabled.
Index this directory	Instructs Microsoft Index Server to include this directory in a full-text index of your Web site. A full-text index enables users to quickly search for words or phrases in documents on your Web site. This feature is available only on Windows NT Server.
FrontPage Web	Creates a FrontPage web for this directory. Clear this check box to delete the FrontPage web from this directory.

The Application Settings group defines all the directories and files in a directory marked as an application starting point until another application starting point is reached. If you make your site's home directory an application starting point, every virtual directory and physical directory within your site can participate in the application. To make this directory an application starting point (and thus create an application), click the Create button. To disassociate this home directory from an application, click the Remove button.

Documents

The Documents property sheet, a model of perfection in Figure 6-16, lets you control which document appears when a browser request doesn't request a specific HTML filename. This is the default document that appears when a user enters a URL such as www.angell.com. The Web server searches the directory for the default documents, following the order in which the names appear in the list. The default entry is the document listed at the top of the list. The Enable Document Footer enables your Web server to automatically insert the specified file to any Web page. This footer is typically a logo image and identifying text that is appended to every page leaving the Web server.

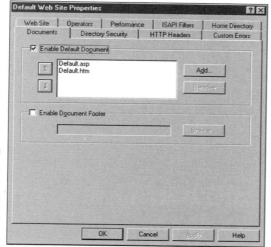

Figure 6-16:
The
Documents
property
sheet.

Directory security

The Directory Security sheet, frolicking into view in Figure 6-17, includes settings for managing your Web server's security. Anonymous Access and Authentication Control lets you set features to configure your Web server to confirm the identity of users before granting access. By default, this setting uses the IIS default setting IUSR_*computername,* which enables on a Windows NT Server computer anonymous logging on. When you installed the server, Setup created the account IUSR_*computername* in Windows NT User Manager for Domains.

The Secure Communications setting lets you set your Web server's Secure Sockets Layer (SSL) secure communications feature. You can use this security feature to encrypt your private communications with users who have SSL Certificates enabled. The IP Address and Domain Name Restrictions setting enables you to let or prevent specific users from accessing this Web site, directory, or file.

HTTP headers

The HTTP Headers property sheet, somberly displayed in Figure 6-18, lets you set a variety of values that are returned to the Web browser in the header of the HTML page. The settings for the HTTP Headers property sheet follow:

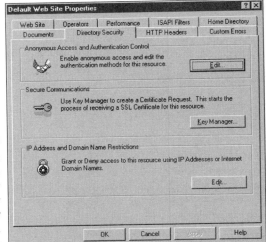

Figure 6-17:
The
Directory
Security
property
sheet.

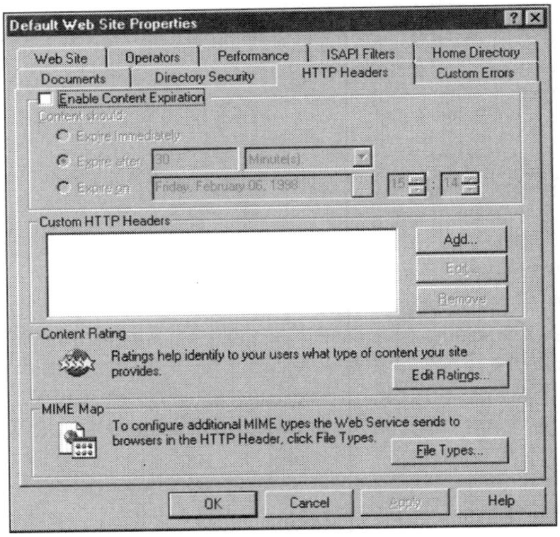

Figure 6-18:
The HTTP
Headers
property
sheet.

✔ The Enable Content Expiration setting includes a dating of time-sensitive information. The Web browser receives this information and compares the current date to the expiration date to determine whether to display a cached page or request an updated page from the server.

✔ The Custom HTTP Headers setting lets you send a custom HTTP header from the Web server to the client browser. To have your Web server send a header, click Add, and then type the name and value of the header in the Add Custom HTTP Header dialog box.

✔ The Content Rating setting enables you to configure your Web server's content rating features to embed descriptive labels in your Web page's HTTP headers. Web browsers can then detect these content labels to help users identify potentially objectionable Web content. Click Edit Ratings to set content ratings for this Web site, directory, or file. This feature works only with Microsoft Internet Explorer.

✔ The MIME Map setting enables you to configure Multipurpose Internet Mail Extensions (MIME) mappings. These mappings set the various file types that the Web service returns to browsers. Clicking the File Types button displays any registered file types installed on Windows NT Server and lets you add your own.

Custom errors

The Custom Errors property sheet, unmasked in Figure 6-19, lists what is returned to the browser when an HTTP error occurs. You have the option of using the default HTTP 1.1 error messages or customizing these error messages with your own information. The HTTP error code is listed as well as the output type, which can be the default HTTP 1.1 error message, an HTML file, or a URL. If the default HTTP 1.1 error is used, the contents of the error message appear under the Contents column of the table. If a file or a URL is used, the path to that file or URL appears under the Contents column of the table. All default HTTP 1.1 errors and their corresponding HTML document files are listed in the Custom Errors property sheet.

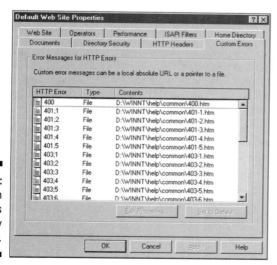

Figure 6-19:
The Custom
Errors
property
sheet.

Touring the FTP Server Properties

Like Web servers, each FTP server has a collection of properties you can use
to configure the server. The Default FTP Site is a good place to check out the
FTP server property sheets. In the results pane, right-click Default FTP Site,
and then choose Properties to open the Default FTP Site Properties dialog
box. An FTP server has five property sheets. Table 6-6 describes the primary
role of these property sheets. The following sections go into more detail
about the controls in these property pages to give you an overview of the
organization of FTP site properties. You'll note that many of these properties
are the same as the Web site property sheets.

Table 6-6	Property Sheets in the FTP Properties Dialog Box
Property Sheet	**What It Does**
FTP Site	Configures FTP Site identification, maximum connections, and logging
Security Accounts	Configures anonymous access and FTP Site operators
Messages	Configures welcome, exit, and maximum connection messages
Home Directory	Configures home directory and directory listing style
Directory Security	Configures access restrictions

FTP site

The FTP Site property sheet, appearing with great aplomb in Figure 6-20, lets
you set the identification parameters for your FTP server. This is the default
property sheet that appears when you open the FTP Properties dialog box.
Table 6-7 describes the settings in the FTP Site property page.

Table 6-7	Settings in the FTP Site Property Sheet
Control	**What It Does**
Description	Names your FTP site, which can be any name you want for the FTP server. This name appears in the tree view of Internet Service Manager.
IP Address	Responds to all IP addresses assigned to this computer and not assigned to other sites, if you do not assign a specific IP address. For a site IP address to be available in this list, you must install the IP address using the Network applet in the Windows NT Server's Control Panel.

Control	What It Does
TCP Port	Specifies the port on which the FTP service is running. The default port is 21, which is the recognized TCP port for anonymous FTP site access. You can change the port to any unique TCP port number; however, clients must know in advance to request that port number or their requests fail to connect to your server.
Unlimited	Allows an unlimited number of connections to occur simultaneously.
Limited To	Limits the maximum number of simultaneous connections to the site. In the dialog box, type the maximum number of connections permitted.
Connection Timeout	Sets the length of time in seconds before the server disconnects an inactive user. This closes a connection in the event the HTTP protocol fails to close a connection.
Enable Logging	Enables logging of your Web site activities to record details about user activity. You can create logs in your choice of format. The logs tell you which users accessed your Web sites and what information they accessed. After you enable logging, you select a logging format in the Active log format list. The default logging file format is W3C Extended Log File Format.
Properties	Configures the settings for the specified log format.
Current Sessions	Displays a dialog box that lists all currently connected users. You can use this feature to disconnect a user or all users from your FTP server.

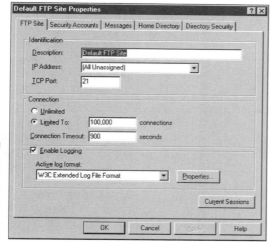

Figure 6-20:
The FTP Site property sheet.

Security accounts

The Security Accounts property sheet, appearing with trepidation in Figure 6-21, lets you control who can use the FTP server and specifies the account used by FTP clients to log on to the FTP server. Table 6-8 describes the settings in the Security Accounts property sheet.

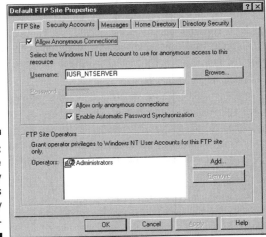

Figure 6-21:
The
Security
Accounts
property
sheet.

Table 6-8   Settings in the Security Accounts Property Sheet

Control	*What It Does*
All**o**w Anonymous Connections	Allows only anonymous connections. With this box selected, users cannot log on with user names and passwords. This option prevents access by using an account with administrative permission; only the account specified for anonymous access is granted access.
<u>U</u>sername	Specifies the username for establishing a connection to the FTP Server. For anonymous connections, the default IUSR_*computername* is used, where *computername* is the name of your NT Server machine.

Control	What It Does
Password	Used if you specify any user account other than anonymous.
Allow only anonymous connections	Prevents access by using an account with administrative permission. With this check box selected, users cannot log on with user names and passwords.
Enable Automatic Password Synchronization	Enables your FTP site to automatically synchronize your anonymous password settings with those set in Windows NT.
FTP Site Operators	Designates members of the Windows NT Administrative group to administer the Web site.

Messages

The Messages property sheet, shown with great clarity in Figure 6-22, lets you create welcome, exit, and maximum connections messages for your FTP server. The welcome message displays the text you enter in the Welcome text box to clients when they first connect to the FTP server. The exit message displays the text you enter in the Exit text box to clients when they log off the FTP server. The maximum connections message displays the text you enter in the Maximum Connections box to clients who try to connect when the FTP service already has the maximum number of client connections allowed.

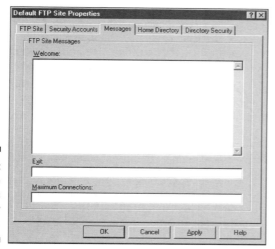

Figure 6-22: The Messages property sheet.

Home directory

The Home Directory property sheet, nestled into Figure 6-23, enables you to change the home directory for your FTP site or to modify its properties. The home directory is the central location for the published files in your FTP site. A default home directory, \Inetpub\ftproot, was created when you installed the FTP service. Table 6-9 describes the settings in the Home Directory property sheet.

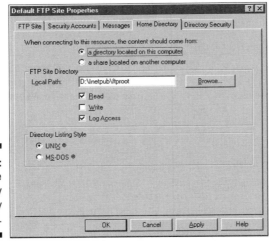

Figure 6-23:
The Home
Directory
property
sheet.

Table 6-9	Settings in the Home Directory Property Sheet
Control	*What It Does*
A directory located on this computer	Specifies the directory used by the FTP server, which is located on the local computer. The path entered in the Local path box uses the standard pathname, for example C:\FTP. The Browse button lets you navigate to the directory.
A share located on another computer	Specifies the directory used by the FTP server, which is located on another computer on the local network. The path entered in the Network Share box uses the Universal Naming Convention (UNC) server and share name, for example \\server\ftp. The Connect As button lets you connect to the machine on your network.
Read	Enables clients to read or download files stored in a home directory or a virtual directory. If a client sends a request for a file in a directory without Read permission, the FTP server returns an error. This permission must be selected for FTP directories.

Control	What It Does
Write	Enables clients to upload files to the enabled directory on your server. Select this permission only for directories that are intended to accept files from users.
Log Access	Lets your FTP site record visits to this directory in a log file. Visits are recorded only if logging is enabled for this FTP site. Logging is enabled by default.
UNIX	Displays files in the FTP site using the standard UNIX directory listing format. Because many browsers expect UNIX format, you should select UNIX for maximum compatibility.
MS-DOS	Lists files in the standard MS-DOS format.

Directory security

The Directory Security property sheet, exhibited with little fanfare in Figure 6-24, sets access by specific IP address to block individuals or groups from gaining access to your server. TCP/IP Access Restrictions lets you control access to your FTP site by specifying the IP address, subnet mask, or domain name of the computer or computers to be granted or denied access. If you choose to grant access to all users by default, you can then specify the computers to be denied access. Conversely, if you choose to deny access to all users by default, you can then specify which computers are allowed access. To add computers that you want to grant access to, click the Granted Access button and then click Add. Conversely, to deny access to certain computers, select the Denied Access button, and then click Add.

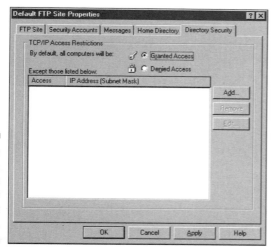

Figure 6-24:
The
Directory
Security
property
sheet.

Chapter 7

Basic Web Site Administration

. . . .

In This Chapter

▶ Adding content to your Web site

▶ Discovering the ins and outs of virtual directories

▶ Handling Web browser redirects

▶ Creating multiple Web servers

. . . .

*W*hen you installed Internet Information Server 4.0, it created the Default Web Site server and started it running on your Windows NT Server computer. This Web site is operating using the default properties defined by the master properties. Now it's time to get started with basic Web site administration using the Web Site Properties dialog box. Working with the Default Web Site is a good place to begin. After you get the basics down, you can add increasingly sophisticated capabilities to your Web server.

Making a Web Site Come Alive with Content

When you tested the installation of Internet Information Server on your system, you used a Web browser to view the default home page in the Default Web Site. This home page, named default.asp, is a placeholder for adding your own home page. If you already have Web pages ready, the first order of business is to add them to a Web site. This is a simple procedure in which you simply copy files to the home directory.

Each Web site must have one home directory, which is the central location for a Web server's content. This directory contains the home page that welcomes users and links to other pages and content on your site. You can use content stored in other directories, but you can have only one home directory.

Microsoft FrontPage 98 and Web content

Microsoft's FrontPage 98 is one of the best HTML authoring tools. FrontPage 98 uses a Microsoft Word-like interface to create sophisticated Web pages without any HTML coding. A powerful Web site content tool,

FrontPage 98 also includes tools to automatically update your Web site as well as manage its content from any PC on your intranet or via the Internet.

The path for the Default Web Site is \Inetpub\wwwroot on the drive where you installed IIS. You can always check the home directory of any Web site by right-clicking the server in the results pane and then choosing Properties from the pop-up menu. In the Web Properties dialog box, click the Home Directory property sheet. The path of your Web site directory appears in the Local Path box.

Using Windows NT Explorer, navigate to the \Inetpub\wwwroot directory. You'll notice that Internet Information Server installed a variety of folders and files in the directory already, as shown in Figure 7-1. You can start publishing documents immediately by simply copying your files into the home directory \Inetpub\wwwroot.

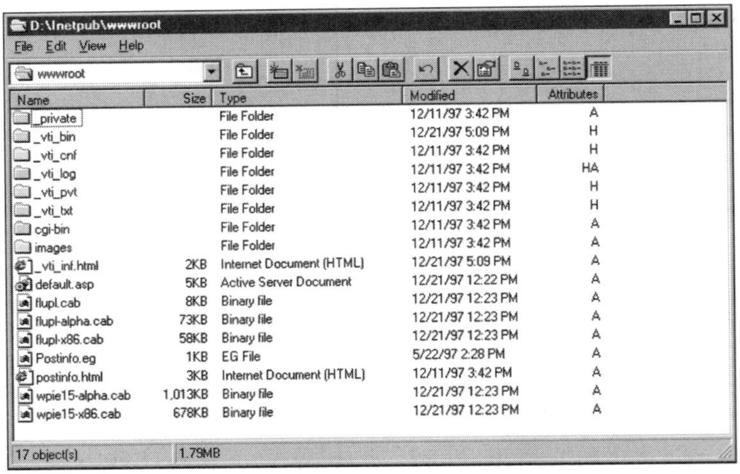

Figure 7-1: The Default Web Site's home directory as it appears in Windows NT Explorer.

Changing the Home Page

After you've added content to your Web site, you need to tell the Web server which page in the home directory is your home page. You can define any HTML or ASP (Active server pages) document as your default document for the Default Web Site server. An HTML document can have an .htm or .html filename extension. An ASP document has the filename extension .asp, the same as the default home page document. Active server pages is a powerful IIS feature that allows you to create dynamic content using scripts embedded in Web pages, which are processed on the server or client side. (See Chapter 14 for information on working with Active server pages and scripts.)

To specify your Web site's home page, do the following:

1. **In the results pane of Internet Service Manager, right-click Default Web Site, and then choose Properties from the pop-up menu.**

   The Default Web Site Properties dialog box appears.

2. **In the Default Web Site Properties dialog box, select the Documents tab.**

   The Documents property sheet appears.

3. **Click the Add button.**

   The Add Default Document box appears.

4. **Type the name of the document that you want as the home page, such as home.htm or default.html.**

   This is the file you created as your home page for the Web site and placed in the home directory.

5. **Click OK.**

   Your document name appears at the bottom of the list. You can specify more than one default document. The Web server returns the first default document it finds, beginning at the top of the list.

6. **Move your default document to the head of the list.**

   Select your default document at the bottom of the list, and then click the Up arrow button until your default document is at the top of the list.

Working with Virtual Directories

To publish from any directory not contained in your home directory, you need to create a virtual directory. A *virtual directory* is a directory that is not contained in the home directory but appears to client browsers as though it were. A virtual directory has an *alias,* a name that client browsers use to access that directory. For example, a Web user might enter `http://www.angell.com` to access the home page in the home directory. To access a virtual directory with the alias `sales`, the user enters the URL `http://www.angell.com/sales/`. The alias name `sales` is detached from the actual directory name and path on your computer or network but takes the user to that directory.

An alias is also more secure; users do not know where your files are physically located on the server and cannot use that information to modify your files. Aliases also make it easier for you to move directories in your site. Instead of changing the URL for the page, you change the mapping between the alias and the physical location of the page. Using virtual directories gives you a great deal of flexibility when it comes to deciding where to store files for your site and effectively lets you expand your site's storage capacity beyond the Windows NT Server machine.

You can create a virtual directory on the Windows NT Server running IIS, or a remote virtual directory located on a networked computer. The only requirement for creating virtual directories on a networked computer is that the remote computer shares the same Windows NT Server domain as the NT Server running Internet Information Server.

Getting from Internet Service Manager to Windows NT Explorer

When you want to create a new Web site or virtual directory, you need to first create the directory you plan to use. Creating new directories is the province of Windows NT Explorer. Internet Service Manager provides two ways to directly access Windows NT Explorer.

Right-clicking a Web server or any folder in the results pane and then choosing Open or Explore displays the Windows NT Explorer window with the directory contents. For example, right-clicking the Default Web Site and then choosing Open from the pop-up menu displays Windows NT Explorer with the home directory `\Inetpub\Wwwroot` as the current directory. You can then create directories in the home directory or navigate to any other directory on your local computer or network.

You can also quickly check out any HTML file from the results pane by right-clicking the file and then choosing Browse from the pop-up menu. Internet Explorer appears with the contents of the HTML file.

Creating directories in Windows NT

Before you can create a virtual directory, you need to create a real directory and place the content files into the folder. You create new folders in Windows NT Server using Windows NT Explorer.

After you create your directories, you then use a wizard in IIS to create the virtual directory. If the directories you want to add to your Web site are already in place, you can skip this section.

Windows NT Explorer is the folder and file-management tool for Windows NT Server. You can use Windows NT Explorer to create a directory by doing the following:

1. **Right-click the server, and then choose Open from the pop-up menu.**

   The Windows NT Explorer window appears with the server's content folders and files.

2. **Navigate to the drive and directory where you want your folder to reside.**

3. **Choose File⇨New⇨Folder from the Windows NT Explorer menu bar or right-click in the left pane to display the pop-up menu.**

   The folder appears with the New Folder label.

4. **Type the new name of the folder, and then press Enter.**

The directory you created uses the default Windows NT Server directory permissions or the default permissions you defined. The default Windows NT Server directory permissions enable open access to the directory by everyone on the Windows NT network and gives them full control over the files in the directory. When you use the Web server properties to take control of the directory as a virtual directory, you can specify a different set of permissions. See Chapter 10 for an explanation of working with permissions.

Creating a virtual directory

After you create the physical directory, you're ready to make it a virtual directory for your Web site. Here's how to create a virtual directory using the Default Web Site:

1. **In Internet Service Manager, right-click the Default Web Site.**

2. **Choose New⇨Virtual Directory.**

   The New Virtual Directory wizard appears, as shown in Figure 7-2.

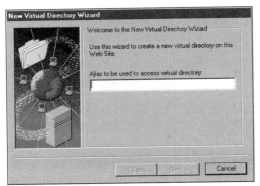

Figure 7-2:
The New
Virtual
Directory
wizard.

3. **Type the alias you want to use, and then click Next.**

For example, entering **sales** in the Alias To Be Used to Access Virtual Directory box means the URL for the directory becomes http://www.angell.com/sales/ for the Web site with a domain name of www.angell.com.

4. **Type the physical path of the directory or click the Browse button and navigate to the directory you want, and then click Next.**

This is the actual path of the directory. If you're entering a path for a directory on another computer, you must specify the directory's Universal Naming Convention (UNC) name and provide a username and password to use for access permission. UNC is a system of naming files among computers on a network so that a file on a given computer will have the same pathname when accessed from any computer on the network. An example of a UNC path is \\ntworkstation\content\.

If you use the Browse button to navigate to a directory on another computer on the network, the wizard automatically enters the UNC path for you.

5. **Choose the access permissions you want to specify for the new directory.**

The default settings, Allow Read Access and Allow Script Access, are fine for most virtual directories. You can change this setting at any time.

6. **Click Finish.**

Managing virtual directories

Any virtual directory you create appears in the listing of folders and files for the specific Web site. For example, if you created the virtual directory with the alias sales in the Default Web Site, double-click the Default Web Site

entry in the results pane and scroll down until you see the sales entry.
Notice in Figure 7-3 that the virtual directory alias appears in the Name
column and the path where the actual directory or file is located appears in
the Path column.

You can configure your virtual directory by right-clicking the alias and then
choosing Properties from the pop-up menu. For example, opening the Sales
alias displays the Sales Properties dialog box shown in Figure 7-4.

Figure 7-3:
In the
results
pane, the
sales alias
appears
along with
its path in
the Web
site listing
of folders
and files.

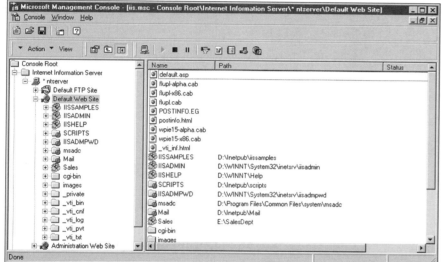

Figure 7-4:
The Sales
Properties
dialog box.

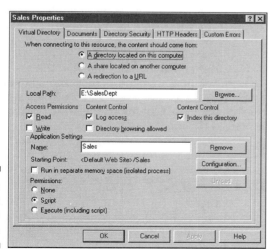

Specifying the home page

Just as you have to specify the home page you want to use for your home directory, you have to specify the home page for your virtual directory. Make sure you copied the Web document into your virtual directory, and then do the following:

1. **In the results pane, right-click the virtual directory name, and then choose Properties from the pop-up menu.**

   The Properties dialog box for the virtual directory appears.

2. **In the Properties dialog box, choose the Documents property sheet.**

3. **Click the Add button.**

   The Add Default Document box appears.

4. **Type the name of the document that you want as the home page, such as home.htm or default.html.**

   This is the file you created as your home page for the Web site and is in the home directory.

5. **Click OK.**

   Your document name appears at the bottom of the list.

6. **Move your default document to the head of the list.**

   Select your default document at the bottom of the list and then click the Up arrow button until your default document is at the top of the list.

7. **Click OK to exit the Properties dialog box.**

Renaming and deleting virtual directories

You can easily rename a virtual directory name by right-clicking its alias, and then choosing Rename from the pop-up menu. Type the new name of your text and press Enter.

To delete a virtual directory, right-click the alias name in the results pane, and then choose Delete from the pop-up menu. A message box appears to confirm the deletion. Click Yes. You can delete an alias also by selecting it in the results pane and then clicking the Delete button (the first button after the View menu) on the MMC toolbar.

Redirecting Web Browser Requests

Redirecting a Web browser request means your Web server forwards a browser request for a particular site or directory to another site or directory. These other locations can be on the local computer, on a directory on another computer connected to your network, or on a remote site on the Internet. Redirecting Web browser requests is a way to preserve the original address of your Web site or virtual directory even if the contents have moved to a new location. Redirecting a URL is useful when you are updating your Web site and want to make a portion of the site temporarily unavailable. Another use of URL redirection is when you change the name of a virtual directory and want links to files in the original virtual directory to access the same files in the new virtual directory.

You can redirect requests at the master properties, server, and folder and file level. In most cases, you'll redirect requests for a particular Web site or directory. The settings for redirecting requests for a directory are the same as for a Web site. For a directory, you use the Virtual Directory property sheet; for a Web site, you use the Home Directory property sheet.

Redirecting requests for specific files is the same as for directories and sites. You use the File property sheet in the File Properties dialog box. You access these properties for directories and folders using the same method. Right-click the folder or file in the results pane, and then choose Properties from the pop-up menu. This section explains how to redirect requests for your Web site; you can use these instructions also for redirecting requests for directories and files.

Redirecting to a local directory

You can easily redirect a Web browser to another directory on the local computer, which is your Windows NT Server computer. For example, the Default Web Site uses the path \Inetpub\wwwroot, which is your home directory. You can specify that whenever a Web browser enters the URL for the Web site, the request goes to another directory on your machine. For example, you might have a directory \temp for routing users to a temporary site while you do some work on the \Inetpub\wwwroot directory. From the users' viewpoint, they see no underlying change in the home directory.

To redirect Web browser requests for a Web site to another directory, do the following:

1. **In Internet Service Manager, right-click the Web site, and then choose Properties from the pop-up menu.**

2. **In the Web properties dialog box, click the Home Directory tab.**

3. **In the Home Directory property sheet, select the option titled A Directory Located on the Computer.**

4. **Enter the path of the directory for which you want to redirect Web browser requests.**

    You can do so in two ways. In the Local Path box, type the directory path. Or click the Browse button to navigate to and select the directory, and then click OK.

5. **Click OK to exit the Web Site Properties dialog box.**

Redirecting to a network share

In Windows NT, a *share* means to make system resources, such as drives and directories, available to users on the network. You can redirect Web browser requests to another drive and directory on any computer connected to the network. Here is how to redirect a Web browser to a directory on another intranet computer:

1. **In Internet Service Manager, right-click the Web site, and then choose Properties from the pop-up menu.**

2. **Click the Home Directory tab.**

3. **Select the option titled A Share Located on Another Computer.**

   The Local Path box changes to the Network Directory box, and the Browse button changes to the Connect As button, as shown in Figure 7-5.

4. **Enter the name of the directory to which you want to redirect requests.**

   You can do so in two ways:

   • In the Network Directory text box, type the name of the shared resource using the Universal Naming Convention (UNC) name for the location of the directory on another machine. The format for UNC is *servername**sharename*.

   • Click the Connect As button to navigate to the computer to select the directory.

5. **Click OK to exit the Web Properties dialog box.**

If you select a directory on a network share, you may need to enter a username and password to access the resource. Use the IUSR_*computername* account. If you use an account that has administration permissions on the server, clients can gain access to server operations. This seriously jeopardizes the security of your network. When you install IIS, it creates an account called IUSR_*computername,* where *computername* is the name of the NT Server computer. This account creates randomly generated passwords and is intended for guest access by the IIS Web, FTP, and other servers. The IUSR_*computername* account is given membership in the Windows NT Domain Users and local Guests groups. The account is also given permission to log on locally.

Redirecting to a URL

Redirecting to another URL (Uniform Resource Locator) means sending the Web browser request to another computer, directory, or file on the Internet. The URL can also point to the same things on your intranet running Microsoft DNS server. When a Web browser requests a page on your Web site, the Web server locates the page identified by the URL and returns it to the browser.

Here is how to redirect a Web browser to another URL on your intranet or the Internet:

1. **In Internet Service Manager, right-click the Web site, and then choose Properties from the pop-up menu.**

2. **Click the Home Directory tab.**

3. **Select the option titled A Redirection to a URL.**

   The Local Path setting changes to the Redirect To box and other settings appear, as shown in Figure 7-6.

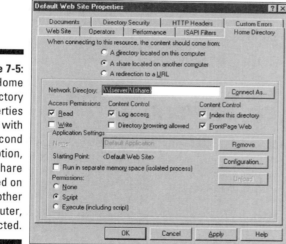

Figure 7-5:
The Home Directory properties page with the second option, A Share Located on Another Computer, selected.

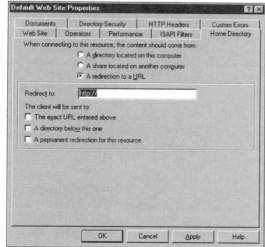

Figure 7-6:
Choosing the A Redirection to a URL option changes the settings in the Home Directory property sheet.

4. **In the Redirect To box, type the URL of the destination directory or Web site.**

   For example, to redirect all requests to a new Web site, enter the domain name. For example, to move `www.angell.com` to `www.bookware.com`, you would enter `http://www.bookware.com` in the Redirect To box.

5. **Select any of the following settings, if needed:**

   - The Exact URL Entered Above setting uses the redirection URL without adding additional information.

   - A Directory Below This One setting redirects the client to a subdirectory below the one in the URL.

   - A Permanent Redirection for This Resource setting makes a permanent redirection and provides the client with the message 301: Permanent Redirect.

6. **Click OK to exit the Web Site Properties dialog box.**

Creating New Web Servers

Internet Information Server 4.0 includes a new capability of supporting multiple Web servers running on a single Windows NT Server computer. This means you can create several Web sites targeted at specific groups of users. Any Web server created beyond the Default Web Site is a virtual Web server. Virtual Web servers allow one physical Web server to act as if it were actually several Web servers. This enables the same Web server to host a Web site with, for example, the domain name `www.angell.com` as well as a Web site with the domain name `www.bookware.com`.

Using redirect variables and wildcards

You use redirect variables and wildcards in the destination URL to precisely control how the original URL is translated into the destination URL. You can use redirection variables to pass portions of the original URL to the destination URL if you type them in the Redirect To text box. For example, if you enter `$V //myserver/scripts/myscript.asp`, the text string is mapped to the destination URL.

You can use redirect wildcards to match any number of characters in the original URL. Insert the wildcard character (*) directly into the Redirect To text box. You begin the destination URL with an asterisk and a semicolon, and separate pairs of wildcards and destination URLs with a semicolon. For example, to redirect all requests for `scripts/filename.asp` to a single file called default.asp, and to redirect all requests for `/scripts/filename.htm` to a single file called default.htm, you would type the following in the Redirect To text box for the /scripts virtual directory: `*;*.asp;/default.asp;*.htm;/default.htm`.

Each Web site has a unique mix of three elements that identify it for receiving and responding to requests. These three identity elements are an IP address, a port number, and a host header name. As long as one of these elements is unique to a specific Web site, it can operate as a virtual Web server. You can create Web sites using the following options and combinations:

- ✔ You can create virtual Web sites that have different assigned IP addresses but share the same default TCP/IP port 80 for anonymous access.

- ✔ You can create multiple Web sites that use the same IP address and port number as long as each site has a different host header name.

- ✔ You can create Web sites that share the same IP address and host header name but have different TCP/IP port numbers.

One of the most useful scenarios for mixing these elements is sharing the IP address and port with other Web sites but having different host header names. Using this strategy, you can operate multiple domain names on one IP address. *Host header names* are instructions returned to the browser via the header of the HTML page. The browser, in turn, uses these HTML commands to process information from the server. Each Web site is differentiated by its host header name, which is processed by the Web client browser. Both Microsoft Internet Explorer (3.01 and higher) and Netscape Navigator (3.01 and higher) support the use of host headers.

Windows NT Server allows you to assign multiple IP addresses to a single network adapter. Using Windows NT Server's Advanced IP Addressing feature, you can add multiple IP addresses to a network adapter card. Then you can host multiple Web sites, each with its own IP address and domain name. You can also add multiple network adapter cards, each of which can have multiple IP addresses assigned to support a number of Web servers. You use the IIS Internet Service Manager and DNS to configure the IP address and domain names. See Chapter 4 for more information on working with Microsoft DNS.

Setting up IP addresses in Windows NT Server

Before you can create a new Web server, you need your network adapter cards and IP addressees set up and working in Windows NT Server. Use the Network applet in the NT Server Control Panel to specify the additional IP addresses. You can bind the IP addresses to a single network card or assign them to multiple network cards. *Binding* is the term for the linking of an IP address to a network card. This section explains how to bind IP addresses to network cards in Windows NT Server.

Adding an IP address to a network card

If you have one or more network adapter cards installed on your system, you can assign a single IP address to each card. Here's how to bind an IP address to one or more network cards.

1. **In the Windows NT Server Control Panel, open the Network applet.**

2. **Click the Protocols tab, and then select TCP/IP Protocol.**

3. **Click the Properties button.**

   The Microsoft TCP/IP Properties dialog box appears.

4. **In the Adapter drop-down list, select the network adapter you want to bind the IP address to.**

5. **Click the Specify an IP Address option.**

6. **Enter the IP address and Subnet Mask IP address in their respective boxes.**

7. **Repeat Steps 4 through 6 for each additional network card you want to bind an IP address to.**

8. **Click OK twice to exit the TCP/IP Properties and Network dialog boxes, and restart Windows NT.**

Binding multiple IP addresses to one network card

Windows NT Server allows you to assign multiple IP addresses to a single network adapter, and you can have multiple network cards running with Windows NT Server. If you're using a single network adapter card and want to bind additional IP addresses to the network card, do the following:

1. **In the Control Panel, double-click the Network applet icon.**

2. **Click the Protocols tab, and then double-click the TCP/IP Protocol entry.**

   The Microsoft TCP/IP Properties dialog box appears.

3. **Click the Advanced button.**

   The Advanced IP Addressing dialog box appears, as shown in Figure 7-7.

4. **Click the Add button.**

   The TCP/IP Address dialog box appears, as shown in Figure 7-8.

5. **Type the IP address and Subnet Mask IP address, and then click Add.**

6. **Click OK three times to return to the Desktop, and then restart Windows NT.**

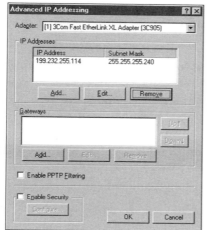

Figure 7-7:
Advanced IP
Addressing
dialog box.

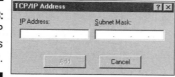

Figure 7-8:
The TCP/IP
Address
dialog box.

Creating a virtual Web server

You can create a new virtual Web site and use any combination of settings to make it unique, or you can change the settings of any existing Web server to ensure that no clashes exist with Web site identities. If you create or change an existing Web site with the exact mix of settings used by another Web site, IIS automatically stops the previous Web server and activates the one you just changed.

Before you create a virtual Web server, make sure you use Windows NT Explorer to create a directory that will be your home directory. When you choose to create a new Web server, IIS uses a wizard to walk you through the configuration process and asks you to specify a path for your Web site. Here is how you create a new virtual Web site:

1. **In the scope pane (the left pane) of Internet Service Manager, right-click the computer name for your Windows NT Server.**

2. **Choose New➪Web Site.**

   The New Web Site wizard appears.

3. **In the Web Site Description box, type the name for the new Web site, and then click the Next button.**

   Remember, the descriptive name appears in Internet Service Manager.

4. **In the Select the IP Address to Use for This Web Site list, choose the IP address you want to assign to the new Web site.**

   All the IP addresses in this list are bound to network cards running on your Windows NT Server computer. If an IP address you installed doesn't appear, enter it in the text box.

5. **In the TCP Port This Web Site Should Use box, type the TCP/IP port you want to use for the Web site.**

   The default TCP/IP Port 80 enables anonymous access to your Web server.

6. **Click the Next button.**

7. **Type the path for the home directory for your new Web site or use the Browse button to navigate to and select the directory.**

8. **Click the Next button.**

9. **Use the default permissions, and then click the Finish button.**

   The Web site is created and appears as an entry in the results pane with the name you gave it. After you create the Web site, you can make any configuration changes to it by opening its Properties dialog box.

Using host headers

Host header names add another way to enable the hosting of multiple Web sites even when these sites share the same IP address and TCP/IP port number, such as 80. Each Web site is differentiated by its host header, which is processed by the Web client browser.

Both Microsoft Internet Explorer and Netscape Navigator support host headers coming from your Web server. If a browser user attempts to contact your Web site with an older browser that does not support host headers, however, the visitor gets the default Web site assigned to the address, which may not necessarily be the site requested. Typically, you should display your home page that references the context for the Web site sought. You can use a script to support the use of host header names for older browsers. Chapter 14 explains how to work with scripts.

To assign a host header name to an existing Web site, do the following:

1. **In the results pane, right-click the Web server you want, and then choose Properties from the pop-up menu.**

2. **In the Web Site property sheet, click the Advanced button.**

   The Advanced Multiple Web Site Configuration dialog box appears, as shown in Figure 7-9.

3. **In the Multiple Identities for This Web Site group, click the Add button.**

   The Advanced Web Site Identification dialog box appears, as shown in Figure 7-10.

4. **Leave the IP Address and TCP Port settings intact, but type your host header name in the Host Header Name box, and then click OK.**

   For example, you could enter the host header name of support.angell.com.

5. **If you'd like to add an additional host header for your Web site, repeat Steps 3 and 4.**

6. **Click OK three times to exit the Web Site Properties dialog box.**

Figure 7-9:
The
Advanced
Multiple
Web Site
Configuration
dialog box.

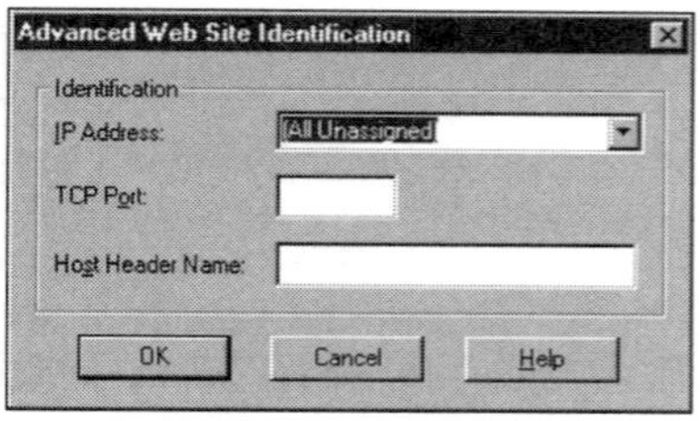

Figure 7-10:
The
Advanced
Web Site
Identification
dialog box.

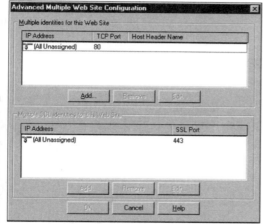

Your host header name must be entered as an entry in the DNS Server on your local Internet or as a registered name on the Internet. See Chapter 4 for more information on configuring the Microsoft DNS Server.

Sailing into TCP/IP ports

The universal port number for anonymous access to a Web site is 80. This means if you want a Web client to have access to your Web site without having to add a port number to the URL, you must use TCP/IP port 80. Otherwise, the Web client must know the unique assigned port number and enter it into the URL. If a Web server is using a different port number than 80, a user who doesn't know the unique TCP/IP port can't access the site. The URL for this nonstandard Web site would be something like: `http://www.angell.com:8001`, where 8001 is the port number. Typically, port numbers above 255 are reserved for private use of the local machine and numbers below 255 are defined as defaults for a variety of universal TCP/IP applications and services.

To convert an existing Web site that shares an IP address, a host header name, and a port number with other sites to a site that has a unique TCP/IP port number (other than 80), do the following:

1. **In the results pane, right-click the Web server your want, and then choose Properties from the pop-up menu.**

2. **In the Web Site property sheet, click the Advanced button.**

   The Advanced Multiple Web Site Configuration dialog box appears.

3. **In the Multiple Identities for This Web Site group, click the Add button.**

   The Advanced Web Site Identification dialog box appears.

4. **In the TCP Port box, enter the TCP/IP port number you want to use.**

5. **Click OK three times to return to Internet Service Manager.**

Chapter 8

More Web Server Management Tools

*I*nternet Information Server includes a number of tools to give you more control over how your Web servers operate. This chapter adds more Web site management tools to your Webmaster's toolbelt.

Limiting Your Connections

Managing your Web server connections helps you prevent it from getting overloaded with Web browser requests, or hits. IIS provides two ways to limit your connections. The first is controlling the number of simultaneous users connected to your Web server at any one time. The second is specifying the time that an inactive connection stays connected to your Web server.

Other factors play a big role in connections

The bandwidth capacity of your intranet or Internet connection, as well as the configuration of your PC hardware, determines your total capacity. However, limiting the number of simultaneous connections and setting other performance values lets you squeeze the most out of what you have. It's a fine art of balancing Web server activities on your intranet with other network activities.

Limiting simultaneous connections

You can easily limit the exact number of simultaneous connections your Web server will support at any one time. Your Web server will reject all connection attempts beyond the connection limit. When limiting connections to individual Web sites, keep in mind that most browsers typically make up to four simultaneous connections to download text and graphics from a page. The default setting is to allow an unlimited number of simultaneous users. The Unlimited option, in the Web Site property page, permits as many simultaneous connections as your bandwidth and processor can support.

To limit the number of simultaneous connections, do the following:

1. **In Internet Service Manager, right-click the Web site you want, and then choose Properties from the pop-up menu.**

2. **On the Web Site tab, select the Limited To option.**

3. **In the connections box, type the maximum number of simultaneous connections you want to allow.**

Cutting them off

Another way to manage connections involves restricting the time that connections are allowed to stay inactive before being cut off. When a browser unexpectedly stops working or a connection is lost in midstream, the site continues to process data for the connection until a timeout value is reached. Setting a timeout value reduces loss of processing resources for broken connections. The default timeout value is 900 seconds, or 15 minutes. In most cases, you'll want to reduce this setting to a more reasonable number. A typical value might be 300 seconds (5 minutes), after which the connection is closed.

To limit the number of seconds that the Web server allows a connection to be inactive, do the following:

1. **In Internet Service Manager, right-click the Web site you want, and then choose Properties from the pop-up menu.**

2. **In the Connection Timeout box, type the connection timeout value in seconds.**

   A good value is 300 seconds or less.

Enhancing Web Server Performance

Beyond limiting connections, you can improve your Web site's performance in another way. To improve your site's capability to handle requests, you can use three settings in the Performance dialog box, which is shown in Figure 8-1. These settings are Performance Tuning, Enable Bandwidth Throttling, and HTTP Keep-Alives Enabled, and this section explains how to work with them.

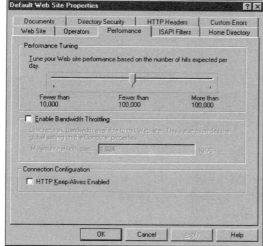

Figure 8-1:
The
Performance
dialog box.

Performance tuning

The Performance Tuning setting enables you to make adjustments to balance memory use against response time by estimating the number of hits, or connections, you expect. You set the slider to the estimated number of connections you anticipate receiving in a 24-hour period. You can adjust the Performance Tuning slider to one of three settings: Fewer than 10,000, Fewer than 100,000, or More than 100,000.

When estimating the Performance Tuning number for your Web site, remember that a single Web page can require several hits from a single Web browser.

If the number you choose is much greater than the actual connection attempts, server memory is wasted, and overall server performance is reduced. Maximizing memory performance may mean slightly slower request responses for users visiting your site. If you set the number slightly higher than the actual number of connections, connection attempts are faster. If you set the number much higher than the actual number of connection attempts, memory is wasted.

Putting the throttle on bandwidth

If a Web server is sharing a network connection with other services, such as an Internet connection for outgoing Web browser traffic, you may want to limit the bandwidth used by your Web server. By limiting the bandwidth available to your Web server, you make the bandwidth available for other services. Throttling bandwidth also comes into play if you're running multiple Web sites on your Windows NT Server computer. You can individually throttle the bandwidth used by each site or control the bandwidth available for all the sites sharing a network card.

If you plan on running multiple Web servers, you may want to start by restricting your first Web server to 50 percent of the available bandwidth measured in Kbps. After you have been in operation for a short time, you can analyze site performance and adjust the bandwidth accordingly.

To throttle the bandwidth on a Web site, do the following:

1. **In Internet Service Manager, right-click the Web site you want, and then choose Properties from the pop-up menu.**

2. **Click the Performance tab.**

3. **Select Enable Bandwidth Throttling.**

4. **In the Maximum Network Use box, type the maximum number of kilobytes per second you want the site to use.**

5. **Click OK.**

Keep 'em alive

The purpose of Keep-Alives is to preserve Web server resources. The less times a server has to create and close a connection, the more users it can effectively serve. By keeping a connection alive for a browser session versus opening and closing it repeatedly, resources are preserved; even though connections are open longer and there are technically fewer connections available, in the end more users are handled more quickly as each user needs fewer connections, and each connection is inherently more efficient. In most cases, you'll want a check mark to appear in the HTTP Keep-Alives Enabled option in the Performance property page, which means it's active.

Taking Advantage of HTTP Headers

HTTP headers are instructions returned to the browser via the header of the HTML page. The browser uses these HTML commands to process instructions from the server. Opening the Web Site Properties dialog box and then clicking the HTTP Headers tab displays the HTTP Header dialog box shown in Figure 8-2. From here, you can enable and specify content expiration, customize HTTP headers, set up a content rating system for your Web site, and map MIME file types.

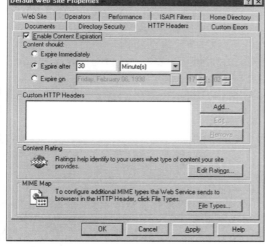

Figure 8-2:
The Enable
Content
Expiration
properties
active in the
HTTP
Headers
dialog box.

You can also apply these HTTP headers to specific folders and files. To use the features in the HTTP Header dialog box for specific folders and files, simply right-click the folder or file in the results pane, choose Properties, and then click the HTTP Headers tab. This section explains how to work with the tools available in the HTTP Headers dialog box.

Freshness dating

Like the freshness dating on food products, you can add freshness dating to your Web content to make sure that outdated information isn't published. You can specify an expiration date for time-sensitive information, which is sent to the Web browser. The browser compares the current date to the expiration date to determine whether to display the cached page or request an updated page from the server.

You can apply content dating at the Web site level or at the folder and file level. In most cases, you use content freshness not for your entire Web site but for specific directories and files. If you want to freshness date your entire Web site, however, click the Enable Content Expiration check box in the HTTP Headers dialog box, which activates the settings for this group. These same settings appear in the HTTP Headers dialog box for a specific folder or file.

With the Enable Content Expiration properties active, you can choose from the following options:

- The **Expire Immediately** setting displays the content once and then expires.

- The **Expire After** setting lets you specify a time period during which the material will be displayed before expiring.

- The **Expire On** setting lets you specify a date and time on which you want the contents to expire.

Rating your content

Internet Information Server uses a rating system developed by the Recreational Software Advisory Council (RSAC), which rates content according to its level of violence, nudity, sexual content, and offensive language. Content rating information is sent by a Web server to the Web browser. Microsoft Internet Explorer supports this content rating system, but Netscape Navigator doesn't.

Before you can establish ratings for your content, you need to understand how the RSAC rating system works. For details, click the More Info button in the Content Ratings dialog box. Here's how to establish your content rating system:

1. **In the HTTP Headers dialog box, click the Edit Ratings button.**

   The Content Ratings dialog box appears with the Rating Service tab selected. Clicking the More Info button provides more information about the RSAC rating service. Clicking the Ratings Questionnaire button lets you complete an RSAC questionnaire to obtain a recommended rating for your Web site content.

2. **Click the Ratings tab.**

3. **Click the Enable Ratings for This Resource check box.**

   All the settings in the Content Ratings dialog box become active, as shown in Figure 8-3.

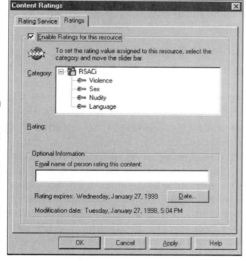

Figure 8-3:
The Content Ratings dialog box with the Enable Ratings setting active.

4. **In the Category list box, select a ratings type.**

   A Rating slider setting appears below the Category list.

5. **Using the slider control, select the rating from 0 to 5 for the category.**

   For example, if you selected the Violence category, level 0 represents no violence and level 5 is defined as "Wanton and gratuitous violence."

6. **In the box titled E̲mail Name of Person Rating This Content, type the e-mail address of the person who rated the material.**

7. **Click the D̲ate button.**

The Select Date to Expire dialog box appears, as shown in Figure 8-4.

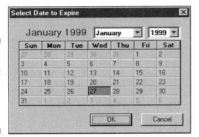

Figure 8-4:
The Select
Date to
Expire
dialog box.

8. **Specify the date, and then click OK.**

Select the month and year in the drop-down lists; select the date by clicking it in the calendar.

9. **Click OK to exit the Content Ratings dialog box.**

MIME mapping

MIME (Multipurpose Internet Mail Extension) is the Internet standard that extends e-mail capabilities beyond just text files to include data such as video, sound, and program files. The sending of binary files is accomplished by the use of MIME types, which describe the content of the document. A MIME-compliant application sending a file assigns a MIME type to the file. The receiving application, which is also MIME-compliant, refers to a standardized list of documents organized into MIME types to interpret the file format. For example, a MIME type of text/html refers to a file written in HTML. MIME is part of HTTP, and both Web browsers and servers use MIME.

If you plan to publish files in multiple formats or files in special proprietary formats, you must be sure that NT Server has a MIME mapping for each file. You do this in Windows NT Server using Windows NT Explorer. Choosing View⇨Options displays the Options dialog box. Clicking the File Types tab displays all the file types recognized by the Windows NT Server. You can use this listing as your guide to what MIME mappings are already in place or for adding new MIME types. The MIME Map setting in the HTTP Headers tab of the Web Site Properties dialog box lets you specify the MIME file types supported by your Web server.

Here is how to do a MIME mapping for a Web site:

1. In the HTTP Headers dialog box, click the File Types button.

The File Types dialog box appears, as shown in Figure 8-5.

Figure 8-5:
The File
Types
dialog box.

2. Click the New Type button.

The File Type dialog box appears, as shown in Figure 8-6.

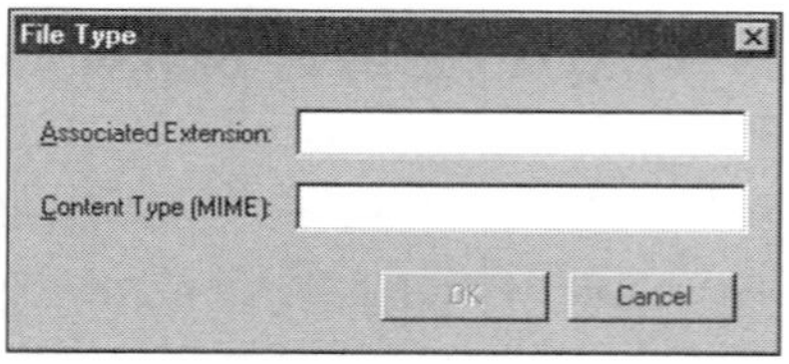

Figure 8-6:
The File
Type dialog
box.

3. In the Associated Extension box, type the filename extension for the file.

4. In the Content Type (MIME) box, type the MIME type.

Use the format *mime type/filename extension.*

5. Click OK twice to return to the HTTP Headers dialog box.

Customizing HTTP headers

The Custom HTTP Headers properties let you create and send a custom HTTP header from the Web server to the client browser. Custom headers allow you to define information outside HTML. Your Web server can use this information to instruct a Web browser to perform activities not yet supported by the official HTML specification.

Here is an example of how to create a Custom HTTP header for your Web server:

1. In the HTTP Headers dialog box, click the Add button.

The Add/Edit Custom HTTP Header dialog box appears, as shown in Figure 8-7.

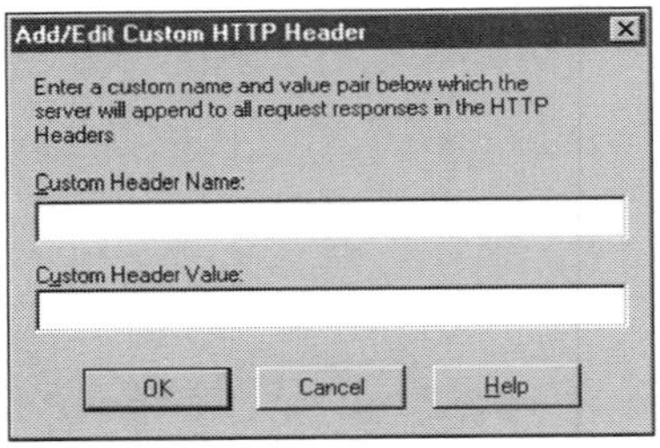

Figure 8-7:
The Add/
Edit Custom
HTTP
Header
dialog box.

2. In the Custom Header Name box, type the name of your custom header.

3. In the Custom Header Value box, type the value of the header.

For example, you might type the following META element:

```
<META HTTP-EQUIV=refresh" CONTENT="60"
        URL="www.angell.com/homepage.html">
```

Microsoft Internet Explorer or Netscape Navigator interprets this as an instruction to wait 60 seconds and then load the new document. You can use this instruction when a document is moved from one location to another.

4. Click OK to return to the HTTP Headers dialog box.

Adding Footers to Web Pages

You can configure your Web server to automatically insert an HTML-formatted file to the bottom of every Web document sent by your Web server. This file can contain HTML formatting instructions to display copyright information, contact information, company logo, or other unchanging information that you want to append to all your Web pages.

Be careful about using document footers on your Web site. Generating these HTML instructions every time a Web browser requests a Web document can reduce Web server performance for busy Web sites.

To add document footers to Web pages in a Web site or directory, do the following:

1. **Create an HTML footer file, and then save it.**

   Your footer file should not be a complete HTML document. The footer should, however, contain the HTML tags necessary for formatting the appearance and function of your footer content. For example, a footer file that adds your organization's name to the bottom of every Web page should contain your text formatted with HTML tags that define the text properties, such as font size and color.

2. **Select a Web site, directory, or file, right-click it, and then select Properties.**

3. **Click the Documents tab, and then select the Enable Document Footer check box.**

4. **In the text box, type the full local path to the footer file or click the Browse button to navigate to and select the file.**

5. **Click OK.**

Maintaining Content Control

The Content Control settings in the Home Directory dialog box let you control what kinds of activities can be accomplished with your Web site content. These properties are Log Access, Directory Browsing Allowed, Index This Directory, and FrontPage Web, and appear when you are working with a local directory or a network share. They're not available if you are redirecting to a URL. A subset of these properties — Log Access, Directory Browsing Allowed, and Index This Directory — is available for a directory in the Directory dialog box. In a File properties dialog box, only the Log Access Property is available.

The following describes the Content Control properties:

- ✓ **Log Access** is active by default, which enables the IIS to record visits to the Web server or directory. IIS records visits only if logging is enabled for the Web site or directory, which it is by default. Working with logging is explained in Chapter 15.

- ✓ **Directory Browsing Allowed** enables a Web browser user to view a hypertext listing of the files and directories in the directory. A hypertext directory listing is generated automatically and sent to the user when the browser request does not include a specific filename and when no default document is in the specified directory. Virtual directories will not appear in directory listings; users must know a virtual directory's alias and type its URL address or click a link in another page to access a virtual directory.

  Because directory browsing reveals your Web site's structure to a user, you should generally leave the Directory Browsing Allowed option disabled.

- ✓ **Index This Directory** instructs Microsoft Index Server to include this directory in a full-text index of your Web site. A full-text index enables users to quickly search for words or phrases in documents on your Web site. Working with the Microsoft Index Server 2.0, which is included with Internet Information Server, is covered in Chapter 12.

- ✓ **FrontPage Web** lets you create a FrontPage web for this Web site. This means you can use Microsoft FrontPage 98, an HTML authoring package, to also manage the content files for your Web site.

Managing Web Sites Remotely

It's not always convenient to perform your Web site administration at the Windows NT Server computer. Internet Information Server lets you perform administration of your Web sites remotely using two different methods. The first method involves using the Internet Service Manager snap-in on another Windows NT Server 4.0 or Windows NT Workstation connected to your network. The second method enables you to remotely access your Web servers using an HTML version of Internet Service Manager. In the HTML-based approach, you access Internet Service Manager using a Web browser on your intranet or the Internet.

You can access the HTML-based Internet Service Manager from your local Windows NT Server computer by choosing Start➪Programs➪Windows NT 4.0 Option Pack➪Microsoft Internet Information Server➪Internet Service Manager (HTML). Internet Service Manager appears in the Internet Explorer Web browser, as shown in Figure 8-8.

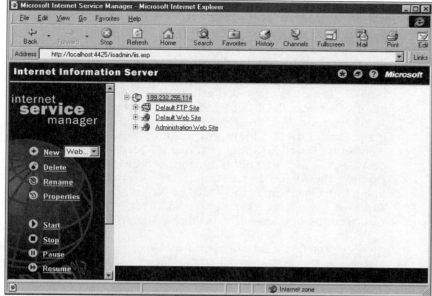

Figure 8-8:
Internet
Service
Manager as
it appears
in the
Internet
Explorer
Web
browser.

Using the Internet Service Manager snap-in remotely

You can install the Internet Service Manager snap-in on any computer on your local network running Windows NT Server 4.0 or Windows NT Workstation 4.0. With the IIS snap-in installed on both the local computer and the Windows NT Server running IIS, you can navigate in the Microsoft Management Console's scope pane to locate the computer running your IIS servers. From the remote computer, you can then remotely manage the sites using Internet Service Manager as if you were sitting at the computer actually running the Web server.

Right-clicking the Internet Information Server folder in the scope pane and then choosing Connect from the pop-up menu lets you connect to another server running Internet Information Server from anywhere on your Windows NT network. If you have TCP/IP and Windows Internet Name Service (WINS) installed on your network, all the computers running IIS on your network appear in the scope pane. If you do not have WINS installed to resolve names, you may see only the installations of IIS that are on the same subnet as the computer you're using.

Setting up for Web browser remote administration

The HTML version of Internet Service Manager uses Administration Web Site as the Web server to gain remote access to your Web servers with a Web browser. During the installation of Internet Information Server, a port number between 2,000 and 9,999 is randomly selected and assigned to the Administration Web Site. Figure 8-9 shows the Administration Web Site with the port number 4425 in the Port column. This means you can access any Web server installed on the Windows NT Server from a Web browser, provided the port number is appended to the address. After the site is reached, the administrator is asked for a username and password to continue. Only members of the Windows NT administrator group can use the site. Web site operators can also administer a Web site remotely. Working with Web site operators is explained in Chapter 10.

Although the HTML Internet Service Manager offers many of the same features as the snap-in, it can't perform some functions. These restricted functions typically involve IIS features handled by Windows NT Server.

You can access the browser-based Internet Service Manager from any computer on your intranet or on the Internet running Microsoft Internet Explorer. To enable remote use of Internet Service Manager (HTML) to administer the Web server, you must configure Internet Service Manager to update the IP address restrictions for the Web site IISADMIN. As a security precaution, Internet Service Manager (HTML) allows access from only the server computer itself. This default IP address is 127.0.0.1 in the IP Address and Domain Name Restrictions dialog box.

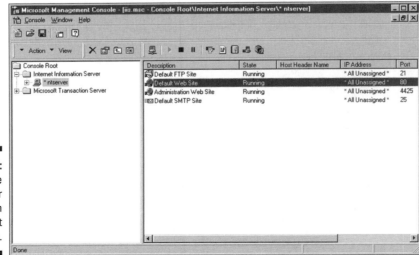

Figure 8-9:
Note the port number of 4425 in the Port column.

To enable the remote use of Internet Service Manager (HTML), do the following:

1. **In the results pane, double-click the Web site you want remote access to.**

2. **Right-click the IISADMIN virtual directory, and then choose Properties from the pop-up menu.**

3. **Click the Directory Security tab.**

4. **In the IP Address and Domain Name Restrictions group, click the Edit button.**

   The IP Address and Domain Name Restrictions dialog box appears, as shown in Figure 8-10.

Figure 8-10: The IP Address and Domain Name Restrictions dialog box.

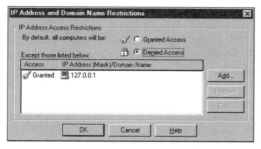

5. **With the Denied Access setting checked, click the Add button.**

   The Grant Access On dialog box appears, as shown in Figure 8-11.

Figure 8-11: The Grant Access On dialog box.

6. **Select the Single Computer option, enter the IP address of the remote computer, and then click OK.**

   Your new entry appears in the Except Those Listed Below list.

7. **Click OK to return to the Web Site Properties dialog box.**

Remotely accessing Internet Service Manager (HTML)

After you enable a Web site for remote administration, you can access the HTML version of Internet Service Manager using a Web browser. You can access the site as a Windows NT Administrator or a Web site operator. Web site operators are a unique class of Windows NT user accounts created by Internet Information Server to allow specified users to have a subset of the Windows NT Administrator access privileges. Establishing Web Site Operators is explained in Chapter 10.

To access the HTML-based Internet Service Manager from a remote computer on your intranet or via the Internet, do the following.

1. **Open the Internet Explorer browser on the remote computer desktop.**

2. **In the URL field of the Web browser, type the URL for the Administration Web Site using the following format:**

   `http://domainname: port number/iisadmin/`

   where *domainname* is the DNS name of the server and *port number* is the port number assigned to the Administration Web Site. For example, you might enter `http://www.angell.com:4425/iisadmin/`.

3. **Press Enter.**

   The Enter Network Password dialog box appears.

4. **Type the Administrative or Web site operator logon username and password, and then click OK.**

   The Internet Service Manager home page appears in your Web browser, as shown in Figure 8-12.

Navigating around the HTML version of Internet Service Manager is straightforward. For example, clicking Default Web Site in the right frame and then clicking Properties in the left frame displays the Web Site dialog box shown in Figure 8-13. The hypertext listing of property sheets is in the left frame.

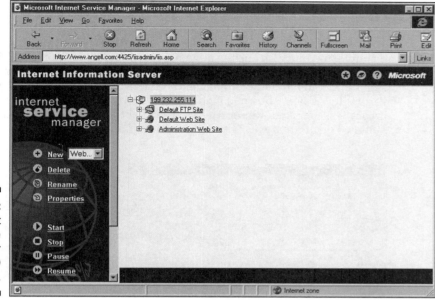

Figure 8-12:
The Internet
Service
Manager
(HTML)
home page.

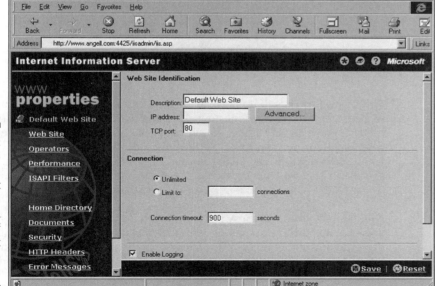

Figure 8-13:
The Web
Site dialog
box as it
appears in
the HTML
version of
Internet
Service
Manager.

Creating Custom Error Messages

You're probably familiar with some standard HTTP error messages. For example, in your Web surfing adventures, the HTTP error code 404: File Not Found has probably popped up in your browser. These generic error messages are cold and impersonal and often leave users guessing. The Custom Errors dialog box, shown in Figure 8-14, lets you specify your own HTTP error messages that are returned to the client browser. This means you can enhance error messages with more information.

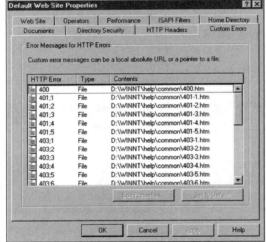

Figure 8-14:
The Custom
Errors
dialog box.

The Custom Errors dialog box lists the HTTP 1.1 error messages used by IIS Web servers. Each error message listed in the Custom Errors dialog box is referenced to an HTML file, which the Web server sends to the Web browser when an error occurs. All these files are stored in the same drive on which you installed Windows NT Server and Internet Information Server. If you installed them on your D drive, the path to these error message files is `D:\\WINNT\help\common\` followed by the filename.

You can use your Web browser to point to a specific file to display the error message as an HTML page. As you might have guessed, you can also edit these files using an HTML authoring tool, such as FrontPage 98, to add more information than just the error message. You can also create an entirely new HTML file and link it to any standard HTTP error message.

The Custom Errors dialog box lets you link any HTML file in any virtual directory on your Web site to a specific error message. Here is how to map a customized error message Web document to a specific error code sent to a Web browser when a particular error occurs. The customized error message can reside as a file on your Windows NT network or on a remote computer via a URL. In most cases, you'll keep the error messages as files on your local network.

Follow these steps to map an error to a file on your Windows NT Server or local network:

1. **Create a file that contains your custom error message or edit the file indicated in the Custom Errors dialog box.**

2. **If you're creating a new HTML file, place it in any virtual directory you want or add it to the** `\WINNT\help\common\` **directory.**

3. **Right-click the Web site, virtual directory, or file you want, and then select Properties from the pop-up menu.**

4. **Click the Custom Errors tab, and then select from the list the HTTP error you want to customize.**

5. **Click the Edit Properties button.**

   The Error Mapping Properties dialog box appears, as shown in Figure 8-15.

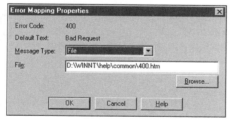

Figure 8-15:
The Error
Mapping
Properties
dialog box.

6. **Make sure the File option appears in the Message Type list, and then in the File box type the path for your new message file or click the Browse button to navigate to and select the file.**

7. **Click OK to exit the Error Mapping Properties dialog box.**

Congratulations, you're now a Webmaster. You know the fundamentals of managing Web sites in Internet Information Server.

Chapter 9

Running an FTP Site

*W*hen you use FTP (File Transfer Protocol), file transfer is efficient and fast. In addition, FTP supports a full range of file types and formats. Web browsers also support FTP file transfers, so users don't even need a separate FTP client. Internet Information Server lets you create FTP sites for transferring files across your intranet or the Internet. This chapter explains the fundamentals of FTP server management.

Setting Up an FTP Site

To set up an FTP server in Internet Information Server, you use many of the same properties you use to configure a Web server. Right-clicking the Default FTP Site and then choosing Properties from the pop-up menu displays the Default FTP Site Properties dialog box, which is shown in Figure 9-1. Like its Web site counterpart, this dialog box lets you manage the settings for the specific FTP site. You can also apply a subset of these properties by opening a folder or file properties dialog box — simply right-click the folder or file and choose Properties from the pop-up menu.

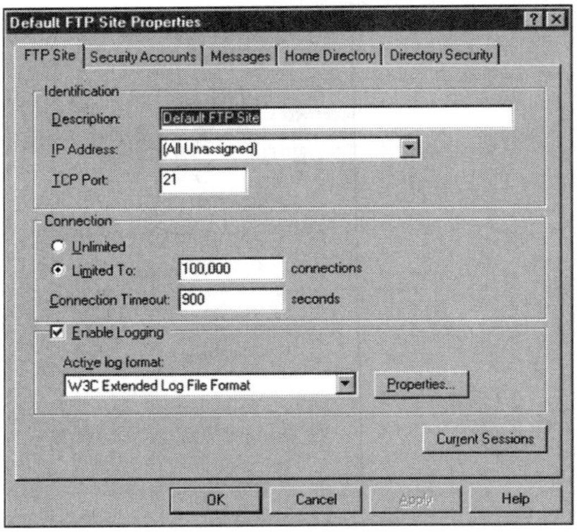

Figure 9-1:
The Default
FTP Site
Properties
dialog box.

Filling up your FTP server

You can easily fill up your FTP site with directories and folders. In the Home Directory dialog box, you can check out the local path for the files connected to the Default FTP Site. Like Web servers, an FTP server has a home directory that is the starting point for the site. When a user connects to the FTP site using the URL ftp://ftp.angell.com/, for example, the contents of the home directory appear in the FTP client.

The directory used for the Default FTP site is \Inetpub\ftproot on your Windows NT Server computer running Internet Information Server. You can add files to the Default FTP Site by simply copying the files into the \Inetpub\ftproot directory using Windows NT Explorer. After you copy the files into the FTP site's home directory, you can point a Web browser to the FTP site to see a hypertext listing of files, as shown in Figure 9-2. Remember, to access an FTP site using a Web browser, you must preface the URL with ftp rather than http. For example, the syntax for most FTP sites on the Web is ftp://ftp.*company*.com/.

Organizing FTP site files

As you add files to your FTP site, you should figure out an organizational structure to make it easier for FTP users to navigate your site. Here are some guidelines for making it easier for visitors to navigate your FTP site:

✔ Create directories with obvious names for specific groups of files and keep the groupings manageable for users.

✔ Each directory can contain an annotation file that the visitor's browser will automatically display. Create the file with the name ~FTPSVC~.CKM, and make it a hidden file so that it does not appear in directory listings.

✔ Include an INDEX.TXT file in each directory to tell visitors exactly what they can expect to find. An index usually contains both the name of the file and a short description.

✔ Add a terms-and-conditions statement. Your legal department may require you to add this material as a reminder to users about copyright and trademark restrictions on the material on the FTP site.

Decompression for your FTP site

Compressed files save space on your hard disk, reduce network traffic, and save users connection times for downloading files from your FTP site. If you use your FTP site as a vehicle for delivering files on the Internet, compressing files is essential.

Data compression squeezes data so that it requires less disk space for storage and less time to transmit during a file transfer. Compression takes advantage of the fact that data contains a lot of repetition; replacing repeated information with a code to represent this information saves space. For many file formats, compression can reduce the file size 30 to 70 percent. Many graphic, video, and sound files, however, are already compressed as part of their file format. For example, GIF, JPEG, MOV, and AVI files already compress data.

The leading compression format used in the PC world is the ZIP format developed by PKware, Inc., in 1989. Any file compressed in the PKZIP format has the file extension .zip. A ZIP file can contain one or more files. ZIP files make it easy to group and transport files. You can compress files into self-extracting files that have an .exe extension. These files can be uncompressed by simply double-clicking the file in Windows Explorer. You can also leave the files with the .zip file extension. However, any client downloading a ZIP format file needs a compression/decompression program to extract the contents of the ZIP file. Fortunately, getting one of these programs is easy. Two leading programs for working with ZIP files are WinZip (www.winzip.com) and Drag and Zip (www.canyonsw.com). Both are available on the Internet.

Always make sure to virus-check any files made available for downloading from your FTP site. You can use any of the popular virus-checking programs, such as Norton AntiVirus from Symantec (www.symantec.com).

On the Internet, other platforms use a variety of file-compression formats, such as ARJ, LZH, GZ, TAR, and Bin/Hex. The popular ZIP compression programs support these file formats as well as ZIP.

Changing your listing style

An FTP server can list files and directories using either the MS-DOS format or a UNIX format. The default setting is the MS-DOS format, which is shown in Figure 9-2.

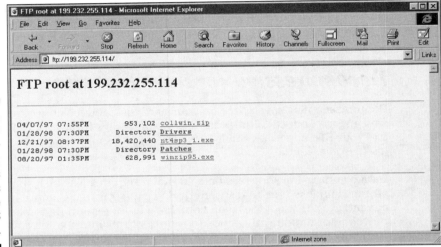

Figure 9-2: An FTP server displaying directories and files in the MS-DOS format.

To change the default MS-DOS format, follow these steps:

1. **Right-click the Default FTP Site, and then choose Properties from the pop-up menu.**

   The Default FTP Site Properties dialog box appears.

2. **Click the Home Directory tab.**

3. **In the Directory Listing Style group, click the UNIX option.**

Figure 9-3 shows the listing of files in an FTP site using the UNIX format.

Because the UNIX format is the most popular on the Internet and most Web browsers expect the file listing in the UNIX format, you should select UNIX for maximum compatibility.

Getting the message out

You can create text messages that appear when three FTP server actions occur. These messages appear in the FTP client to provide helpful information to your FTP site users.

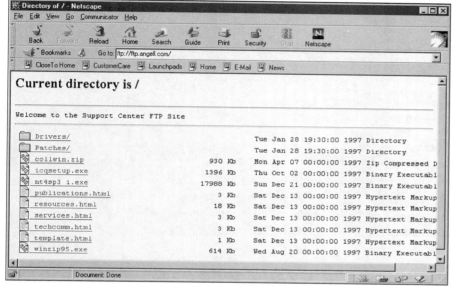

Figure 9-3:
The same
listing of
files as in
Figure 9-2,
but this time
in the UNIX
format.

You can create the following types of messages for your FTP server:

✔ A **Welcome message** that displays to clients when they first connect to the FTP server. The message appears at the top of the file listing.

✔ An **Exit message** that displays when clients log off the FTP server. The Exit message appears only in a text-based Web client.

✔ A **Maximum Connections message** that displays to clients who try to connect when the FTP service already has the maximum number of client connections allowed. You can specify the number of supported connections in the FTP Site dialog box.

To add messages to your FTP site, click the Messages tab in the Default FTP Site Properties dialog box, which is shown in Figure 9-4. The following explains how to add Welcome, Exit, and Maximum Connection messages to your FTP site.

✔ To add the Welcome message, type your text in the Welcome text box. If your message fills the box, the scroll bar on the right side of the text box becomes active so you can type more.

✔ To add the Exit message, type your text in the Exit text box. If your message fills the box, the text scrolls so you can type more.

✔ To add a Maximum Connections message, type your text in the Maximum Connections text box. If your message fills the box, the text scrolls so you can type more.

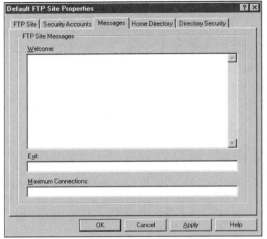

Figure 9-4:
The
Messages
page of
the Default
FTP Site
Properties
dialog box.

Checking out who's connected

You can check out the users connected to your FTP at any time and disconnect an individual user or all users of your FTP site. From the Default FTP
Site Properties dialog box, click the Current Sessions button to display the
FTP User Sessions dialog box, which is shown in Figure 9-5. This dialog box
displays a list of all currently connected users, their IP addresses, and the
amount of time each user has been connected.

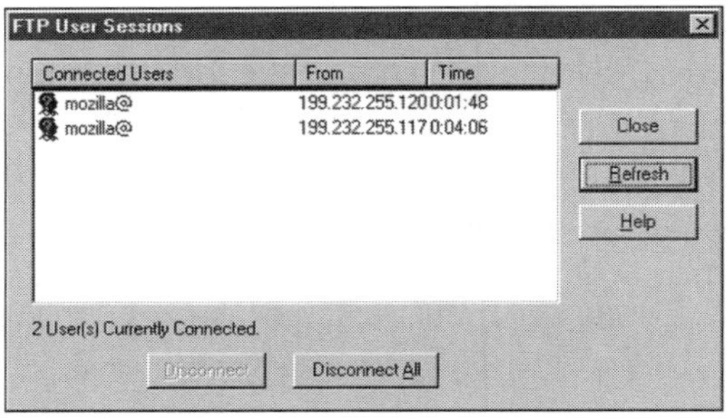

Figure 9-5:
The FTP
User
Sessions
dialog box.

In the FTP User Sessions dialog box, you can do the following:

 ✔ Click the Refresh button to display changes in the users connected to
 your FTP server since the FTP User Sessions dialog box appeared. The
 FTP User Sessions dialog box doesn't automatically update FTP client
 status information; you must use the Refresh button to see changes.

> ✔ Select a user and click the Disconnect button to disconnect a single user from your FTP.
>
> ✔ Click the Disconnect All button to disconnect all users from your site at once.

Be careful about disconnecting users of your FTP site. If an Internet user is in the middle of downloading a large file from your site and you cut the user off, he or she won't be a happy camper.

Changing names

You can change the name of your FTP site as it appears in Internet Service Manager at any time. To do so, you simply right-click Default FTP Site, choose Properties from the pop-up menu, and then click the FTP Site tab. Type the new name in the Description box. This name is completely separate from the DNS or UNC name used to access your FTP site.

Limiting Your FTP Server Connections

You can limit connections to your FTP server using two properties. The first controls the number of simultaneous users connected to your FTP server at any one time. The second specifies the time that an inactive connection remains connected to your FTP server. Because running an FTP server is a data-intensive activity, you should put limits on connections to your FTP site.

Keep in mind that other factors also play a big role in connections. The bandwidth capacity of your intranet or Internet connection, as well as the configuration of your PC hardware, determine your total capacity. However, limiting the number of simultaneous connections and setting other performance values enhances the capabilities of what you have to work with.

Managing simultaneous connections

You can specify the exact number of simultaneous connections your FTP server will support at any one time. Your FTP server will reject all connection attempts beyond the connection limit. The default setting is to allow an unlimited number of simultaneous users. The Unlimited option permits as many simultaneous connections as your bandwidth and computer can support.

To limit the number of simultaneous connections to an FTP site, do the following:

1. **In Internet Service Manager, right-click the FTP site you want, and then choose Properties from the pop-up menu.**

   The FTP Site tab appears by default.

2. **Select the Limited To option.**

3. **In the Limited To connections box, type the maximum number of simultaneous connections you want to allow.**

Cutting them off

You can manage connections also by restricting the time that inactive connections are allowed to stay inactive before being cut off. When an FTP client unexpectedly stops working or a connection is lost in midstream, the site continues to process data for the connection until a timeout value is reached.

The default timeout value is 900 seconds, or 15 minutes. In most cases, you'll want to reduce this setting to a more reasonable value, such as 300 seconds (5 minutes), after which the connection is closed.

To limit the number of seconds that the FTP server keeps an inactive connection active, do the following:

1. **In Internet Service Manager, right-click the FTP site you want, and then choose Properties from the pop-up menu.**

   The FTP Site tab appears.

2. **In the Connection Timeout box, type the connection timeout value in seconds.**

   A good value is around 300 seconds or less.

3. **Click OK.**

Working with Virtual Directories

A *virtual directory* is a directory that is not contained in the home directory but appears to the FTP clients as though it were. A virtual directory has an *alias,* a name that clients use to access that directory. For example, an FTP user might enter `ftp://ftp.angell.com/` to access the home directory. To access a virtual directory with the alias support, the user enters the URL `ftp://ftp.angell.com/support/`. Alias name support is detached from the actual directory name and path on your computer or network but takes the user to that directory.

An alias is also more secure because users do not know where your files are physically located on the server and therefore can't use that information to modify your files. Aliases also make it easier for you to move directories in your site. Instead of changing the URL for the directory, you change the mapping between the alias and the physical location of the files. By using virtual directories, you gain a great deal of flexibility in deciding the location of file storage for your site and can effectively expand your site's storage capacity beyond the Windows NT Server machine.

You can create a virtual directory on the Windows NT Server running IIS or on a networked computer. The only requirement for creating virtual directories on a networked computer is that the remote computer share the same Windows NT domain as the NT Server running Internet Information Server.

Getting from Internet Service Manager to Windows NT Explorer

Whenever you want to create a new FTP site or virtual directory, you need to create the directory that will contain the files using Windows NT Explorer. Internet Service Manager provides two ways to directly access Windows NT Explorer.

Right-clicking an FTP server or any folder in the results pane and then choosing Open or Explore from the pop-up menu displays the Windows NT Explorer window with the directory contents. For example, right-clicking the Default FTP Site and then choosing Open displays Windows NT Explorer with the home directory `\Inetpub\ftproot` as the current directory. You can then create directories in the home directory or navigate to any other directory on your local computer or network.

Creating directories in Windows NT

You create new folders in Windows NT Server using Windows NT Explorer. After you create your directories, you use IIS to create the virtual directory using a wizard. If the directories you want to add to your FTP site are already in place, you can skip this section.

Windows NT Explorer is the folder and file-management tool for Windows NT Server. You can use Windows NT Explorer to create your directories by doing the following:

1. **Open Windows NT Explorer from Internet Service Manager by right-clicking any server in the scope or results pane and then choosing Explorer from the pop-up menu.**

   The Windows NT Explorer window appears.

2. **Navigate to the drive and folder where you want your folder to reside.**

3. **Choose File⇨New⇨Folder from the Windows NT Explorer menu bar or from the pop-up menu.**

   The folder appears with the New Folder label.

4. **Type the new name of the folder, and then press Enter.**

The directory you created uses the default Windows NT Server directory permissions or the default permissions you defined. The default Windows NT Server directory permissions enable open access to the directory by everyone on the Windows NT network and give them full control over the files in the directory. When you use the FTP server properties to take control of the directory as a virtual directory, you'll be able to specify a different set of permissions. Chapter 10 explains working with permissions.

Creating virtual directories

After you create the directory on your hard drive, you're ready to make it a virtual directory for your FTP site. Internet Information Server uses a wizard to guide you through the process of setting up a virtual directory. Here's how to create a virtual directory using the Default FTP Site:

1. **In Internet Service Manager, right-click the Default FTP Site.**

2. **Choose New⇨Virtual Directory.**

   The New Virtual Directory wizard appears

3. **Type the alias you want to use, and then click Next.**

   For example, entering *sales* in the Alias to Be Used to Access Virtual Directory box means the URL for the directory becomes `ftp://ftp.angell.com/support/` for the FTP site with a domain name of `ftp.angell.com`.

4. **Type the physical path of the directory, or click the Browse button and navigate to the directory you want, and then click Next.**

   This is the actual path of the directory. If you're entering a path for a directory on another computer, you must specify the directory's Universal Naming Convention (UNC) name and provide a username and password to use for access permission. UNC is a system of naming files among computers on a network so that a file on a given computer will have the same pathname when accessed from any computer on the network.

   You can use the Browse button to navigate to a directory on another computer on the network, and the wizard automatically enters the UNC path for you.

5. **Specify the access permissions for the new directory.**

   If you want your FTP virtual directory to allow users to only download files, use Allow Read Access. If you want users to both download and upload files, select both the Allow Read Access and Allow Write Access properties.

6. **Click Finish.**

Managing virtual directories

Any virtual directory you create appears in the listing of folders and files in a specific FTP site. For example, if you created a virtual directory with the alias Support in the Default FTP Site, double-click the Default FTP Site entry in the results pane, and you'll see the Support alias entry. Notice that the virtual directory alias appears in the Name column, and the path where the actual directory or file is located appears in the Path column.

You can configure your virtual directory by right-clicking the alias and then choosing Properties from the pop-up menu. For example, right-clicking the Support alias, and then choosing Properties from the pop-up menu displays the Support Properties dialog box.

You can easily rename the alias by right-clicking the alias and then choosing Rename from the pop-up menu. Type the new name of your text, and then press Enter.

To delete a virtual directory, right-click the alias name in the results pane, and then choose Delete from the pop-up menu. A message box appears to confirm the deletion. Click Yes. You can also delete an alias by selecting it in the results pane and then clicking the Delete button (the first button after the View menu) on the MMC toolbar.

Redirecting FTP Clients

Redirecting a client means your FTP server takes a request for a particular home directory or virtual directory and forwards the request to another directory on the local computer or to a directory on another computer connected to your network. Unlike working with a Web server, you cannot redirect an FTP request to a remote computer via a URL.

Redirecting FTP clients is a way to preserve the original address of your FTP site or virtual directory, even if the contents have moved to a new location. Redirecting is useful when you are updating your FTP site and want to make a portion of the site temporarily unavailable. Another use of redirection is when you change the name of a virtual directory and want links to files in the original virtual directory to access the same files in the new virtual directory.

You can redirect requests at the master properties, server, and folder and file level. In most cases, you'll redirect requests for a particular FTP site or directory. The settings for redirecting a directory request are the same as those for an FTP site. You use the Virtual Directory dialog box to redirect a directory request and the Home Directory dialog box to redirect an FTP site request.

You redirect requests for specific files in the same way you redirect requests for directories and sites. You use the File tab in the File Properties dialog box. Right-click the file in the results pane, and then choose Properties from the pop-up menu. This section explains how to redirect clients for your FTP site, but you can also use these instructions for redirecting requests for directories and files.

Redirecting to a local directory

You can redirect an FTP server to another directory located on the local Windows NT Server running Internet Information Server. For example, the Default FTP Site uses the path \Inetpub\ftp, which is your home directory. You can specify that whenever an FTP client enters the URL for the FTP site, the request goes to another directory on your computer. For example, you might have a directory \temp for routing users to a temporary site while you do some work on the \Inetpub\ftproot directory. From the users' viewpoint, they don't see the underlying change in the home directory.

To redirect an FTP client to another directory on your local computer, do the following:

1. **In Internet Service Manager, right-click the FTP site, and then choose Properties from the pop-up menu.**

2. **Click the Home Directory tab.**

3. **Select the A Directory Located on the Computer option.**

4. **Type the path of the directory you want to redirect FTP clients.**

   You can also click the Browse button to navigate to the directory you want on the NT Server computer. In the Browse for Folder dialog box, select the directory.

5. **Click OK.**

Redirecting to a network share

A *share* in Windows NT means to make resources, such as drives and directories, available to others on the network. You can redirect FTP clients to another drive and directory on any computer connected to the network. Here is how to redirect an FTP client to a directory on another intranet computer:

1. **In Internet Service Manager, right-click the FTP site, and then choose Properties from the pop-up menu.**

2. **Click the Home Directory tab.**

3. **Select A Share Located on Another Computer.**

   The Local Path box changes to the Network Directory box, and the Browse button changes to the Connect As button.

4. **In the Network Directory text box, enter the share using the Universal Naming Convention (UNC) name for the location of the directory on another machine.**

   The format for UNC is *servername**sharename*. You can also use the Connect As button to navigate to the computer to select the directory.

5. **Click OK to exit the FTP Site Properties dialog box.**

If you select a directory on a network share, you may need to enter a username and password to access the resource. If you use an account that has administration permissions on the server, clients can gain access to server operations. This seriously jeopardizes the security of your network. To safeguard your network, use the IUSR_*computername* account. When you install IIS, it creates an account called IUSR_*computername,* where *computername* is the name of the NT Server computer. This account creates randomly generated passwords and is intended for guest access by the IIS Web, FTP, and other servers. The IUSR_*computername* account is given membership in the Windows NT Domain Users and local Guests groups. The account is also given permission to log on locally.

Creating New FTP Servers

Internet Information Server 4.0 lets you set up and run multiple FTP servers on the same Windows NT Server computer. Unlike creating new Web servers, however, you can't create FTP servers that share both the same IP address and TCP/IP port number. In the case of Web servers, you can use the host header to differentiate a site that uses the same IP address and TCP/IP port number. Creating a new FT___ ___r requires you to assign it to a unique IP address or a unique TCP/IP p_____ ___ou want to run two FTP servers that both allow anonymous acc____ __ TCP/IP port 21, each server must have its own IP address.

Windows NT Server allows you to assig___ ___ple IP addresses to a single network adapter. Using Windows NT Se____ ___dvanced IP Addressing feature, you can add multiple IP addres____ __ network adapter card. After you add the IP addresses to the specifi____ __ork adapter card, you can host multiple Web sites, each with its o___ ___ddress and domain name. You can also add multiple network adapter ___ ___ each of which can have multiple IP addresses assigned to supp____ __mber of Web servers. You use the IIS Internet Service Manager and DNS to configure the IP address and domain names. See Chapter 4 for more information on IP addresses.

Setting up IP addresses in Windows NT Server

Before you can create a new FTP server, your network adapters and IP addresses must be installed and configured in Windows NT Server. Use the Network applet in the NT Server Control Panel to specify the additional IP addresses. You can bind the IP addresses to a single network adapter card or assign them to multiple network adapter cards. The processing of connecting an IP address to a network card is referred to as a *binding*. Chapter 7 explains how to bind IP addresses to network cards in Windows NT Server.

Creating new FTP servers

Before you create a site, make sure you use Windows NT Explorer to create a directory that will be your home directory. Internet Information Server uses a wizard to walk you through the process of creating a new FTP site. You can create a new FTP site using either a different IP address or a different TCP/IP port than the Default FTP Site. In most cases, you'll use a different IP address while using the same TCP/IP port 21 for anonymous FTP service. If you create an FTP site with the exact mix of settings used by another FTP site, IIS automatically stops the existing FTP server and activates the one you just created.

Here is how you create a new FTP server:

1. **In the scope pane of Internet Service Manager, right-click the computer name for your Windows NT Server.**

2. **Choose New⇨FTP Site from the pop-up menu.**

   The New FTP Site wizard appears.

3. **Type the name for the new FTP site, and then click Next.**

   This descriptive name appears in Internet Service Manager.

4. **From the drop-down list, select the IP address you want to assign to the new FTP site.**

   All the IP addresses you specified in Windows NT appear in the list.

   If you want to use the standard TCP port 21 for your new FTP server as well as for another FTP server, you must have at least two IP addresses installed on your system. Otherwise, one FTP server cannot run.

5. **Type the TCP/IP port you want to use for the FTP site, and then click the Next button.**

   In most cases, you'd use the default TCP/IP port 21 for anonymous connections.

6. **Type the path for the home directory for your new FTP site or use the Browse button to navigate to and select the directory you want for your Web site.**

7. **Click Next.**

   A page appears, asking you to define access permissions for your home directory.

8. **Choose one of the following:**

   - If you want users to download files only, use the Allow Read Access property.

   - If you want users to be able to upload as well as download files, use the default Allow Read Access and click the Allow Write Access check box.

9. **Click Finish.**

   Your new FTP site appears as a new entry in the right pane of the Internet Service Manager window.

Sailing into port

The universal TCP/IP port number for anonymous access to an FTP site is 21. This means if you want FTP clients to have access to your FTP site without having to add a port number to the URL, you must use TCP/IP port 21. Otherwise, the FTP client must know the unique assigned port number and enter it in the URL. The URL for this nonstandard FTP site would be something like `ftp://ftp.angell.com:8001`, where 8001 is the port number. Typically, port numbers above 255 are reserved for the private use of the local machine, and numbers below 255 are defined as defaults for a variety of universal TCP/IP applications and services.

To convert an existing FTP site to one that shares an IP address but has a unique TCP/IP port number (other than 80), do the following:

1. **In the results pane, right-click the FTP server you want, and then choose Properties from the pop-up menu.**

   The FTP Site Properties dialog box appears.

2. **In the TCP Port box, type the TCP/IP port number you want to use.**

3. **Click OK to exit the FTP Site Properties dialog box.**

Chapter 10

Taking Security Precautions

• •

In This Chapter

▶ Understanding how IIS and Windows NT security work together

▶ Setting permissions in IIS and Windows NTFS

▶ Checking user authentication

▶ Using TCP/IP server access restrictions

▶ Assigning site operators

▶ Working with SSL and digital certificates

• •

*W*eb and FTP servers deliver exciting new ways to share information within your organization, whether these servers are connected to your intranet or the Internet. These powerful capabilities, however, come with increased security risks. Your security configuration is crucial for protecting the information on your Web and FTP servers. Using a combination of Internet Information Server and Windows NT Server security features, you can protect your IIS servers as well as your local network from Internet intruders. This chapter tells you how to enhance your IIS servers with added security protection.

IIS and Windows NT Security Synergy

Internet Information Server and Windows NT Server provide three important security tools for your Web and FTP sites. The first tool is NTFS (New Technology File System), which provides folder and directory security through the file system. The second tool is the Windows NT user account, which controls access at the system level. The third tool is the Internet Information Server IUSR user account, which enables anonymous access to your Web and FTP sites. These tools combine to grant users access to your Web and FTP sites while preventing unauthorized access of your private files and directories. Windows NT Server manages security permissions relating to files and directories, and controls access to programs through assigning users and groups privileges.

NTFS

NTFS (New Technology File System) is the new file system designed by Microsoft specifically for Windows NT. It enables you to protect folders and files by using access permissions that specify the privileges (access) a user or group of users has with specific directories and files. For example, you can use permissions that enable only designated people to update the contents of the Web site. You can work with file permissions through Internet Information Server or Windows NT Explorer.

The User Manager for Domains

The User Manager for Domains, shown in Figure 10-1, manages the authentication of users on a Windows NT network and works with NTFS permissions. You use the User Manager for Domains to define the permissions that users have to access network resources. A user who wants to access content must have a valid NT user account. You can configure your Web and FTP server's authentication features to prompt users for valid Windows NT account credentials, or usernames and passwords, before connecting them to restricted content.

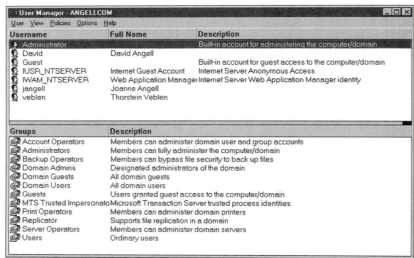

Figure 10-1:
The User Manager for Domains window.

The IUSR user account

When you install Internet Information Server, it adds a user account named IUSR *computername* in User Manager for Domains, where *computername* is the name of the Windows NT Server running IIS. (IUSR, by the way, stands for Internet user.) For example, if your computer is named "ntserver," the anonymous user account is IUSR_ntserver (refer to Figure 10-1).

This Windows NT user account forms the basis for anonymous access to Web and FTP sites running on Windows NT Server. Anonymous access — the default and preferred access control method for most Web and FTP server installations — allows users to visit your sites while preventing them from gaining access to your server's critical administrative features. When your server receives an anonymous logon request, it logs on the user with an anonymous or guest account, which is a valid Windows NT user account. By default, your Web and FTP servers will log on all users by using the IUSR account.

Using the NTFS permissions can further enhance this anonymous account like any Windows NT user account. When you configure anonymous access for your servers based on the IUSR account, you automatically apply some default NTFS permissions to prevent ordinary users from accessing private files and directories.

Setting Permissions in IIS

Internet Information Server provides the interface for defining NTFS permissions. You can control user access to specific sites, directories, or files from Internet Service Manager. As with other IIS properties for Web and FTP servers, permissions are available at the master, individual server, or individual folder and file property levels. When you set security properties for a specific site, you automatically set the same security properties for all directories and files belonging to that site unless the security properties of the individual directories and files have been previously set. Likewise, you can change the settings of individual directories and files within a site so that they are different from the settings governing the entire site.

IIS prompts you for permission to reset the properties of individual directories and files when you attempt to set security properties for your site. If you choose to reset these properties, your previous security settings will be replaced by the new settings. The same condition applies when you set security properties for a directory containing subdirectories or files with previously set security properties.

Setting Web server permissions

Setting permissions at the server level involves specifying whether a user has read and write permissions. The read permission enables Web clients to read or download files stored in a home directory or a virtual directory. The write permission enables Web clients to upload files to the enabled directory on your server or to change content. Only browsers that support the Put feature of the HTTP 1.1 protocol can take advantage of the write permission. Both Microsoft Internet Explorer and Netscape Navigator support HTTP 1.1.

For more flexibility in setting permissions, you can set read and write permissions at the directory level by right-clicking the folder in the results pane and choosing Properties from the pop-up menu. Then specify the read and write permissions in the Directory tab of the Directory Properties dialog box. Likewise, you can set read and write permissions for specific files using the File tab.

Changes made to folders and files take precedence over the settings in the next level but only for the specific folder or file. For example, you can specify that your Web site have read-only access, but specific files or folders in it can have write permissions.

In the Web Site Properties dialog box, the Home Directory tab includes two access permissions you can set for the entire Web site. In the Access Permissions group, you see Read and Write settings. The Read setting, which enables the viewing of files, is active (contains a check mark) by default. The Write setting, which allows the changing of files, is inactive by default.

Disabling a Web server permission restricts all users regardless of their Windows NT user account permissions and user rights. Enabling a permission allows all users access unless Windows NT permissions restrict access. If both Web server permissions and Windows NT permissions are set, the permissions that explicitly deny access take precedence over permissions that grant access.

To set Web server permissions for your entire Web site, do the following:

1. **In Internet Service Manager, right-click the Web site, and then choose Properties from the pop-up menu.**

2. **Click the Home Directory tab.**

3. **In the Access Permissions group, choose Read, or Write, or both.**

   The Read permission enables Web clients to read or download files stored in a home directory or a virtual directory. This is the default setting for Web sites. The Write permission enables Web clients to upload and overwrite files to the enabled directory on your server or to change content. Write can be accomplished only with a browser that supports the Put feature of HTTP 1.1 protocol standard.

4. Click OK.

If you select the <u>W</u>rite property and check the E<u>x</u>ecute check box in the Permissions group, you enable users to upload and execute programs on your Web or FTP server. This means that users can inadvertently or intentionally upload and execute a potentially destructive program on your server.

Controlling directory browsing

The Home Directory tab includes another setting that affects the security of your Web site. If you enable the Directory Browsing Allowed check box in the Content Control group, a Web browser displays a hypertext listing of the files and subdirectories in your Web site directories. A hypertext directory listing is generated automatically and sent to the user when a browser request does not include a specific filename and when no default document is in the specified directory. Virtual directories will not appear in this listing. If you do not specify a default.htm document for your Web server, and the Directory Browsing Allowed check box is not selected, the Web server returns an access forbidden error message to the user's browser.

Because directory browsing reveals your Web site's structure, you should generally leave the Directory Browsing Allowed option disabled.

Setting FTP server permissions

You can define read and write permissions for your entire FTP site using the Home Directory tab of the FTP Site Properties dialog box. Only the Read setting, which is active by default, enables users to download files from your FTP site. If you want users to be able to upload files to your entire FTP site, click the Write check box.

In most cases, it's best to use the Read setting for your entire FTP site and set Write permissions for specific folders. That way, you can control which folders files can be uploaded to, thus isolating those files from other files on the site. You can also turn off read permissions on the upload directories so others can't see what's been uploaded until the files are reviewed, virus-checked, and "merged" with the rest of the site's content.

Setting folder and file permissions

You can also define permissions for every folder and file. You access these properties by right-clicking the folder or file in the results pane of Internet Service Manager. These properties allow you to make changes on a folder-by-folder or file-by-file basis.

Right-clicking a file or folder in the results pane and then choosing Properties in the pop-up menu displays the Properties dialog box for that specific file or folder. Then click the File tab or the Directory tab to display the Access Permissions group with the Read and Write permissions.

NT File Permissions

The entire motivation behind user accounts and permissions is to ensure that the appropriate user gets access to the proper network resources. Every network resource has a list of user and group accounts with access to the resource, along with the access level for each account.

You can use the security features of the Windows NT File System (NTFS) to limit access to your Web or FTP site's folders and files. These settings control permissions for determining the level of access granted to a particular user account or user group. For example, you can configure your Web server so that only a specific user group has permission to view and execute a particular file, while excluding all other users from accessing that file.

Unlike Web or FTP server permissions, which apply to all users, you can use NTFS permissions to precisely define which users can access your content and how those users can manipulate that content. These permissions combine read and write permissions with Windows NT user accounts in User Manager for Domains. At the User Manager for Domains level, you define which users or groups have which types of NT file permissions.

You can control access to your Web server's directories and files by setting Windows NT File System access permissions. You can use permissions to define the level of access that you want to grant to specific users and groups. For example, you can set up permissions to allow some users to view and modify a particular file, while preventing other users from copying, moving, or executing the same file. Proper configuration of file and directory permissions is crucial for preventing unauthorized access.

The default access settings for NTFS directories and files grants Full Control access to the Everyone user group, which includes all users. This means that until you set permissions, all users have permission to modify, move, and delete files or directories and to change NTFS permissions.

If conflicts exist between your NTFS and Web server permissions, the most restrictive settings are used. Therefore, permissions that explicitly deny access always take precedence over permissions that grant access.

You can configure these permissions using Windows NT Explorer tools, which you can access directly from Internet Service Manager. To set access permissions for a directory or a file, do the following:

1. **In Internet Service Manager, right-click a folder, and then choose Explorer from the pop-up menu.**

   The directory contents appear in the Windows NT Explorer window.

2. **In Windows NT Explorer, right-click a directory or a file you want to secure with permissions, and then choose Properties from the pop-up menu.**

3. **Click the Security tab, and then click the Permissions button.**

   The File Permissions dialog box or Directory Permissions dialog box (see Figure 10-2) appears.

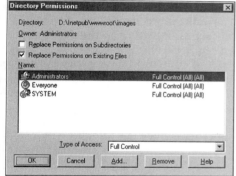

Figure 10-2:
The
Directory
Permissions
dialog box.

4. **Click the Add button.**

   The Add Users and Groups dialog box appears, as shown in Figure 10-3.

5. **In the List Names From box, select a computer or a domain.**

6. **In the Names box, select a user or a group to whom you want to grant access to your file or directory.**

7. **In the Type of Access box, set the access permission level for the selected user or group.**

8. **Click OK twice.**

Figure 10-3:
The Add
Users and
Groups
dialog box.

Authentication Control

Normally, all users attempting to establish a connection with your Web server or FTP server do so as anonymous users. When a user establishes an anonymous connection, your server must log on the user with the anonymous IUSR account. You can require users attempting to establish an FTP or a Web connection with restricted content to have a valid Windows NT account username and password. Each time a user attempts to access restricted content, your server *authenticates,* or checks, the user's identity to ensure that the user has a valid Windows NT account. User authentication occurs only when anonymous access is disabled or when NTFS permissions require users to identify themselves with a valid Windows NT account username and password.

IIS provides two authentication methods beyond the IUSR anonymous authentication account for Web servers. These two methods are Basic and Windows NT Challenge/Response. Your Web server will refuse to establish an anonymous connection and attempt to identify users with the authentication method you have enabled if, as before, anonymous access is disabled or NTFS permissions require a valid account username and password. By enabling different combinations of these authentication methods, in addition to setting up the anonymous user account, you can establish various levels of security for your server's content.

You configure authentication for an FTP server differently than you do for a Web server. FTP server security includes a few important additions to provide stricter security. IIS adds these settings because FTP has the potential to be more of a security risk than a Web server does. When users log on to the FTP service from the Internet, their usernames and passwords are vulnerable to detection.

When you set security properties, as with other IIS properties, for a specific site, you automatically set the same security properties for directories and files belonging to that site, unless the security properties of the individual directories and files have been set previously. Your server will prompt you for permission to reset the properties of individual directories and files when you attempt to set security properties for your site. If you choose to reset these properties, your previous security settings will be replaced by the new settings. The same condition applies when you set security properties for a directory containing subdirectories or files with previously set security properties.

Usernames in Windows NT domains

A username in Windows NT includes a domain name in addition to the actual user account username. This domain name identifies a computer or a group of computers administered by your Web server as a single entity. This means a username appears as *domain/username,* where *domain* is the Windows NT security domain and *username* is the logon name for the user on the Windows NT network. For example, a user account called David Angell on the Bookware domain would log on as Bookware/David Angell.

The term *domain name* refers to the Windows NT security system. Don't confuse it with the DNS (Domain Name System) name resolution system for TCP/IP networks.

Basic authentication

The Basic authentication method is widely used for collecting username and password information on the Internet. When Basic authentication is enabled on a Web server, the user's Web browser renders a dialog box in which users can enter their previously assigned Window NT account usernames and passwords. The Web browser then attempts to establish a connection by using this information. If the server rejects the information, the Web browser continues to prompt the user until the user enters a valid username and password or chooses to close the dialog box. After your Web server verifies that the username and password correspond to a valid Windows NT account, the user can establish a connection.

The big problem with using the Basic authentication method is that it transmits usernames and passwords as clear, unencrypted text across the Internet. Someone attempting to access your Web server content could use a network-monitoring tool to intercept username and password information.

To enable Basic authentication for your Web site, folder, or directory, do the following:

1. **In Internet Service Manager's results pane, right-click a Web site, a folder, or a file, and then choose Properties from the pop-up menu.**

2. **For a Web site or a folder, click the Directory Security tab. For an individual file, click the File Security tab.**

3. **In the Anonymous Access and Authentication Control group, click the Edit button.**

   The Authentication Methods dialog box appears, as shown in Figure 10-4.

Figure 10-4:
The
Authen-
tication
Methods
dialog box.

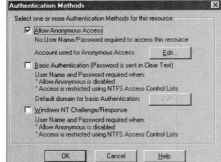

4. **Click the Basic Authentication check box.**

   A message box appears, warning you of the risks of using this authentication method.

5. **Click Yes.**

6. **Click the Edit button.**

   The Basic Authentication Domain dialog box appears, as shown in Figure 10-5. This box lets you define the Windows NT Domain used for Basic Authentication. The default is the local domain that the Web server is running.

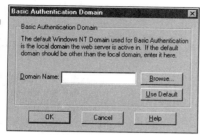

Figure 10-5:
The Basic
Authen-
tication
Domain
dialog box.

7. Click OK to exit the Authentication Methods dialog box.

Users authenticated with Basic authentication must log on with a valid
Windows NT username and password.

Windows NT Challenge/Response authentication

IIS Web servers support Windows NT Challenge/Response authentication,
which authenticates users without requiring the transmission of passwords
across a network. When you enable Windows NT Challenge/Response
authentication, the user's Internet Explorer browser proves its knowledge of
the password through a cryptographic exchange with your Web server. The
actual password never travels over the network. Microsoft Internet Explorer
is the only Web browser that supports this authentication method. The
Windows NT Challenge/Response authentication method is most useful
when both the user and Web server computers are in the same Windows NT
Server domain.

You can configure the Windows NT Challenge/Response authentication
feature to verify a user's identity and grant access to Web sites, directories,
or files. When you set security properties for a specific Web site, you
automatically set the same security properties for directories and files
belonging to that site, unless the security properties of the individual
directories and files have been set previously. Your Web server will prompt
you for permission to reset the properties of individual directories and files
when you attempt to set security properties for your Web site. If you choose
to reset these properties, your previous security settings will be replaced by
the new settings. The same condition applies when you set security properties for a directory containing subdirectories or files with previously set
security properties.

To enable Windows NT Challenge/Response authentication, do the following:

**1. In Internet Service Manager's results pane, right-click a Web site, a
directory, or a file, and then choose Properties from the pop-up menu.**

2. **For a Web site or a folder, click the Directory tab. For an individual file, click the File Security tab.**

3. **In the Anonymous Access and Authentication Control group, click the Edit button.**

   The Authentication Methods dialog box appears.

4. **Click the Windows NT Challenge/Response check box.**

5. **Click OK to exit the Authentication Methods dialog box.**

FTP server security

FTP server security doesn't include support for the Windows NT Challenge/Response authentication feature available for Web servers. The Security Accounts tab (Figure 10-6) in the Default FTP Site Properties dialog box, however, includes two other security settings. The Allow Anonymous Connection setting lets you specify the account used for anonymous client requests to log on to the computer. Allow Anonymous Connections allows users with the username *anonymous* to log on to your FTP server. Typically, anonymous FTP users use *anonymous* as the username and their e-mail address as the password. The FTP server then uses the IUSR_*computername* account as the logon account for permissions.

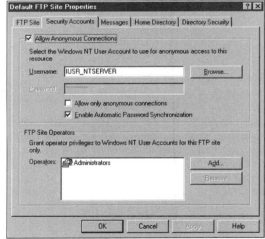

Figure 10-6:
The
Security
Accounts
tab of the
Default FTP
Site
Properties
dialog box.

The Enable Automatic Password Synchronization option makes sure that your FTP site and Windows NT password settings are identical. This option is active by default for any anonymous FTP server, which enables your FTP site to automatically synchronize your anonymous password settings with those set in the IUSR_*computername* account. Whenever you create a different FTP server authentication account, you must make sure that your FTP site and Windows NT password settings are identical.

Allow only anonymous connections

Clicking the Allow Only Anonymous Connections option restricts access to only anonymous connections. This means users cannot log on with their Windows NT usernames and passwords. You should take advantage of this property because it prevents access by user accounts with administrator permissions over your Windows NT Server.

If you select Allow Only Anonymous Connections and later decide to de-select it, an Internet Service Manager information dialog box appears, warning of the dangers of not using the anonymous only option, as shown in Figure 10-7. If you still want to disable the setting, click the Yes button.

Figure 10-7:
The Internet
Service
Manager
message
appears
when you
disable the
Allow Only
Anonymous
Connections
option.

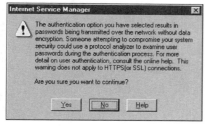

The IIS FTP server does not support Windows NT Challenge/Response authentication. When a user logs on to the FTP service from the Internet using any other username and password than those for an anonymous logon, that information is sent as clear text (unencrypted). Anyone with a sniffer program on an intermediate system can determine the username and password and can then use them to log on to your system.

Creating a private FTP server

You can create a private FTP site on your local intranet by defining the Windows NT user accounts that will have access to the site; these accounts replace the default IUSR anonymous account. This type of FTP service is only for users who already have an account on your Windows NT Server, and they must log on with a username and a password. They can download any file they would be permitted to read if they logged on locally, and they can upload to any directory for which they have write access.

To make the FTP site available to only a selected user account defined in User Manager for Domains, do the following:

1. **Right-click the FTP site you want, and then choose Properties from the pop-up menu.**

2. **Click the Security Accounts tab.**

3. **In the Allow Anonymous Connections group, click the Browse button.**

   The Select Windows NT User Account dialog box appears, as shown in Figure 10-8.

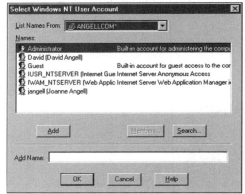

Figure 10-8:
The Select Windows NT User Account dialog box.

4. **Select the user account you want, click Add, and then click OK.**

   The Allow Anonymous Connections group in the Security Accounts tab displays Username and Password boxes, as shown in Figure 10-9.

5. **In the Password box, type the password for the Windows NT user account.**

   This account must have a password. This password is used only within Windows NT; anonymous users do not log on using this username and password.

6. **Click OK.**

   The Confirm Password dialog box appears.

7. **Type the password again, and then click OK.**

8. **Click OK to exit.**

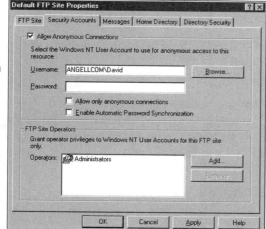

Figure 10-9:
The
Security
Accounts
tab
displaying
Username
and
Password
boxes.

Restricting Access via TCP/IP

You can configure your Web and FTP servers to prevent specific computers, groups of computers, or entire networks from accessing a server. This security is based on TCP/IP information, including IP addresses and domain names. When a user initially tries to access your Web site server content, the server checks the IP address of the user's computer against the server's IP address restriction setting. You can configure these settings to grant access to all computers or groups, or to all but specific computers or groups. Or you can restrict access to all computers or all groups except those to whom you specifically allow access. You can restrict access by TCP/IP elements through the Directory Security tab of the Web Properties or FTP Properties dialog box.

Although you can create a private Web or FTP site using the TCP/IP restrictions for denying access to everyone but designated IP addresses, this approach makes your site vulnerable to attacks known as *spoofing*. Chapter 5 explains this type of Internet-based attack.

Granting access to specific computers

You restrict access based on TCP/IP information using the same properties for both Web and FTP servers. The location of these properties, however, is different for Web and FTP servers. The following steps explain granting access to specific computers for either a Web or an FTP site:

1. **Right-click the Web or FTP site you want, and then choose Properties from the pop-up menu.**

2. **Do one of the following:**

   - For an FTP server, click the Directory Security tab.

   - For a Web server, click the Directory Security tab. Click the Edit button. The IP Address and Domain Name Restrictions dialog box appears, as shown in Figure 10-10.

Figure 10-10:
The IP
Address and
Domain
Name
Restrictions
dialog box.

3. **Choose the Denied Access option.**

   When you select this option, you deny access to all computers and domains, except those you specifically grant access to in this dialog box.

4. **Click Add.**

   The Grant Access On dialog box appears, as shown in Figure 10-11.

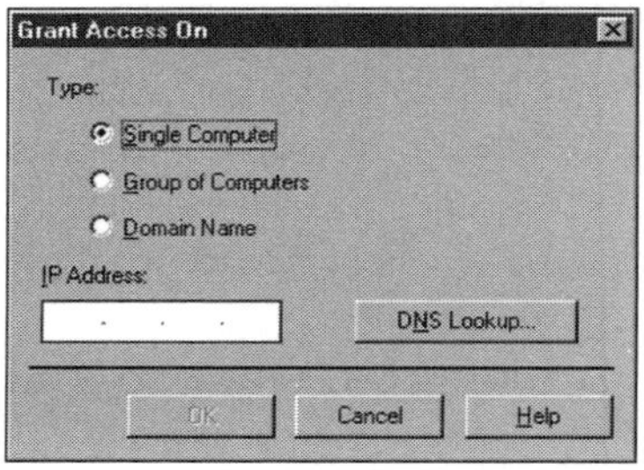

Figure 10-11:
The Grant
Access On
dialog box.

5. Select the **S**ingle Computer option.

6. In the **I**P Address box, type the IP address of the remote computer.

   You can click the DNS Lookup button to find a computer by its domain name rather than by its IP address.

7. **Click OK.**

   The IP address appears in the list of computers that are granted access.

Restricting access to only specific computers

The opposite of restricting access to all computers except the ones you list is to grant access to all computers except the ones you specify. The following steps explain denying access to specific computers for either a Web site or an FTP site:

1. **Right-click the Web or FTP site you want, and then choose Properties from the pop-up menu.**

2. **Do one of the following:**

   • For an FTP server, click on the Directory Security tab.

   • For a Web server, click on the Directory Security tab. In the Directory Security property sheet, click on the **E**dit button. The IP Address and Domain Name Restrictions dialog box appears.

3. **Choose the G**ranted Access option.

   When you select this option, you grant access to all computers and domains except those you specifically deny access to in this dialog box.

4. **Click A**dd.

   The Deny Access On dialog box appears.

5. **Select the S**ingle Computer option.

6. **In the I**P Address box, type the IP address of the remote computer.

   You can click the DNS Lookup button to find a computer by its domain name rather than by its IP address.

7. **Click OK**

   The IP ___ ___ ears in the list of computers that are denied access.

Assigning Site Operators

Site operators are a special Windows NT user group that has limited administrative privileges for individual Web and FTP sites. They do not have access to properties that affect the running of Internet Information Server, the Windows NT server hosting IIS, or the network. Site operators are based on existing Windows NT user accounts but have added permissions to perform Web and FTP site administration activities. By using site operators, you can assign responsibilities to other users on your Windows NT network to help administer your organization's Web and FTP sites. Site operators don't need to be members of a Windows NT administrators group.

Site operators can change or reconfigure a variety of Web and FTP site functions. A Web site operator can set Web site access permissions, enable logging, change the default document or footer, set content expiration, and enable content rating features. The Web site operator is not permitted to change the identification of the Web site, configure the anonymous username and password, throttle bandwidth, create virtual directories, or change the path of virtual directories. FTP site operators cannot change the identification of the FTP site, configure the anonymous username and password, create virtual directories, or change the path of virtual directories.

To assign an operator for either a Web or an FTP server, do the following:

1. **In Internet Service Manager, right-click the Web or FTP site, and then choose Properties from the pop-up menu.**

2. **For a Web site, click the Operators tab. For an FTP site, click the Security Accounts tab.**

3. **Click the Add button.**

   The Add Users and Groups dialog box appears.

4. **Select the user account you want to add to the Operator list for your Web or FTP site, and then click the Add button. Repeat for each additional user account you want to enter as an operator.**

5. **Click OK.**

   The selected users appear in the Operators list.

Keeping Secure with SSL

Keeping your network secure from outside attacks is one thing; keeping your communications secure over the Internet is another. If you want to create a secure Web server where specified users can work with sensitive, private information, you need to use Secure Sockets Layer (SSL) and digital certificates. The SSL protocol, created by Netscape, provides a way to send encrypted Web data over the Internet. Secure Sockets Layer provides the following services:

- Authentication to assure the Web client that the data is actually being sent to the right server and that the server is secure.

- Encryption/decryption to transform the data so that it can't be read by anyone other than the intended Web browser.

- Data integrity to ensure that the data stream isn't altered or tampered with in any way.

Keys and certificates

For the client and the server to send and receive encrypted data, both sides must know the secret to decrypting the data. This is where public and private keys come into play. Public key algorithms use a pair of keys — a public key and a private key — to encrypt and decrypt messages. Anyone can use the public key to encrypt data, but a private key is required to decrypt the data.

Digital certificates (also referred to as simply *certificates*) are the means for getting your security keys. A *digital certificate* is a short text file created by a special algorithm that combines a private key with a message. The recipient then verifies the digital certificate using the sender's public key and the message. The digital certificate is secure in the sense that it is virtually impossible to find another message that will produce an identical certificate. The degree of encryption strength is measured in bits. The greater or longer the number of bits that make up the session key, the greater the level of encryption and security of the communication session.

With SSL, your Web server can authenticate users by checking the contents of their client certificates, which function as driver's licenses or passports. Client certificates can contain detailed identification information about the user and organization that issues the certificate. With client certificates, you can configure your Web server to automatically connect, or map, users logging on with certificates to their matching Windows NT user accounts.

Both the server and the clients get their certificates from a mutually trusted third-party organization known as a Certificate Authority (CA). The leading CA on the Internet is VeriSign (www.verisign.com). The important point to keep in mind when using certificates is that you must purchase digital certificates for both the Web server and any Web clients for whom you want to provide secure access to the Web server. Here are some other important things to keep in mind about using SSL and certificates:

- After SSL is enabled and configured with digital IDs, only SSL-enabled Web browsers will be able to access your SSL-protected directories.

- URLs that point to an SSL-protected directory or Web site must use https:// instead of http://.

- If your site offers both secure and public content, you should set up two sets of directories, one for each kind of content. Do not configure an unsecured directory not protected by SSL as a parent for a secure directory.

- Certificates are sold as annual subscriptions that can quickly add up to serious money because you must have certificates for both the Web server and any Web browsers for which you want to have secure communications.

What certificates cost

Acquiring an SSL digital certificate requires several steps, including contacting the Certificate Authority (CA). VeriSign (www.verisign.com), a spin-off from RSA Data Security, acts as a trusted third-party certificate authority. RSA owns the public key encryption algorithms upon which the public key encryption is based.

VeriSign provides digital certificates and certificate-management services, including issuing several classes of certificates. What class you use depends on the types of applications the certificates are used with and the level of assurance required regarding the user's identity. Purchasing a digital certificate for your Web server costs $349 for the initial year. You can add additional certificates for other servers for $249 each. After the first year, the renewal fee is $75. You can purchase a Class 1 or Class 2 digital ID. The Class 1 digital ID costs $9.95 for one year. The Class 2 digital ID with greater security for electronic transactions costs $19.95 a year.

You can get a trial version of both server and client certificates from the VeriSign Web site. The trial server certificates last 14 days, and the trial client certificates last 60 days. If you're not sure whether you want to go the SSL route, try out the test certificates.

The Microsoft Certificate Server

Internet Information Server includes the Certificate Server, which allows you to create your own private key pairs. These key pairs, however, are not usable on an Internet Web site because there is no way to prove who you are and the identity of the users connecting to your Web site from the Internet. The use of the Certificate Server is limited to adding security for intranets.

Getting and Setting Up Certificates

Setting up Internet Information Server for SSL requires a number of steps. The following lists the operations you need to perform to enable SSL on a Web server:

- Use Key Manager to generate a key pair.
- Contact a certification authority and request a certificate for your security keys.
- Install the certificate you obtained from the certificate authority on your server.
- Activate SSL for Web servers and directories that require security.

Getting a Dun & Bradstreet number

To purchase a certificate digital ID for a Web server, you should get a Dun & Bradstreet (D&B) number for your business. Getting a D&B number doesn't cost anything except the time to apply. Using a D&B number makes the process of applying for a certificate much easier. Without a D&B number, you must fax or mail copies of your company's information, such as Articles of Incorporation, partnership papers, business license, DBA (doing business as) license, or federal tax number. Your business may already have a D&B number, which you can check as part of the application process.

To get a D&B number, you need to fill out a three-page online form with information about your business. It takes a few days to get your D&B number, so do this before actually purchasing your server certificates. You don't need a D&B number to get a sample server certificate or client certificates. The following steps show you how to get a D&B number online through the VeriSign Web site.

You can point your browser to `www.dnb.com/aboutdb/Verisigndunsform.htm` to bypass navigating the VeriSign site.

1. **Point your browser to** `digitalid.verisign.com/dnd_query.htm`.

2. **Click the Continue button at the bottom of the page.**

3. **In the online form, type your company name, choose the state where it's located, and type your city.**

4. **Click the Submit button.**

   A listing of businesses with some matching elements appears.

5. **If your business is in the Dun & Bradstreet database, select your business record by clicking the radio button.**

   The D&B number appears in the text at the top of the screen. Make a note of the number and go on to the next section.

6. **If you need a D&B number, click the Request D-U-N-S Number link.**

   A DUNS Number Request form appears. Complete the form with information about your business.

7. **Click the Send Form button.**

Generating a key pair

Key Manager enables you to create a key request file that you will eventually upload to VeriSign (the certificate authority). Key Manager is already installed on your system as part of Internet Information Server, and you access it from Internet Service Manager. The following steps explain how to create the request file you need:

1. **In the MMC window, click the Key Manager button.**

   It's the fifth button from the right on the Internet Service Manager toolbar. The Key Manager window appears, as shown in Figure 10-12.

2. **Select the server type WWW on the server where you want to add SSL support.**

3. **Choose Key⇨Create New Key.**

   The Create New Key wizard appears, as shown in Figure 10-13.

4. **Click the option titled Put the Request in a File That You Will Send to an Authority, and then click Next.**

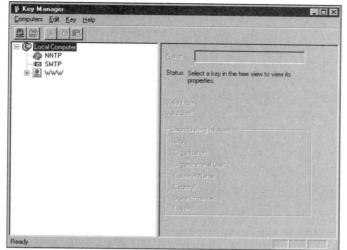

Figure 10-12:
The Key
Manager
window.

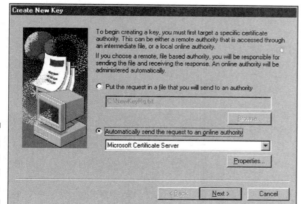

Figure 10-13:
The Create
New Key
wizard.

5. **In the Key information page, complete the following, and then click Next:**

   - In the Key Name box, enter a descriptive name so you can identify the key later.

   - In the Password box, enter a password and then confirm it in the Confirm Password field.

   - Leave the Bit Length setting at 512.

6. **In the Organizational information page, do the following, and then click Next:**

   • In the Organization field, type your company name.

   • In the Organizational Unit field, type your department within your company, such as Marketing.

   • In the Common Name field, type the domain name of your Web server as it will appear in your URL, such as www.angell.com.

7. **Fill in the following information, and then click Next.**

   • Type your two-letter country name abbreviation or select it from the list.

   • Type your state or province name.

   • Type your city or locality.

Spell out the entire state and city or locality name. Don't use abbreviations or the certificate application will be rejected at VeriSign, and you'll have to create a new key pair.

8. **In the Administrator contact information page, do the following, and then click Next.**

   • Type your name.

   • Type your e-mail address.

   • Type your phone number.

9. **Click Finish.**

   A message box appears, telling you that the file is created.

10. **Click OK.**

Applying for the certificate

What you created using Key Manager in Internet Information Server was a key pair and a Certificate Signing Request (CSR). You now need to use this information to apply for a certificate at VeriSign (www.verisign.com). You can apply for a free 14-day trial certificate for your server, or you can purchase a certificate. The following sections explain how to do both.

The VeriSign Web site, like other Web sites, changes frequently, so the procedures for purchasing and getting a free 14-day trial certificate may change.

Buying a server certificate online

The easiest way to get your server certificate is to purchase it online at the VeriSign Web site. Here is how VeriSign certifies you with your purchase of a certificate for the first year:

1. **In Notepad or any text editor, open the NewKeyRq.txt file.**

   Figure 10-14 shows the NewKeyRq.txt file in Notepad.

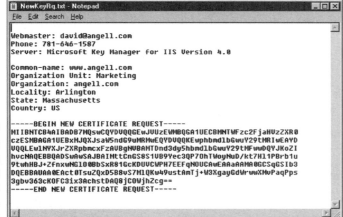

Figure 10-14:
The
NewKeyRq.txt
file in
Notepad.

2. **Point your Web browser to** https://digitalid.verisign.com/.

3. **Click the Enroll button.**

   A Web page appears, asking you to select the type of digital ID you want.

4. **Under Organizations, click Web Servers.**

5. **Choose I Want a Secure Server Digital ID to Run SSL on My Server.**

6. **Select Microsoft from the list of server software vendors, and then click the Select button.**

   A page of registration information appears.

7. **Click the Continue button at the bottom of the page.**

8. **Cut the CSR text from the Notepad window, paste it into the text box, and then click Continue.**

9. **Do the following:**

- Verify that your CSR information is correct. If any information is wrong, you must generate a new CSR with the appropriate information.

- From the list, choose Microsoft as your server software vendor.

- Type a Challenge Phrase that is easy for you to remember and hard for someone else to guess. You'll need this phase later if you want to revoke your digital ID.

- Enter names and contact information for a Technical Contact, an Organizational Contact, and a Billing Contact.

- Choose the option titled This Is the First VeriSign Digital ID My ORGANIZATION Has Requested-USD 349.00.

- Choose the way you want to pay — credit card, purchase order, or check.

- In the DUNS Number box, type your DUNS number.

10. **Click the Accept button.**

Your technical and organizational contacts will receive an e-mail message confirming your enrollment. The message will include a PIN and a URL where you can use that PIN to check the status of your certificate request. When your certificate is approved, VeriSign sends it to your technical and organizational contacts by e-mail. When you receive your digital ID, make a backup copy of it and store it on a labeled floppy disk, noting the date you received it. You're now ready to install the certificate in Internet Information Server.

Getting a free test certificate

VeriSign also offers a test certificate for your Web server that you can try out for 14 days. You create a Key Pair and Certificate Signing Request in the same way you do for purchasing a certificate, and then fill out an online form. Unlike getting the real thing, you don't need a Dun & Bradstreet number to get a test certificate.

Here's how to get a test certificate for a Web server:

1. **Generate a Key Pair and Certificate Signing Request (CSR) by following the steps under "Generating a key pair."**

2. **Point your Web browser to** www.verisign.com.

3. **Click Server IDs.**

4. **Click the Try It button.**

5. **Click the Begin button at the bottom of the page.**

6. **Use your Web browser to cut and paste your CSR into the Enrollment form.**

   You can open up the text file containing your CSR information.

7. **Verify your Distinguished Contact Information, and then enter the Contact Information.**

8. **Click the Accept button under the Digital ID Subscriber Agreement.**

9. **Click the Install button.**

   The file download process begins.

10. **Save the file on a floppy disk for backup and to a directory on your Windows NT Server machine running IIS.**

VeriSign will e-mail the test certificate, which you should then install on your Web server using the IIS Key Manager.

Backing up your certificate

Your certificate is a valuable piece of information. It's a good idea to back up the certificate file and keep it in a safe place, in case you ever have to reinstall it. You can use Key Manager to create a ready-to-use backup file by doing the following:

1. **In Key Manager, choose Key⇨Export⇨Backup File.**

2. **Read the warning about downloading sensitive information to your hard disk.**

3. **In the File Name box, type the key name.**

4. **Click Save.**

The file is given a .req filename extension and is saved to your hard disk drive. You can copy it to a floppy disk or magnetic tape after you have completed all the key setup steps; just don't forget the password you gave the key file.

Adding a certificate to your Web server

After applying for a certificate with a certification authority, you will receive a signed certificate. A certificate is a text file with a long string of coded letters. The following steps explain how to add the certificate information to your IIS server:

1. **Make sure your certificate information is in a separate text file.**

2. **Open Key Manager, and highlight the key for which you want to install a certificate.**

3. **Choose Key➪Install Key Certificate.**

   The Open dialog box appears.

4. **Locate your certificate text file and open it.**

   Key Manager asks for your password.

5. **Type your password, and then press Enter.**

   The Server Bindings dialog box appears, as shown in Figure 10-15.

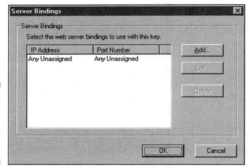

Figure 10-15:
The Server
Bindings
dialog box.

6. **Choose the specific IP address for your certificate.**

   You can also use the Any Unassigned option to apply the certificate to all unassigned IP addresses. Click the Add button to enter any additional IP addresses.

7. **Click OK.**

   Key Manager installs your certificate and activates the key. The red line through the key disappears.

8. **Choose Computers➪Commit Changes Now to make the changes permanent.**

9. **Close Key Manager.**

Activating SSL on your Web server

After you install the certificate using Key Manager, you're ready to activate SSL for your Web server. You can apply SSL security to any virtual directory on the Web server. To activate SSL for any directory or Web server, do the following:

1. **Start Internet Service Manager.**

2. **Right-click the Web server or directory you want to use, and then choose Properties from the pop-up menu.**

3. **Click the Directory Security tab, and then click the Edit button in the Secure Communications group.**

   The Secure Communications dialog box appears, as shown in Figure 10-16.

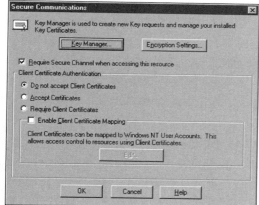

Figure 10-16: The Secure Communications dialog box.

4. **Click the Require Secure Channel When Accessing This Resource check box.**

   This enables SSL support from the server site.

5. **Choose a client certificate option from the following:**

   - The Do Not Accept Client Certificates option means no client certificates are required.

   - The Accept Certificates option means the Web server will accept a client certificate if one is available.

   - The Require Client Certificates option means the client must provide a certificate before your Web server will allow access.

- The Enable Client Certificate Mapping option maps your client certificate information to Windows NT user accounts, which gives clients access to the restricted Windows NT resource. To display the Account Mappings dialog box, which is shown in Figure 10-17, click the Edit button.

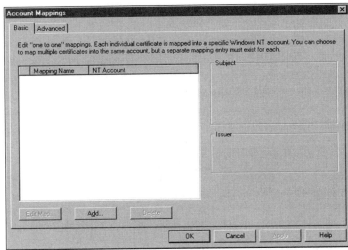

Figure 10-17:
The Account
Mappings
dialog box.

6. **Click the Encryption Settings button.**

   The Encryption Settings dialog box appears, as shown in Figure 10-18. The default setting is 40 bit, which enables international access to your Web server.

7. **If you want to require a browser to be capable of 128-bit encryption to connect with your server, select the Require 128-bit Encryption check box.**

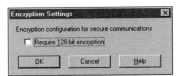

Figure 10-18:
The
Encryption
Settings
dialog box.

If you use the 128-bit setting, you effectively restrict access to your secure server to Internet users from the United States and Canada. The 128-bit key strength encryption feature is available only in the United States and Canada and restricted for export. International versions of Web browsers don't support the 128-bit encryption.

8. Click OK.

Certificate Server

Certificate Server, which comes with Internet Information Server, allows you to create your own certificates. Because these certificates don't come from a Certificate Authority, however, you can use them only as part of securing internal, intranet communications. You must install Certificate Server using the Windows NT 4.0 Option Pack Setup program.

To access the information maintained in this database, you can use the Certificate Server Administration Tools, a Web-based package. But before you can use this package, you must be logged on as an Administrator, and the Certificate Server must be running.

In your Web browser, open the default.htm file in the \WINNT\System32\ CertSrv\ directory. The Microsoft Certificate Server home page appears, as shown in Figure 10-19.

Figure 10-19: The Certificate Server administration page.

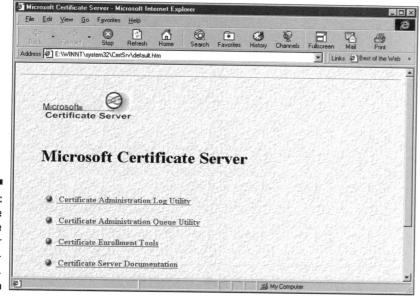

The Certificate Server Administrator includes the following four options:

- ✔ Certificate Log Utility lets you look at the Certificate Log Administration Page. Each row contains a database record for each certificate, and the rows are displayed in the order in which the certificates were created.

- ✔ Certificate Queue Utility allows you to look at the Certificate Queue Administration Page, where each row contains information on requests for a certificate, and the rows are displayed in the order in which the requests were received.

- ✔ Certificate Enrollment opens the Certificate Server Enrollment Page.

- ✔ Certificate Server Documentation opens the extensive documentation package that accompanies Certificate Server; this documentation also includes information for application programmers working to create custom modules to use with Certificate Server.

Security Guidelines

You can achieve a reliable security configuration only by properly setting your Web server and Windows NT security features. To properly safeguard your Web server content, your security practices should include carefully managing passwords on your network and limiting the access to your Web server's Administrative group.

Unauthorized individuals can gain access to your Web server by stealing or guessing user account passwords. You must make sure that all passwords, especially those used for protecting Administrative privileges, are difficult to guess. To select strong passwords, use the following guidelines:

- ✔ Avoid selecting common words as passwords.

- ✔ Require that passwords be greater than eight characters and contain both uppercase and lowercase characters, numbers, and even non-standard characters.

- ✔ Require users to regularly change passwords or add password expirations to user accounts to force password changes.

- ✔ Change all passwords at least every 90 days and be sure that all passwords are removed from the system.

- ✔ Always remove user accounts of terminated employees as well as all unused accounts.

Be sure to limit access to your Web server's Administrative group. Members of the Administrative group have complete control over your entire Web server and its security features. The best advice here is to grant Administrator privileges only to trusted individuals and periodically change the Administrator account password.

Part III
Beyond the Fundamentals

The 5th Wave   By Rich Tennant

"We're researching molecular/digital technology that moves massive amounts of information across binary pathways that interact with free-agent programs capable of making decisions and performing logical tasks. We see applications in really high-end doorbells."

In this part . . .

This part taps into Internet Information Server's power tools. You set up the Microsoft News Server to create a Usenet message-based conferencing server to host discussion newsgroups like the ones on the Internet. You also set up Microsoft Index Server to let users search the contents of your Web and News servers as a searchable database. Adding to your Webmaster toolkit, you delve into publishing interactive content using Active server pages, scripting languages (VBScript and JScript), and ActiveX components. On the database front, you find out how to connect Microsoft Access and Microsoft SQL Server databases to your IIS Web sites to create updateable Web pages from database queries. This part ends with how to work with logging to record the activity going on at your sites and how to create graphical usage analysis reports.

Chapter 11

Conferencing with Microsoft News Server

. . . .

In This Chapter

▶ Setting up Microsoft News server

▶ Managing newsgroups

▶ Establishing expiration policies

▶ Setting up moderated newsgroups

▶ Changing the location of newsgroups

▶ Controlling Microsoft News server remotely

. . . .

*I*nternet Information Server includes Internet NNTP Service, which uses the Network News Transport Protocol (NNTP) to create a Usenet message-based conferencing server. Users from the Internet or on your intranet can read and post messages to these newsgroups using any newsreader program, such as Microsoft Outlook Express. This chapter tells you how to set up and run your own NNTP server in Internet Information Server.

About Microsoft News Server

The Microsoft NNTP Service — referred to as *Microsoft News server* — provides a convenient means for accessing a simple tool that enables communication between groups of users. The News server manages both moderated and unmoderated threaded discussion groups. These discussion groups can be made available via an intranet or to Internet users. You can make each newsgroup a public or private newsgroup as well as control what articles get posted to a newsgroup. You can create a public newsgroup that anyone can read but to which only selected individuals can post.

Newsgroups are popular because they create an electronic forum where people with common interests can share views and information. These forums, known as *threaded discussion groups,* support streams of conversation among multiple users that can occur over extended periods. Users can start their own conversation threads, or they can follow or respond to existing threads at their convenience. Users can access and use your newsgroups with Microsoft Outlook Express, which comes with Internet Explorer, or any other program.

The Microsoft NNTP Service does not support Usenet news feeds to or from other network news servers on the Internet. Usenet is the Internet-based bulletin board system of special-interest discussion groups, which number in the thousands.

After a user writes a news article in a newsreader, the user initiates a connection to the News server and sends a request to post the article to one or more newsgroups. The news client usually connects to the News server through access port 119, which is the default anonymous connection TCP/IP port. (However, any port not used by another server or service can be used.) The News server receives the connection request, verifies authentication of the user account, and determines whether the user can post to the intended newsgroups. Upon authentication, the NNTP service receives the article and places it into news storage, where other users can access it. You manage your NNTP server using Internet Service Manager in the Microsoft Management Console. Like other servers in Internet Information Server, a variety of administration functions can be performed from the server's properties dialog box.

Installing Microsoft News Server

You install Microsoft News server using the Windows NT 4.0 Option Pack Setup program. At least one Internet Information Server service, such as a Web or an FTP server, must be installed so that files required by the NNTP service are properly configured. Here's how to install the Microsoft News server:

1. **Click Start⇨Programs⇨Windows NT 4.0 Option Pack⇨Windows NT 4.0 Option Pack Setup.**

   The Microsoft Windows NT 4.0 Option Pack Setup wizard appears.

2. **Click Next, and then click the Add/Remove button.**

3. **In the Components list, double-click the Internet Information Server (IIS) item, or select it and then click the Show Subcomponents button.**

   A listing of subcomponents for Internet Information Server appears.

4. In the Suḇcomponents of Internet Information Server (IIS) list, click the Internet NNTP Service check box, and then click OK.

5. Click N̲ext.

6. Use the default setting "C:\Inetpub\Nntproot" entry in the N̲ntpFile Directory setting for the root directory of Network News Server, and then click N̲ext.

7. Click F̲inish.

Basic News Server Administration

Setting up Microsoft News server involves updating and configuring its properties in a similar manner used for Web and FTP sites. To access the News server properties, right-click Default NNTP Site in Internet Service Manager's results pane. The Default NNTP Site Properties dialog box appears, as shown in Figure 11-1. You'll notice some familiar and some new tabs in the NNTP Properties dialog box. Four tabs — News Site, Home Directory, Security Accounts, and Directory Security — include similar properties used by the Web and FTP servers. The two additional tabs — Groups and NTTP Settings — are unique to the NTTP Site Properties dialog box.

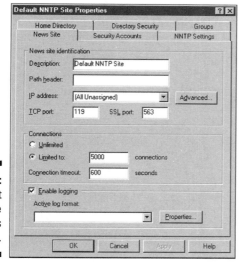

Figure 11-1: The Default NNTP Site Properties dialog box.

Managing connections

Managing your NNTP server connections helps prevent the server from becoming overloaded. You can control the number of simultaneous users connected to your server at any one time, as well as restrict the time that an inactive connection stays linked to your News server. By default, a news server restricts the number of simultaneous connections to 5,000 users, which you can change by simply entering a new number in the Limited to Connections box of the News Site tab.

Setting a timeout value in the Connection Timeout box reduces loss of processing resources for broken connections. The default time-out value is 600 seconds, or 10 minutes. In most cases, you'll want to reduce this setting to a more reasonable setting. A typical value might be 300 seconds (5 minutes) or less, after which the connection is closed.

Handling News server security

The Security Accounts and Directory Security tabs in the NNTP Properties dialog box let you manage security for your NNTP server. These settings are the same ones available in the Web Site Properties dialog box. The Security Accounts tab, shown in Figure 11-2, is used to specify a Windows NT Server user account for anonymous access. The default is the same anonymous user account used by the Web and FTP sites: IUSER_*computername*. You can also specify, in the News Site Operators group, other Windows NT Server user accounts that will have privileges to provide limited management of the NNTP server.

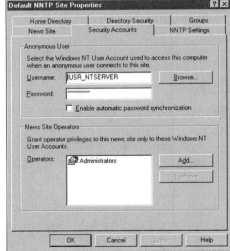

Figure 11-2: The Security Accounts property sheet.

The Directory Security tab enables you to specify security access to your NNTP directories, including three authentication options for your news server. The default setting allows anonymous access, in which no username or password is required to access the News server. The two other, more restrictive security options are the Basic and Windows NT Challenge/ Response authentication methods. You can also deny or grant access to a News server directory by TCP/IP address. By default, all directories are accessible for all TCP/IP addresses. You can, however, either grant or deny access to specified TCP/IP or domain name addresses. Chapter 10 explains working with these security properties.

Changing the home directory

During the setup of Microsoft News server, you specified a home directory for the storage of news articles. The default location is `C:\InetPub\NntpRoot`. You can use the Home Directory tab to specify another directory for news storage. Before you can specify a new home directory, though, you need to create the directory using Windows NT Explorer.

The Home Directory includes two options for changing your home directory location:

- **A Directory Location on This Computer.** Select this option if the directory you want for your home directory is on the local NT Server. In the Local path box, enter the path to the directory or use the Browse button to navigate to and select the directory.

- **A Share Located on Another Computer.** Select this option if the location of the directory storing your news messages is located on another computer on your local network. In the Network directory path, enter the network path or click the Connect As button to navigate to the computer on your network. You need to enter the username and password to log on to the other computer.

Setting restrictions and content controls

The Home Directory tab also provides four settings for access restrictions and content control. These settings follow:

- The Allow Posting setting in the Access Restrictions group allows news clients to post articles to newsgroups in the directory.

- The Restrict Newsgroup Visibility setting in the Access Restrictions group restricts the viewing of newsgroup lists in this directory to users who have access permissions for newsgroups. This option adds processing overhead and should not be used for newsgroups that allow anonymous access.

✔ The Log Access setting in the Content Control group generates a log of news client access to this directory. To enable logging, you must also select the Enable Logging check box in the News Site tab, which by default is active.

✔ The Index News Content setting in the Content Control group lets you index the newsgroups in this directory with Microsoft Index Server, which allows users to search for specific text.

Testing your News server

The best way to test that Microsoft News server is working properly is to make a connection with a newsreader. When you're connected, you should be able to read articles and post messages to a newsgroup. To test the NNTP server, you can use Outlook Express, which comes with Microsoft Internet Explorer. Here's how to configure the Outlook Express newsreader to access your NNTP server:

1. Do one of the following:

- If you're using the Outlook Express newsreader for the first time, the Internet Connection wizard will walk you through the configuration of the newsreader. Go to Step 4 to begin your configuration.

- If your newsreader is already configured for a news server, open the newsreader in Outlook Express, which you can do from the main screen by clicking the Read News icon. If you're in the e-mail client, you can choose Go⇨News. Either way, the Outlook Express Newsreader appears, as shown in Figure 11-3.

Figure 11-3:
The Outlook Express Newsreader.

2. Choose Tools⇨Accounts.

   The Internet Accounts dialog box appears.

3. Click the News tab.

4. Click the Add button, and then select News.

   The Internet Connection wizard appears.

5. In the Display Name box, type the name you want to display in your posting's From box, and then click Next.

6. In the E-mail Address box, type your e-mail address, and then click Next.

7. In the News (NTTP) Server box, type the domain name or IP address of your NTTP server.

8. If your NNTP server requires a username and password to log on, click the My News Server Requires Me to Log On.

9. Click Next.

10. In the Internet News Account Name box, enter a descriptive name to make it easier for you to identify the news server. Click Next.

11. Choose the Connect Using My Local Area Network (LAN) for Any Computer on Your Local Network. Click Next, and then click Finish.

    Your new news server entry appears in the Internet Accounts dialog box.

12. If you want the news server to be your default news server, select the server you just entered, and click the Set as Default button.

13. Click the Close button.

    Outlook Express asks whether you want to download newsgroups from your news server.

14. Click Yes.

    The Newsgroups running on your NNTP server appear in the Outlook Newsgroups dialog box, as shown in Figure 11-4.

15. For each newsgroup you want to subscribe to, select the newsgroup and click the Subscribe button.

    You can click the Unsubscribe button to not subscribe to any previously subscribed newsgroup.

16. Click OK.

    All the articles for the selected newsgroups are available for reading in the Outlook Express Newsreader.

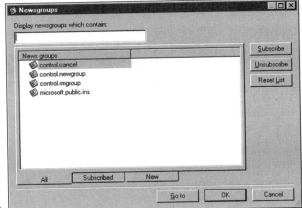

Figure 11-4:
The Outlook
Express
Newsgroups
dialog box.

Monitoring current sessions

You can check the status of the current NNTP server session at any time. Expanding the Default NNTP site in the scope pane of Internet Information Server displays the Current sessions object. Clicking Current sessions displays in the results pane all the users connected to your NNTP, including the username and address and the time they connected.

You can disconnect a single connected user by right-clicking its entry in the results pane and then choosing Terminate from the pop-up menu. To disconnect all users currently connected to your News server, right-click any entry in the results pane, and then choose Terminate All.

Working with Newsgroups

The NNTP Settings tab and the Groups tab in the Default NNTP Site Properties dialog box include the properties for creating, modifying, and deleting your newsgroups. These tabs also provide properties for managing postings to your newsgroups. You can configure newsgroups to operate without a moderator or have a moderator who accepts or rejects news articles. This section explains how to create and manage your newsgroups.

Creating newsgroups

You create newsgroups using the Create New Newsgroup button in the Groups tab, which is shown in Figure 11-5. You can create as many newsgroups as you want for the News server. For your newsgroups, you can use the same DNS format that's used by newsgroups on the Internet, such as bookware.public.news and bookware.employee.benefits.

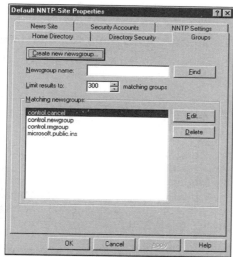

Figure 11-5:
The
Groups tab.

To create newsgroups, do the following:

1. In the Default NNTP Site Properties dialog box, click the Groups tab.

2. Click the Create New Newsgroup button.

The Newsgroup Properties dialog box appears, as shown in Figure 11-6.

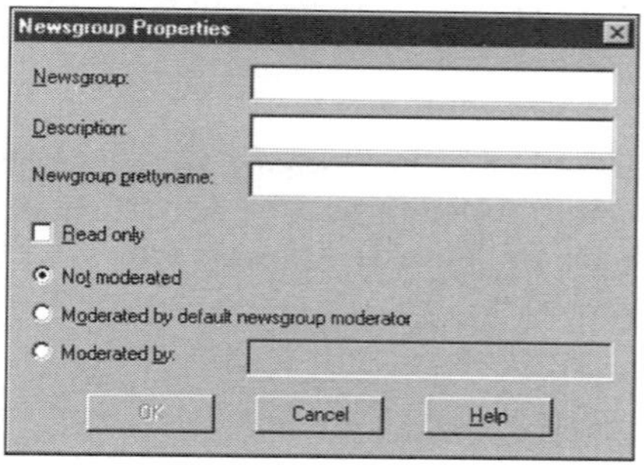

Figure 11-6:
The
Newsgroup
Properties
dialog box.

3. **In the Newsgroup text box, type the name for the newsgroup.**

   For example, you can use a DNS style name entry such as water.cooler.updates. Optionally, in the Description text box, you can enter a comment that describes the newsgroup.

4. **If you want to prevent messages from being posted to the newsgroup, click the Read Only check box.**

   Keep in mind that this restricts the newsgroup to one-way communication.

5. **Click OK to return to the Groups tab.**

6. **Repeat Steps 2 through 5 for each newsgroup you want to create.**

   Your newsgroups appear in the Matching Newsgroups list.

Editing and deleting newsgroups

Editing and deleting newsgroups is straightforward using the Groups tab. If you have a large number of newsgroups, you can find a particular newsgroup by entering the first few characters of the newsgroup name (or the entire name) in the Newsgroup Name text box and then clicking the Find button. Any matching newsgroup appears in the Matching Newsgroups list. The Limit Results To option defines the maximum number of newsgroups to be displayed using a Find query. The default is 300 newsgroups.

You can select multiple newsgroups in the Matching Newsgroups list. Hold down the Ctrl key while clicking newsgroups to select multiple newsgroups in the list. If you want to select a contiguous group, click the first newsgroup, scroll to the last newsgroup you want, press Shift, and click that newsgroup.

You can edit any newsgroup entry by selecting the newsgroup in the Matching Newsgroups list and then clicking the Edit button. The Newsgroup Properties dialog box appears (see Figure 11-6), which is the same dialog box you use to create a newsgroup. The only difference is that the Newsgroup text box is not available for changing the name of the newsgroup. You must create a newsgroup and delete the old one to change the name of a newsgroup.

You can delete a newsgroup by selecting the newsgroup in the Matching Newsgroups list and then clicking the Delete button. A confirmation box appears, asking whether you want to delete the newsgroup; click Yes to delete the selected newsgroup.

Managing postings

The NTTP Settings tab, shown in Figure 11-7, provides several properties for managing postings and limiting the amount of data transferred in a session. By default, the Allow Client Posting check box is checked as well as the Limit Post Size and Limit Connection Size settings. Clicking Allow Client Posting bars users from posting any articles directly to the News server, and deactivates the related Limit Post Size and Limit Connection Size settings.

You can limit the size of an article posting by clicking the Limit Post Size check box and then specifying the size in kilobytes. The default is 1000K. The Limit Connection Size setting lets you limit the maximum amount of data that can be transferred in one session. The maximum is 400MB, and the default setting is 20MB.

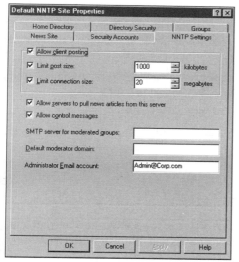

Figure 11-7:
The NTTP
Settings
tab.

Creating an expiration policy for newsgroups

An *expiration policy* lets you keep the contents of newsgroups current automatically by weeding out old postings. For example, you can define an expiration policy to delete all news articles older than 14 days from all newsgroups. Similarly, you can define an expiration policy to allow a total of no more than 500MB of news articles on your News server. When the limit is reached, the News server begins removing the oldest articles and replacing them with newly posted articles to keep the size at 500MB. To set an expiration policy, do the following:

1. **In Internet Service Manager's results pane, right-click NNTP Site, and then choose New➪Expiration Policy from the pop-up menu.**

   The New Expiration Policy wizard appears.

2. **In the Expiration Policy Description text box, type a descriptive name for your expiration policy, and then click Next.**

3. **Choose one of the following:**

   - Select All Newsgroups on This Site, and then click Next.
   - Select Only Selected Newsgroups on This Site, and then click Next. The next page prompts you to specify the newsgroups you want to be affected by this expiration policy.

4. **Click the When Articles Become Older Than setting, and specify the number of days you want to keep the messages on the server before they expire.**

5. **Click the When the Combined Group Size Exceeds setting; in the megabytes setting, enter the maximum size.**

6. **Click Finish.**

   After you create an expiration policy, it appears under the Expiration policies folder in the scope pane of Internet Service Manager.

Setting up moderated newsgroups

If you want control over what articles are posted to a newsgroup, you can create a moderated newsgroup. Articles submitted to a moderated newsgroup are not posted until the moderator for the newsgroup approves them. When a user submits an article to a moderated newsgroup, Microsoft NNTP service sends the article to a newsgroup moderator. The moderator can either approve the article and send it back to the NNTP server to be posted, or discard the article. For discarded articles, the moderator can send a message to the article's author to explain why the article was rejected.

SMTP and moderated newsgroups

To use moderated newsgroups, you have to specify either a SMTP (Simple Mail Transfer Protocol) mail server for sending articles directly to the moderators or a directory where the articles are stored for the moderators. SMTP is the universal standard for electronic mail on the Internet. The Microsoft SMTP server that comes with Internet Information Server and is already installed in Internet Service Manager handles the message-forwarding requirements of moderated newsgroups. The Default SMTP Site in IIS only forwards e-mail messages; it's not a full-blown POP3 (Post Office Protocol 3) server, which provides the full range of e-mail services. Microsoft Exchange Server is a POP3 server that receives and routes e-mail as well as manages user e-mail boxes.

For running the NNTP service, the default configuration settings for the SMTP server do the job. You can, however, make changes to the Default SMTP Site in Internet Service Manager. Like any IIS server, its properties can be displayed by right-clicking the Default SMTP Site in the results pane and then choosing Properties from the pop-up menu. The Default SMTP Site Properties dialog box appears, as shown in Figure 11-8. For more information on working with the SMTP Server, check out the IIS documentation by choosing Start⇨Programs⇨Windows NT 4.0 Option Pack⇨Product Documentation.

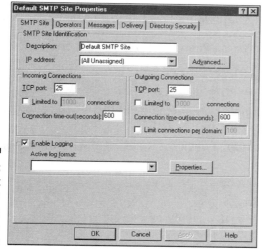

Figure 11-8: The Default SMTP Site Properties dialog box.

Enabling moderated newsgroups

Before you create a moderated newsgroup, you need to specify the SMTP server to use for your newsgroup. You also can specify a default moderator domain, which is used as the basis of each moderator's e-mail address. If you choose to use the default moderator for a News server, articles are sent to `newsgroup_name@default-domain`. To enable moderated newsgroups, do the following:

1. **In the Default NNTP Site Properties dialog box, click the NNTP Setting tab.**

2. **In the SMTP Server for Moderated Groups text box, type either the DNS name or the IP address of the Default SMTP Site server, or enter the path to the directory where articles are to be stored for the moderators.**

The directory path must be a local directory. You should normally set this value to the pickup directory of the SMTP Server, which by default is `\Inetpub\Mailroot\Pickup`.

3. **In the Default Moderator Domain text box, type the e-mail domain for default moderators.**

    For example, angell.com might be the domain.

4. **Type the e-mail account you want to use for the receipt of moderated newsgroup articles that cannot be delivered to the designated moderator, which is typically the server NTTP server administrator.**

5. **Click OK.**

Creating a moderated newsgroup

You can create a moderated newsgroup or convert an existing newsgroup into a moderated newsgroup. Here's how to create a moderated newsgroup:

1. **In the Default NNTP Site Properties dialog box, click the Groups tab.**

2. **Click the Create New Newsgroup button.**

    The Newsgroup Properties dialog box appears.

3. **In the Newsgroup box, type the name of the newsgroup you want to create.**

4. **In the Description box, type a brief description of the newsgroup function.**

5. **Choose one of the following:**

    - Click the Moderated by Default Newsgroup Moderator option if you want to use the default newsgroup moderator as defined in the NTTP Settings property sheet.

    - Click the Moderated By option, and then type the e-mail address of the moderator in the box.

6. **Choose OK.**

Adding New Identities to Your News Server

You cannot create additional NNTP servers, as you can with IIS Web and FTP servers. You can, however, create additional identities for the NNTP server to make it appear as though it were more than a single news server. This enables the same NNTP server to host a news site with the domain name news.angell.com as well as a news site with the domain name of news.bookware.com. You can create virtual news sites with each one using a different assigned IP address that shares the same TCP/IP port 119 for anonymous access. You also can create multiple news site identities using the same IP address but a different port number. Using any TCP/IP port besides 119, however, requires the port number be added to the News server address in the client newsreader.

Setting up IP addresses

Before you can create a virtual News server, your network adapter cards and IP addresses must be set up and working in Windows NT Server. Windows NT Server allows you to assign up to five multiple IP addresses to a single network adapter. Use the Network applet in the NT Server Control Panel to specify the additional IP addresses. You can bind the IP addresses to a single network card or assign them to multiple network cards. After you add the IP addresses to the specified network adapter card, you can host multiple News sites, each with its own IP address and domain name. See Chapter 7 for information on setting up IP addresses in Windows NT Server.

Creating a virtual News server

When you've finished setting up additional IP addresses to network cards, you're ready to create virtual News servers using the Default NNTP Site Properties dialog box. Here is how you create a virtual News server using different IP addresses, which you set up in Windows NT:

1. **In Internet Service Manager, right-click the Default NNTP Site, and then choose Properties.**

    The News Site tab appears by default.

2. **In the News Site tab, click the Advanced button.**

    The Advanced Multiple News Site Configuration dialog box appears, as shown in Figure 11-9.

3. **Click the Add button.**

    The Advanced News Site Identification dialog box appears.

4. **In the IP Address drop-down list, select an IP address different than the one you're using for the Default NNTP site.**

5. **In the TCP Port box, type 119 for anonymous access.**

6. **Click OK three times to exit the Default NNTP Site Properties dialog box.**

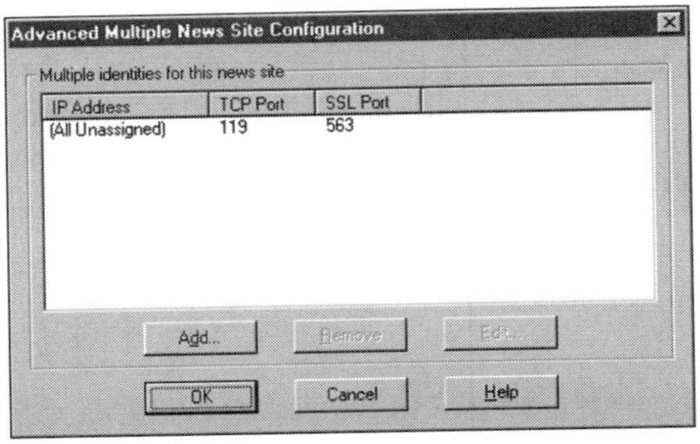

Figure 11-9:
The
Advanced
Multiple
News Site
Configuration
dialog box.

Working with Virtual Directories

Virtual directories consist of a physical directory path and a virtual directory alias. The use of virtual directories makes it easy for you to change the physical location of newsgroups without having to change the location that clients use to access newsgroups. The alias appears in the news service Uniform Resource Locator (URL) and can remain the same regardless of where the files are stored. You can create any number of virtual directories for a News server.

Use the Directories folder in the Default NNTP Site Properties dialog box to create subdirectories for storing specific newsgroups. For example, you can create a virtual directory to store all the content related to corporate news on one disk drive, and all water cooler content on another. To create a virtual directory for the News server, do the following:

1. **In Internet Service Manager's results pane, right-click Default NNTP Site, and then choose New⇨Virtual Directory from the pop-up menu.**

2. **Type the newsgroup subtree that will be stored on this virtual directory (such as rec.golf), and then click Next.**

3. **Type the path for the local directory or the UNC path for the network directory.**

   You can also click the Browse button and navigate to and select the directory.

4. **Click Finish.**

   The alias for the Newsgroup subtree appears in the Directories folder in the scope pane.

Remote Control of the NNTP Service

You can operate the Microsoft NNTP Service remotely using the HTML version of Internet Service Manager. To run Internet Service Manager (HTML) to manage the NNTP service, do the following:

1. **Start Internet Explorer.**

2. **In the Address box, type the following address:**

   ```
   http://server_name/News/Admin/
   ```

   where *server_name* **is the Domain Name System (DNS) name or IP address of the NTTP server.**

   Internet Service Manager with the Default NNTP Site properties appears in your browser (see Figure 11-10).

3. **In the left pane, select Properties, and then select the tab you want to view or modify.**

4. **In the right pane, change options as needed.**

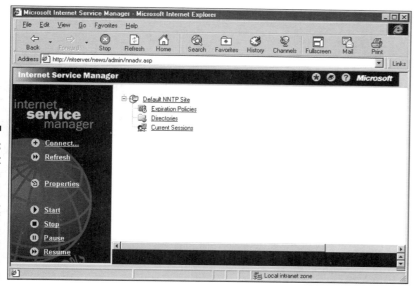

Figure 11-10: The Default NNTP Site properties in the HTML version of Internet Service Manager.

Chapter 12

Searching Your Content

In This Chapter

▶ Using Index Server to let users search your Web site

▶ Discovering the ins and outs of working with catalogs and directories

▶ Managing catalog properties

▶ Making queries in Index Server

*T*he more content your Web site contains, the more you need Microsoft Index Server 2.0, which is included in the Windows NT 4.0 Option Pack. Index Server lets users make queries to search the contents of your Web and News servers as a searchable database. This chapter takes you through the process of setting up and using Index Server as a powerful search engine for your Web and News sites.

Getting Started with Index Server

Index Server 2.0 is a database application that indexes the contents of your Web documents. It then lets users search your Web site for specific information. Index Server comes complete with its own lingo, which you need to understand if you want to work with the program. Table 12-1 describes the common terms to illuminate your way through Index Server.

Table 12-1	Index Server Terms
Term	*What It Is*
Catalog	A directory that contains all Index Server indices and cached properties for a scope. Each catalog is completely self-contained. A query is limited to a single catalog.
Corpus	The entire collection of documents indexed by Index Server, which can include multiple IIS sites.

(continued)

Table 12-1 *(continued)*

Term	What It Is
Index	A data structure that contains words or phrases extracted from searched documents. An index applies only to a defined set of directories and any subdirectories branching from that set.
Query	Any search request made by a client.
Scanning	The process by which files and directories are checked for any changes.
Scope	A set of documents searched by a query.

Index Server gives you access to a full set of document-indexing features, including the following:

- All the HTML-based content on your Web site
- All documents prepared by Office and BackOffice applications and by applications that use compatible formats and text files
- Multiple languages, including English, Dutch, French, German, Italian, Spanish, and Swedish
- Complete indexing of document properties, such as HTML tags and other formatting
- Automatic updating of content as it's added to a Web or News server

The querying, or user side, of Index Server consists of making search queries to target specific information. Index Server gives you complete control over which documents are searched, how they are searched, and how the results of the search are shown to users. Index Server query features include the following:

- Queries can be limited to specific documents
- Users can search document content or properties
- Content queries can search for specific words or phrases in a document or for related words or phrases
- Searches can use wildcards, Boolean and relational expressions, or regular expressions
- Free-text queries can search for document content that matches the meaning rather than the wording of a query
- Vector queries allow searches of documents to find those with content that matches a list of words or phrases

Checking out Index Server

By default, Index Server is running on your system and has already indexed a variety of directories and your Web sites. Choosing Start⇨Programs⇨ Windows NT 4.0 Option Pack displays the Microsoft Index Server submenu, which includes the following entries:

- ✔ Index Server Manager
- ✔ Index Server Manager (HTML)
- ✔ Index Server Sample Query

You can try out Index Server by opening the samples of user query forms that come with Index Server. You can choose from several different samples for conducting different types of searches. To try out Index Server by doing a query, do the following:

1. **Choose Start⇨Programs⇨Microsoft Index Server⇨Index Server Sample Query Form.**

   You see the search query page in your Web browser, as shown in Figure 12-1.

2. **Using the Sample ASP search form, enter a string of text in the Enter Your Query Below box.**

   Use a text string that you know exists in your Web site so that a list of matches will appear. Clicking the Tips for Searching link displays information on how to make effective queries (see Figure 12-2).

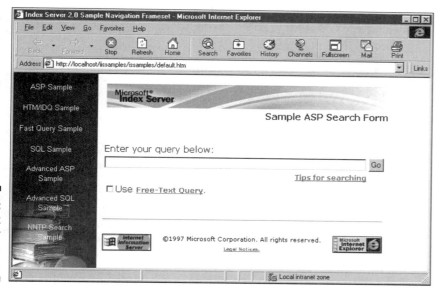

Figure 12-1:
The Index Server sample query page.

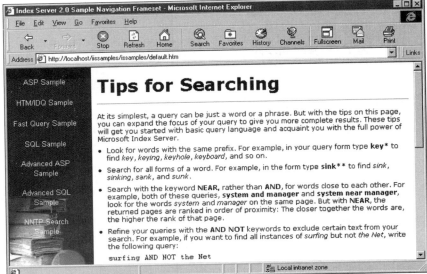

Figure 12-2:
Tips for
Searching a
Web
document.

3. **After entering your query text, click the Go button.**

   Index Server returns a numbered list of references for the query,
   including the item number, a short text abstract, the URL or location of
   the file, and the file size and time. See Figure 12-3 for an example.

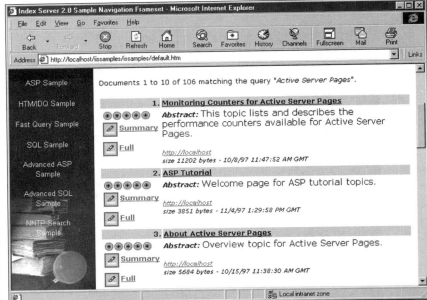

Figure 12-3:
An example
of Index
Server
query
results.

4. **Index Server returns the results of the query in batches of ten; to see the next group of documents (if any additional were found), click the Next 10 Documents button.**

Working with Index Server Manager

You already are familiar with Microsoft Management Console (MMC) as the context for working with Internet Service Manager. Index Server Manager is also installed as a Microsoft Management Console (MMC) snap-in. To open Index Server Manager, choose Start⇨Programs⇨Windows NT 4.0 Option Pack⇨ Microsoft Index Server⇨Index Server Manager. The MMC window with Index Server Manager as a snap-in appears, as shown in Figure 12-4.

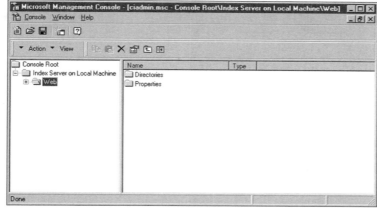

Figure 12-4:
The Index
Server
Microsoft
Management
Console
snap-in.

Note that Index Server Manager is the only snap-in that appears in the MMC window. You can make life easier by adding Index Server as a snap-in in the MMC window that houses Internet Service Manager. This way, you can have everything in one handy place. To add Index Server to the same Microsoft Management Console window as Internet Information Server, do the following:

1. **Choose Start⇨Programs⇨Windows NT Option Pack Setup⇨ Microsoft Internet Information Server⇨Internet Service Manager.**

    The MMC window appears with the Internet Information Server snap-in.

2. **Choose Console⇨Add/Remove Snap-in.**

    The Add/Remove Snap-in dialog box appears, as shown in Figure 12-5.

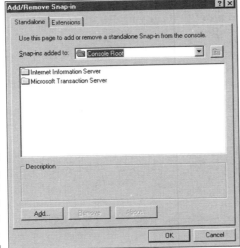

Figure 12-5:
The Add/
Remove
Snap-in
dialog box.

3. **Make sure the <u>S</u>nap-ins Added To list displays Console Root, and then click the A<u>d</u>d button.**

The Add Standalone Snap-in dialog box appears, as shown in Figure 12-6.

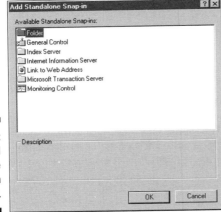

Figure 12-6:
The Add
Standalone
Snap-in
dialog box.

4. **Select Index Server, and then click OK.**

The Connect to Computer dialog box appears.

5. **Use the default Local Computer: (the Computer This Console Is Running On) setting, and then click the Finish button.**

   Index Server on Local Machine appears in the Add/Remove Snap-in dialog box.

6. **Click OK.**

   Index Server on Local Machine appears in the Microsoft Management Console window as a snap-in with Internet Information Server.

The Microsoft Management Console's scope pane displays the Index Server on Local Machine snap-in. Selecting this entry displays a variety of Index Server statistics in the results pane, under column headers that are described in Table 12-2. The initial display provides a list of statistics for the currently selected Index Server catalog.

Table 12-2   Column Heads for the Index Server Statistics List

Statistic	What It Does
Catalog	Lists the names of all catalogs associated with Index Server. Index Server maintains separate statistics for each catalog.
Location	Displays the root path for the catalog in question. This is normally the first directory that appears in the directories listing for that catalog.
Size (MB)	Indicates the amount of space required to hold an index for the cataloged items. This statistic is changed only when the index is optimized, so it may not reflect how much disk space is actually in use.
Total Docs	Indicates the total number of documents in the catalog directory. This isn't necessarily the total number of indexed documents because you have to include documents in a filter before they'll appear in the index.
Docs To Filter	Displays the number of filtered documents. Filtered documents usually appear in the catalog index.
Wordlists	Indicates the number of temporary word lists that Index Server has created for the catalog. As users make requests of Index Server, it creates a temporary word list to service that need. When there are between 14 and 20 temporary word lists, Index Server merges them into the persistent (permanent) index.

(continued)

Table 12-2 *(continued)*

Statistic	What It Does
Persistent Indexes	Shows the number of persistent (permanent) indexes for the catalog. In most cases, you'll have only one persistent index for any catalog. Sometimes, however, Index Server creates additional persistent indexes. At some point, these other indexes are merged into the master index.
Status	Indicates that the catalog isn't up to date or is malfunctioning. The only time you'll see an entry in this column is if Index Server is doing something to the catalog in question. A variety of messages can appear in this column. The only time you have to take any action when you see a message in the Status column is if you see a Scan message, which means you need to rescan the directories in the catalog.

Working with Catalogs and Directories

At the heart of Index Server are catalogs and directories. An Index Server *catalog* is a collection of directories and properties that you want to index as one database entity. You can add to and remove from a catalog any directories you specify.

Index Server Manager provides a number of tools for working with catalogs and their directories. In addition, properties in Internet Information Server define which sites and directories are indexed. This section explains how to work with catalogs and manage their directories in Index Server Manager and IIS.

Creating catalogs

Every installation of Index Server starts out with the default Web catalog, which was created when you installed IIS. Normally, it references the Default Web site. You can use Index Server Manager to add other catalogs for other virtual Web sites on your system. Before you create a catalog, you need to specify the directory that will contain the catalog. Make sure you have created the directory using Windows NT Explorer before you create a catalog.

You must stop Index Server before you add a new catalog. After you create a catalog, you restart Index Server to bring the new catalog online.

To create a catalog, do the following:

1. **In the MMC scope pane, right-click Index Server on Local Machine, and then choose Stop from the pop-up menu.**

   You must always stop Index Server before adding a new catalog.

2. **In the MMC scope pane, right-click Index Server on Local Machine, and then choose New⇨Catalog.**

   The Add Catalog dialog box appears.

3. **In the Name box, type a descriptive name you want to use for the new catalog.**

   For example, you could type **Intranet** to identify the search engine as connected to your company's intranet Web site.

4. **Type the directory path where you want to locate the catalog.**

   You can also click the Browse button to find and select the directory you want to use for the catalog.

5. **Click OK.**

   A New Catalog Created message box appears, telling you the catalog will remain offline until you restart Index Server.

6. **Click OK.**

7. **In the MMC scope pane, select Index Server, and then choose Start from the pop-up menu to restart Index Server.**

What's in a catalog?

To display directories indexed by a specific catalog, double-click Index Server on Local Machine in the MMC scope pane, and then double-click the catalog name. For example, double-click the Web catalog in the scope pane. The Directories and Properties folders appear under the Web catalog. Double-click the Directories folder in the MMC scope pane. The MMC displays a list of directories in the results pane. These are the directories currently included as part of the catalog.

Figure 12-7 shows the directories that together make up the scope of the default Web catalog. In the results pane, the three columns of information are as follows:

✔ The **Root** column displays the list of physical directory paths, which are included in the catalog. All the files below these directories are indexed.

✔ The **Alias** column displays any alias returned to a client computer when a query is issued to Index Server. This entry appears in the URL of the user's Web browser after the search results are returned.

✔ The **Exclude Scope** column displays the status of the directory as to whether it's part of the scope or excluded. A No entry in this column indicates that the directory is included in the scope, which means its contents are indexed. A Yes entry in this column indicates that the directory is part of the catalog but its contents aren't indexed.

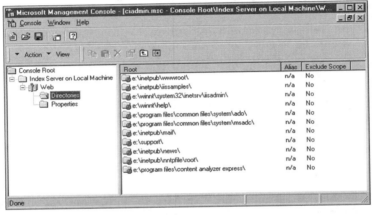

Figure 12-7: The Web catalog directories as they appear in the MMC window's results pane.

Adding directories to catalogs

Your catalog isn't complete until you define what directories you want to include as part of the catalog. Before you add a directory to a catalog, the directory must already exist. If you need to create a directory, use Windows NT Explorer.

Indexing is at the directory level, so you can't restrict a single file in a directory from appearing in the index. To add a directory to a catalog, do the following:

1. **In the MMC window's scope pane, right-click the catalog where you want to create a directory, and then choose New⇨Directory.**

   The Add Directory dialog box appears, as shown in Figure 12-8.

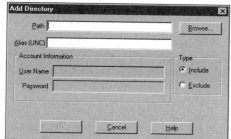

Figure 12-8:
The Add
Directory
dialog box.

2. **Type the path to the directory, or click the Browse button to find and select the directory.**

3. **In the Alias (UNC) box, type the server name and path for this directory, using the format *servername**directory_alias*.**

4. **Click OK.**

   The new directory appears in the results pane.

Scanning directories

Index Server handles the indexing of directories automatically to track changes to files. This means updates, index creation, and many other functions take place automatically without your intervention. After you add a directory to your catalog, however, no one can search the directory until Index Server indexes it. The process of indexing a directory is referred to as *scanning*.

Before scanning a directory, make sure Index Server is running. Remember, when you add a directory to the catalog, you turn off Index Server. To restart Index Server, right-click Index Server on Local Machine in the MMC scope pane, and then choose Start from the pop-up menu.

To scan a new directory, do the following:

1. **In the MMC scope pane, select the catalog, and then double-click Directories.**

2. **In the right pane, right-click the directory you want to scan, and then choose Rescan from the pop-up menu.**

   A message box appears, asking whether you want to do a full rescan.

3. **Click Yes.**

Excluding directories from indexing

You can remove a directory from being indexed as part of a catalog but keep the directory available to include at a later time. This procedure differs from deleting a directory, which eliminates the directory from the catalog. The following steps explain how to exclude a directory from a catalog.

Before excluding a directory, make sure Index Server is not running. To stop Index Server, right-click Index Server on Local Machine in the MMC scope pane, and then choose Stop from the pop-up menu.

1. **In the scope pane of the MMC window, right-click the catalog where you want to create a directory, and then choose New➪Directory.**

   The Add Directory dialog box appears (see Figure 12-8).

2. **Type the path to the directory, or click the Browse button to find and select the directory.**

3. **In the Alias (UNC) box, type the server name and path for this directory.**

4. **In the Type group, click the Exclude option.**

5. **Click OK.**

   After the directory is excluded, a Yes appears in the Exclude column in the results pane.

Deleting catalog directories

Deleting a directory from a catalog doesn't remove the physical directory from your computer; it removes the directory from being part of an Index Server catalog. Before deleting a directory, make sure Index Server is not running. To stop Index Server, right-click Index Server on Local Machine in the MMC scope pane, and then choose Stop from the pop-up menu. To delete a directory, right-click the directory you want to remove from the catalog, and then choose Delete from the pop-up menu.

Managing indexing from IIS

The Directory tab in the Web Site Properties and Folder Properties dialog boxes lets you control whether a Web site or folder is included or excluded in an index. Clicking to add a check mark to the Index This Directory check box tells Index Server to index the Web site or folder's contents. Clearing the Index This Directory check box tells Index Server not to index the server or folder.

You can also control the indexing of newsgroup articles for your News server by clicking to add a check mark to the Index News Content check box in the Home Directory tab of the NNTP Site Properties dialog box. Clearing the Index News Content check box tells Index Server not to index the server. You can do the same for any directory of messages in your News server.

Managing Index Server Properties

Index Server allows you to set properties at the server level or the catalog level. Most of these properties, however, are available only at the catalog level. To access the Properties dialog box for a catalog, right-click the catalog you want to configure, and then choose Properties from the pop-up menu. For example, right-clicking the default Web catalog and then choosing Properties from the pop-up menu displays the Web Properties dialog box shown in Figure 12-9. This section describes the tabs in the Properties dialog box for a catalog.

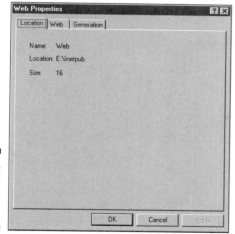

Figure 12-9:
The Web
Properties
dialog box.

Location properties

The Location tab (see Figure 12-9) doesn't contain any configurable settings. The purpose of this tab is to tell you about the catalog you're viewing. The following describes the information in the Location tab.

✔ **Name.** The name of the catalog as it appears in the Index Server Manager dialog box.

✔ **Location.** The physical location of the catalog on the Web server. This is the location of the catalog's data, not the main directory for which the catalog holds an index. The actual index files are in the \Inetpub\ Catalog.wci folder.

✔ **Size.** The size of the catalog in megabytes as determined by the size of the catalog when Index Server last checked it.

Web properties

The Web tab, shown in Figure 12-10, enables you to define the Web server that the catalog is indexing. Each Web server you want to index must have a separate catalog. Choose the Track Virtual Roots option, and then select from the Virtual Server drop-down list the virtual server you want to work with. You can also associate your catalog with a news server by choosing the Track NNTP Roots check box and then selecting from the NNTP Server drop-down list the NNTP server you want to work with. This enables the indexing of messages from the news server. When the user requests a search of the catalog, the news items you've cataloged are returned as part of the search results.

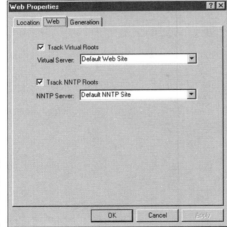

Figure 12-10:
The Web tab.

Make sure you choose at least one tracking option (either Track Virtual Roots or Track NNTP Roots) on the Web page. Otherwise, the catalog will simply use up processor cycles indexing material that the user will never see.

Generation properties

The Generation tab, shown in Figure 12-11, lets you define the way an index is generated, which can be at the catalog level or the server level. This is the only tab available at the Index Server level. The following are the properties in the Generation tab:

- **Filter Files with Unknown Extensions.** A Web server directory can contain much more than just content files. It can contain executable files as well as multimedia files of various formats. The Filter Files with Unknown Extensions option prevents these types of files from appearing in the results pane of the MCC window.

- **Generate Characterizations.** This option tells Index Server that you want to create a summary for every file in a search result. A summary can give users some idea of what to expect when they click the link to the information. Generating the summary, however, consumes processor cycles and may not provide any more information than the document title for some users. Whether you use this option or not depends a great deal on what types of searches the visitors to your site perform.

- **Maximum Size.** This property determines the maximum number of characters that are returned in a summary. It helps you further define how much of a summary the user gets. Sites with complex documents with a lot of similar names may require fairly large summaries to allow users to find what they need. On the other hand, large summaries reduce the number of result links you can display on a page and also increase the amount of processing time required to generate the result list. Some users simply don't need a large summary to determine whether the link you've provided is the one they want.

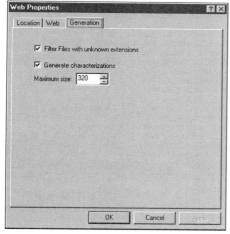

Figure 12-11:
The
Generation
tab.

Speeding Up Queries with the Index Server Cache

A *cache* (pronounced "cash") is a method for improving system performance by keeping data in memory for faster processing. You can add search properties to the Index Server's cache to speed up access to frequently queried values; this helps to decrease response time for typical queries. To access a property to the cache on your system, do the following:

1. **In the MMC scope pane, expand the catalog you want to configure by clicking the plus sign to the left of the catalog name.**

2. **In the scope pane, double-click the Properties folder.**

   In the MMC results pane, you see a list of the properties available on your system, such as that shown in Figure 12-12.

3. **Right-click the property you want to add to the cache, and then choose Properties from the pop-up menu.**

   The Properties dialog box appears, as shown in Figure 12-13. Use the Friendly Name column shown in Figure 12-12 to identify the property.

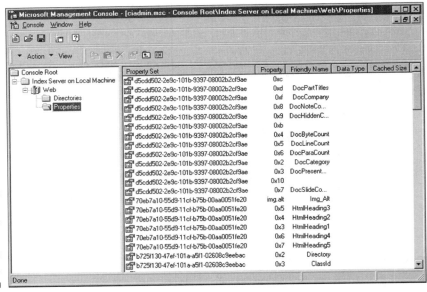

Figure 12-12:
A list of properties in the results pane.

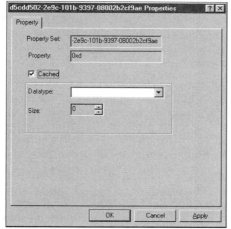

4. **Click to add a check mark to the Cached check box.**

5. **In the Datatype list box, select the appropriate type for the property. In the Size box, type the number of bytes to use for this property.**

   You can also use the default data type and the default size of 8 bytes.

6. **Click OK to return to the main MMC display.**

To remove a property from the cache, follow the preceding steps but clear the Cached check box. Changes made to cache settings do not take effect immediately, and it's a good idea to make all your changes at once. When you're finished, right-click the Properties folder in the scope pane, and choose Commit Changes from the pop-up menu. When the status bar at the bottom of the MMC window displays Done, all your changes have been committed.

Making Index Server Queries

Index Server uses a database query language to structure requests. Index Server's query language enables a variety of searches based on different criteria. Web users can choose from the following types of queries:

✔ **Free Text.** You use free text queries to find pages that contain a match for a word or a phrase you type in the search field. To enter multiple words, separate them with commas. Index Server looks for all occurrences of the words. To combine these words into a phrase, enclose the words in quotation marks. You can also make content searches, which find pages that match the meaning of your query rather than its exact wording. All content queries must be prefixed with $contents. Free-text queries are among the most useful features of Index Server because you can refine query restrictions using sets of words or phrases or even a complete sentence.

✔ **Vector Space.** A variation on a free-text query is the vector space query. This is a complicated-sounding name for a search that ranks the results of a query according to a weighting system, in which the rank of each page indicates how well the result matches the query. Separate the individual components in a vector space query with commas, and specify the weighting by adding a number in square brackets, for example, lassie[500], eddie[400].

✔ **Wildcards.** You can use wildcard queries to find words with a common prefix. For example, the query ball* finds *ball, ballplayer, ballroom,* and so on. You can also look for words with a common root or stem. The query talk** takes the wildcard operator a step further by allowing you to specify words with the same stem. This search will find pages containing words based on the same root, such as *talking, talked,* and *talker.*

✔ **Regular Expressions.** Queries based on regular expressions are a little more complex. The term *regular expression* originated in the UNIX world. A regular expression is a sequence of characters that can match a set of fixed-text strings used in searching text.

✔ **Boolean.** These queries let you use one of the three Boolean operators — AND, OR, or NOT — and the proximity queries let you use a similar operator — NEAR. You can write these queries out in full, such as apples and oranges or you can use symbols instead of operators, such as david & brent. If a Boolean or proximity query operator occurs in a free-text query, enclose the whole query within quotation marks. This allows Index Server to look for pages containing the phrase *David and Brent* rather than the Boolean expression of David AND Brent.

✔ **Property Value.** Property values are elements stored as part of documents and include such attributes as file size, creation date, modification date, filename, file author, and ActiveX properties.

Using ready-made query forms

Index Server comes with several ready-made query forms complete with interactive searching capabilities built in. Choosing Start➪Programs➪ Microsoft Index Server➪Index Server Sample Query Form displays the ASP sample search form in your Web browser. Clicking the Advanced ASP Sample link displays a more advanced search form, as shown in Figure 12-14.

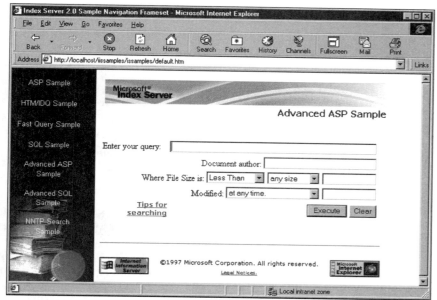

Some sample search forms offer a Use Free-Text Query check box. Clicking this box tells Index Server to perform a different type of search than those offered by other Web servers. Although a free-text search isn't strictly the same as a natural language search, the user enters a sentence to make the request. This has the advantage of allowing the user to express a request in terms that are easier to understand and more likely to produce the desired results when making a complex query. A free-text search takes more time to complete than a standard search does.

Users enter a query in the Enter Your Query Below box, and click Go to begin the search of the catalog. A query results page shows matches listed with a title, rating, and abstract (see Figure 12-3). The rating system uses five bullets to define just how close you got to the requested search criteria. Note that you can also choose between a full or summary view of the matches. Just click the appropriate link for the match. Clicking the title takes you to the matched Web page so you can review the requested information.

Playing by the rules

Index Server uses rules called *query syntax* to define how queries are structured. Clicking the Tips for Searching link in any sample search form displays the Tips for Searching page (see Figure 12-2), which explains your search options. To find out how to do more complex searches, scroll to the bottom of the Tips for Searching page and click the Query Language link at the bottom of the page. Here, you can find out more about Index Server's query language capabilities and structure. The following highlights common searching features in Index Server:

- All queries are case insensitive; uppercase and lowercase queries produce the same results.

- A group of consecutive words is treated as a complete phrase and must appear in a document in the same order. To qualify as a hit, those same words must appear in the same order in the document.

- Words in Index Server's exception list — which in English contains *a, an, and, as, the,* and others — are ignored by Index Server in conducting queries. However, Index Server considers such words to be delimiters in phrase and proximity queries.

- You can use the Boolean operators AND, OR, and NOT as well as the proximity operator NEAR. The operator NEAR resembles AND in returning a match if both operands are in the same page, but NEAR differs from AND in assigning a rank to hits based on the proximity of words. The operator NOT can be used only after the operator AND in content queries. AND has a higher precedence than OR, so queries or parts of queries containing AND are executed before queries or parts of queries containing OR.

- You can use a wildcard character to match words with a particular prefix.

- Common punctuation marks such as the period, comma, colon, and semicolon are ignored in searches. To use punctuation marks that have a special meaning, such as &, |, #, @, or square or round brackets, enclose the entire query in double quotation marks.

- You can search for a phrase already containing quotation marks by enclosing the phrase in two sets of quotation marks.

- You can search file properties. Property names must be preceded by an at sign (@) in relational queries or by a pound sign (#) in a regular expression that is part of a query.

- Free-text queries must begin with the string $contents. The properties that may be searched for in any type of file include contents, filename, size, and write (the last time the file was modified).

Using the NNTP search form

Index Server doesn't stop at allowing you to search the Web site for data; you can also search the various newsgroups on your server. Index Server provides a sample form for NNTP that you can use as a basis for creating your own search form, as shown in Figure 12-15. For the NNTP search form to appear as a sample form, you must install NNTP Server. This form lets you make queries to search articles in newsgroups.

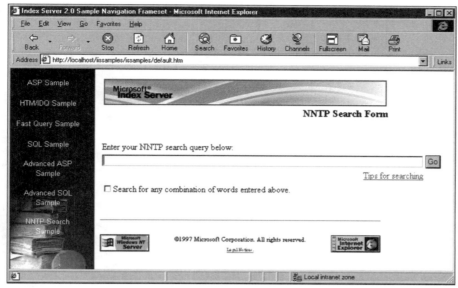

Figure 12-15:
The NNTP
search form.

This form looks deceptively simple — you can use it to create very complex queries. As with Web search pages, you can use a variety of search operators and query syntax options. These include Boolean and proximity search operators such as OR, AND, and NOT, wildcard characters, free-text queries, vector space queries, and property searches.

The NNTP search form has a unique feature not available for Web queries. Unlike the Web search forms, the NNTP search form assumes that you want to find all the search words in the newsgroup message. You can click the Search for Any Combination of Words Entered Above option to search for any of the words you've entered. The NNTP search form also provides a different result page than the Web search pages. You see a table containing a list of common news server headings, along with a location. The following describes each table entry:

✓ **Group:ArticleID.** Indicates the name of the group where the article appeared and its identifier (message number in most cases) within that group. This information helps you find the article you're looking for.

✓ **From.** Tells who wrote the message. Because this is a public forum, you can't guarantee that the person named is the person who actually wrote the message.

✓ **Subject.** Contains the subject line from the message so that you know what the message was about.

- ✔ **Date.** Indicates the date the message was accepted at the server. This doesn't necessarily reflect the date the user submitted the message, especially in a moderated newsgroup. In addition, this date doesn't reflect propagation delays that the message may have suffered in transit when you use this form on an Internet site.

Chapter 13

Active Server Pages and Scripting

● ●

In This Chapter

▶ Understanding the difference between CGI and Active server pages

▶ Scripting language options for IIS 4

▶ Creating Active server pages

▶ Adding VBScript and JScript to your Web pages

▶ Finding out about Active server page objects and applications

▶ Using ASP objects to create interactive and dynamic pages

▶ Saving time by using ActiveX components

▶ Including files and information with Server Side Includes

▶ Understanding the Internet Server Application Program Interface (ISAPI)

● ●

To really tap the power of Internet Information Server, you'll want to deliver pages with dynamic content so that your Web site can interact with visitors. This chapter gives you an overview of the programming and scripting alternatives available for creating and publishing interactive content through IIS. It explains the process of using Active server pages, scripting languages, and ActiveX components.

CGI versus Active Server Pages

The Common Gateway Interface (CGI) was created as a way to extend the HTTP protocol to enable servers and external programs to communicate. Although people generally refer to these external programs as CGI programs, CGI is not a programming language; it is a standard. The word *gateway* is a broad term that refers to the common variables and conventions used to pass information to and from a server. The Common Gateway Interface lets you create your own programs using any programming language that can run on the Web server. Most CGI programs are written in the Practical extraction reporting language (PERL) or the C programming language. Using a CGI program written in PERL or C, you can store or display the information entered in a form or display a random image when a page is loaded.

In the recent past, you had to use CGI and master a language such as PERL or C to create dynamic Web pages or interact with users. Beginning with Internet Information Server 3.0, Microsoft introduced Active server pages (ASP) technology as a server-side scripting alternative to using CGI. ASP is really an Internet Server Application Program Interface (ISAPI) filter that checks the file extension of all files requested by clients. If the extension is .asp, the page is passed to the Active Server. ISAPI and ISAPI filters are explained later in this chapter.

Active server pages are files that contain HTML tags, text, and script commands. When the Active Server receives a request for a file, it executes any scripts in the file and delivers the results to the client. Writing scripts to create ASP pages is a lot easier than learning to write CGI programs with PERL or C. Besides running scripts, ASP also lets you run ActiveX server components on the server that run faster and more efficiently than CGI programs. Even using ActiveX server components, you can create pages that display the same on all browsers. Like CGI programs, ASP lets you create interactive and dynamic pages to perform such tasks as processing a form's data or connecting to a database to display up-to-date information on a Web page.

Dynamic HTML: Panacea or problem child?

Today, some CGI tasks used to create interactive and dynamic pages can be accomplished with Dynamic HTML (DHTML). Dynamic HTML lets you create or update interactive Web pages without requiring the client to reconnect to the server. *Dynamic HTML* encompasses several technologies but is primarily based on what is called a Document Object Model (DOM). The DOM defines each element that makes up a page as an object. As the browser encounters each element on the page, it notes what the element is and where it is located.

To manipulate the objects on a page, you use a scripting language, such as JScript or VBScript. Cascading style sheets and cascading style sheet positioning are also important parts of DHTML. Cascading style sheets (CSS) let you define attributes for HTML elements and apply those attributes to a section of a page, the entire page, or the entire Web site. For example, using CSS, you could change the font for all your headings in your Web pages

from Times New Roman to Arial by changing a single style.

Cascading Style Sheets Positioning (CSS-P) lets you control the absolute and relative position of elements on your page. CSS-P also includes Z-indexing, which lets you hide or overlap elements. Using CSS-P and a scripting language, you can create expanding and collapsible documents or let users drag an object, such as an image, from one part of a page to another.

The big problem with DHTML is that Microsoft and Netscape vary in the way they implement it. Because DHTML runs on the client side, it doesn't work the same way for both Netscape Navigator 4 and Microsoft Internet Explorer 4. Until Microsoft and Netscape follow a single standard, to present the same style of pages for these two types of browsers you will have to create two sets of pages and learn the idiosyncrasies of both Microsoft's and Netscape's implementations of DHTML. Not an easy way to go.

IIS 4 Scripting Language Options

IIS 4 supports two scripting engines: Microsoft Visual Basic Scripting Edition (VBScript) and Microsoft JScript. The default scripting language is Microsoft VBScript. IIS 4 also supports any other ActiveX scripting language for which you have an engine. A *scripting engine* is simply a program that processes commands written in a particular language. For example, you can install and use engines for other languages, such as PERL.

JScript, ECMAScript, and JavaScript

Netscape created JavaScript. It was the first scripting language created for browsers. Microsoft's version of JavaScript is JScript. To help standardize scripting on the Web, JavaScript was turned over to a European standards committee. The results were called ECMAScript. ECMA is an acronym for the European Computer Manufacturers Association standards committee. Although the language standard is called ECMAScript 262, most people still refer generically to both JScript and ECMAScript as JavaScript. It's important to note that although JScript 3.1 is Microsoft's implementation of the ECMA 262 language specification, it also includes enhancements that work only with Microsoft Internet Explorer. JScript is an interpreted, object-based scripting language. You cannot write standalone applications in JScript; for example, JScript has little capability for reading or writing files. JScript scripts are run using an interpreter. The latest JScript interpreter is built into the IIS 4 server and the Internet Explorer 4 browser.

You can find documentation on JScript at www.microsoft.com/scripting. The complete ECMA-262 specification is located at www.ecma.ch/stand/ecma-262.htm.

VBScript

Looking to leverage its investment in the Visual Basic language and the large number of Visual Basic programmers, Microsoft created VBScript. VBScript is a subset of Microsoft Visual Basic and is compatible with Visual Basic for Applications (VBA), which is shipped with Microsoft Office applications. Most of the exclusions from the Visual Basic language are to make VBScript fast and safe.

VBScript is the default language for creating Active server pages. The biggest limitations of using VBScript are that it isn't a cross-platform language and it doesn't work with Netscape Navigator for client-side processing. Because Active server pages are run on the server side, however, ASP generates only HTML. This means Active server pages containing VBScript appear the same on both Netscape Navigator and Internet Explorer browsers. This means also that a client never sees your VBScript code — the client sees only the resulting HTML. Like JScript, VBScript can't be used to write standalone applications.

You can get more information about using VBScript at `www.microsoft.com/scripting/`.

Client-Side and Server-Side Scripts

As mentioned, you can add scripts to HTML pages to be run on the client side or on the server. For client-side scripts, you place the script in the head portion of the HTML document, and the script is executed when the page is loaded. Because Netscape Navigator doesn't directly support VBScript, JavaScript is the most common scripting language for client-side scripting. The following shows a client-side script written in JavaScript:

```
<HTML>
<HEAD>
<TITLE>A Page with JavaScript</TITLE>
</HEAD>
<SCRIPT LANGUAGE="JavaScript">
 <!-- Begin hiding the script from old browsers
 Your JavaScript code goes here...
 // End hiding the script contents here. -->
</SCRIPT>
```

Note that the two forward slashes on the line before the closing `</SCRIPT>` tag indicate a JavaScript comment.

Unlike client-side scripts, ASP pages are run on the server and then delivered to the browser. You don't use the HTML `<SCRIPT>` element to enclose expressions for ASP pages. Instead, you use the `<SCRIPT>` element to define procedures in languages other than the primary scripting language, which is explained in the following section.

How Do I Create an Active Server Page?

Active server pages such as HTML pages are ASCII text files. To create an ASP page, you can use a text editor such as Notepad, a word processor such as Microsoft Word, or an HTML editor such as FrontPage 98 to insert script commands into an HTML page. If you are using a text editor or a word processor, be sure to save the file as ASCII text. ASP files end with the .asp filename extension. The .asp extension indicates to the server that the file contains script commands.

Don't convert all your HTML pages into ASP pages. ASP files require extra processing. Only the files that will have script commands need to have the .asp extension.

To show you what an ASP page looks like, the following example creates a simple ASP page that when requested from the server displays the words "Hello World Wide Web!" in five font sizes:

```
<%@ LANGUAGE = "VBScript" %>
<HTML>
<BODY>
<% For i = 3 To 7 %>
<FONT SIZE=<% = i %>>
<P>Hello World Wide Web!</P>
</FONT>
<% Next %>
</BODY>
</HTML>
```

The first line sets the scripting language to VBScript. By default, the primary scripting language of IIS 4 is VBScript. To set the primary scripting language to JScript for a single page, add the `<%@ LANGUAGE=JSCRIPT %>` directive to the beginning of your .asp file.

Script commands are enclosed within `<%` and `%>` characters, which are called *delimiters*. Text within the delimiters is processed as a script command. Any text following the closing delimiter is displayed as HTML text in the browser. In this example, the script command begins a VBScript loop that controls the number of times the phrase "Hello World Wide Web!" is displayed. The first time through the loop, the counter variable (`i`) is set to 3. The second time the loop is repeated, the counter is set to 4. The loop is repeated until the counter reaches 7.

Each time through the loop, the font size is set to the current value of the counter variable (`i`). The first time the text is displayed, the font size is 3; the second time, the font size is 4; the third time, the font size is 5, and so on until the font size changes to 7. Note that a script command can be enclosed within an HTML tag. The last VBScript command, `Next`, repeats the loop until the counter reaches 7.

You can store your ASP and HTML files in the same directory. Save the document as hello.asp in the Web server directory (`Inetpub/wwwroot`). To view the results of an Active server page, you must use the HTTP protocol and enter the path to the Active server page. For example, start your browser and enter the URL `http://localhost/hello.asp`. The browser displays your Web page with "Hello World Wide Web!" presented five times, each time in a larger font size, as shown in Figure 13-1. If you change and save a file that is open in an editor, click Refresh to view your changes.

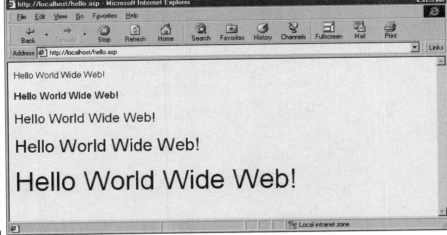

Figure 13-1:
The results
of the
hello.asp
Active
server page
example.

Microsoft's Web development arsenal

Microsoft offers a powerful arsenal of different Web-publishing tools to make creating sophisticated Web sites easier than coding everything from scratch. On the low end, FrontPage 98 includes prebuilt components and a Script wizard to save you from some scripting tasks. On the high end, Visual InterDev is a development tool that contains wizards for creating ASP pages and tools for building ActiveX database Internet or intranet applications. InterDev also includes tools for integrating your own Visual C++ and Visual Basic components, as well as scripts.

Web pages created with FrontPage 98 can be opened and edited by Visual InterDev and vice versa. Visual InterDev can be a great asset for creating and maintaining Web sites. It enables a group of individuals to work together on the same Web site project. Another software package that works with InterDev is Visual SourceSafe. Using Visual InterDev with Visual SourceSafe, you can manage and protect files that are being worked on by different group members. This allows programmers, HTML authors, and graphic designers to effectively work on the same Web site pages at the same time.

Microsoft also publishes Microsoft Visual Studio, which includes Visual C++, Professional Edition; Visual J++, Professional Edition; Visual Basic Professional Edition; Visual InterDev; Visual FoxPro Professional Edition; and the MSDN Library Developer Reference CD. At the top tier is the Microsoft Visual Studio Professional Edition, which includes Visual C++, Enterprise Edition; Visual Basic; Enterprise Edition Transaction Server; SQL Server Developer Edition; Visual SourceSafe, and the kitchen sink. You can get more information on Visual Studio at www.microsoft.com/vstudio.

Using multiple scripting languages in one page

The ASP primary scripting language is the language used to process commands inside the <% and %> delimiters. For your primary scripting language, you can use any scripting language for which you have a script engine. You can set the primary scripting language on a page-by-page basis, or for all pages in an ASP application.

Multiple scripting languages can be used in the same Active server page. A script tag is inserted in the file with the language name parameter and the RUNAT="SERVER" attribute as follows:

```
<SCRIPT Language="JScript" RUNAT="Server">
```

The closing Script tag, </SCRIPT>, must follow the end of each section of code for the specified language.

When you use two scripting languages in the ASP file, the secondary language executes first, followed by the primary language. The following shows an ASP file with alternating lines from the primary and secondary scripting languages. VBScript is set as the primary script language, and JScript is the secondary language. Notice in Figure 13-2 that both the JScript lines appear before the VBScript lines. Because JScript is the secondary language, it runs first; then VBScript is executed.

```
<%@ LANGUAGE="VBSCRIPT" %>
<HTML>
<HEAD>
<TITLE>Multiple Script Language Example</TITLE>
</HEAD>
<BODY>
<%response.write ("<P>This VBScript line is at the top of
           the ASP file.</P>")%>
<SCRIPT LANGUAGE="JScript" RUNAT="Server">
Response.Write ('<P>This JScript line is after the first
           VBScript line in the ASP file.</P>');
</SCRIPT>
<%response.write ("<P>This VBScript line is after the first
           JScript line in the ASP file.</P>") %>
<SCRIPT LANGUAGE="JScript" RUNAT="Server">
Response.Write ('<P>This JScript line is at the end of the
           ASP file.</P>');
</SCRIPT>
</BODY>
</HTML>
```

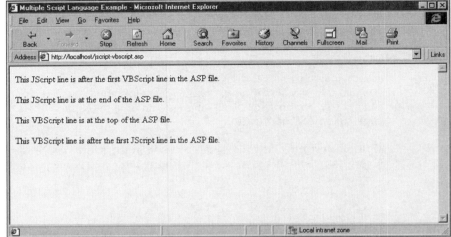

Figure 13-2:
An ASP file
containing
both
JScript and
VBScript.

Changing the default scripting language

By default, the standard scripting language is set to VBScript. If you plan to do most of your project using another scripting language, such as JScript, you should change the default. To set the primary scripting language for all pages in an application, you need to set the Default ASP Language property on the App Options tab in Internet Service Manager. The following steps explain how to change the default language from VBScript to JScript:

1. **Choose Start➪Programs➪Windows NT Option Pack Setup➪Microsoft Internet Information Server➪Internet Service Manager.**

   The Microsoft Management Console appears.

2. **Double-click the Internet Information Server folder and right-click the Web site or the starting point directory of the application for which you want to change scripting languages.**

   The directory's property sheets appear.

3. **Click the Home Directory, Virtual Directory, or Directory tab.**

4. **Click the Configuration button.**

   The Application Configuration dialog box appears.

5. **Click the App Options tab.**

   The application options appear, as shown in Figure 13-3.

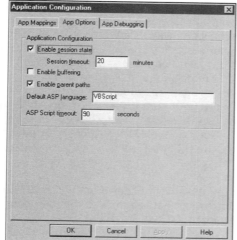

Figure 13-3:
The App Options tab lets you change the default scripting language.

6. **In the Default ASP Language text box , type** JScript.

7. **Click OK twice to close the Application Configuration dialog box and the Default Web Site Properties dialog box.**

8. **Choose Console⇨Save to save your change.**

9. **Choose Console⇨Exit to close the Microsoft Management Console.**

Remember, if you are changing to a language other than JScript or VBScript, the ActiveX script engine for the language must be installed on your server. Be sure to use the exact keyword required for your engine as documented by your script engine provider.

Active Server Applications

One of the basic problems you can face with publishing a Web site is how to keep track of a user during a session. The interaction between IIS and a browser is *stateless,* which means the server doesn't keep track of the state, or any information, about a user. IIS serves up a Web page to the client and then breaks the connection. Each request for a Web page from the server is as though it is the first request.

ASP makes it possible to have the server keep the connection open to keep track of the user. For example, you may want to track whether a user has visited your site previously or seen a certain ad banner. To do this, ASP creates what is called an Active server application and an Active server session.

An *Active server application* is really just a virtual directory and all of its pages. The word *application* is a little misleading because Active server applications don't work in the same way as a Windows application. To run a Windows application, the user starts a program, and data can be stored in variables and recalled until the user exits the program. Using an Active server application, you aren't really running a program; you're simply loading pages in your browser. A user may load a page at your site, jump to another site, and then return to your site. If the user requests a Web page from a virtual directory, the user has started an Active server application. This application is given the same name of the directory or page the user has loaded. So if users enter the URL www.somesite.com/fun/, they start the fun application.

A *session* refers to an individual browser accessing the same Web pages. A session for an individual browser lasts as long as the user continues to request Web pages from the virtual directory. If the user stops requesting Web pages for 20 minutes, the session ends. You can change the amount of time from 20 minutes to any amount of time you choose by displaying the Application Configuration dialog box and clicking the App Options tab. To do this, simply perform Steps 1 through 5 listed in the preceding section, "Changing the default scripting language," and change the number of minutes in the Session Timeout box.

Active Server Page Objects

Creating ASP pages with scripts can be limiting. VBScript, for example, is not a fully functional programming language — it can't open text files and lacks built-in functions to allow access to any external data sources, such as a database. To use ASP to perform advanced functions such as working with files and accessing a database, you need to supplement your VBScript with ASP objects and components.

ASP objects and components are simply ActiveX components. ActiveX is a set of technologies that enables software components to interact with one another in a networked environment, regardless of the programming language in which the components were created. ActiveX was developed by Microsoft and is primarily designed for developing interactive content for the Web. The difference between an ASP object and an ASP component is that ASP objects are always available to VBScript. ASP objects let you handle events, such as triggering an action to take place the first time a user loads a page from the Web, getting information from a user, or setting properties for the user's session. ASP supports five built-in objects: Application, Session, Request, Response, and Server. This section explains these objects and shows simple examples of how they are used.

The Request and Response objects

Every time you type a URL to request a file, additional information is sent to the server. For example, if you just filled out a form and clicked the Submit button, the script specified by the ACTION statement in the form is requested and all the data you input in the form is sent to the server. The Request object contains values that are passed by the browser to the server with the request for a file. Five types of variables can be passed to your application through the Request object:

- **Form.** The values of the data the user entered in a form.
- **Cookies.** The values of cookies. A *cookie* is data that a Web site stores on the visiting person's hard disk. The data is added to a file named cookies. Cookies let you store data that would otherwise be lost, so you can maintain the state, or information, about a user.
- **ServerVariables.** The values of Web server environment variables, such as the IP address and the browser being used.
- **QueryString.** The values of variables being passed to a server. These values appear in the URL after the question mark.
- **ClientCertificate.** The values of fields stored in the client certificate.

Each of these types of variables has a *collection,* which is data associated with a particular Request object. For example, you can access variables by referring to the Request object, then the collection, and then the particular variable you're trying to access. When retrieving a variable, naming the collection is optional. If you don't include the collection, all the collections are searched for the variable. The ServerVariables collection contains the values of the environment variables. For example, the following returns the user agent string, a fancy term for the type of browser viewing the page:

```
<%Request.ServerVariables ("HTTP_USER_AGENT")%>
```

The Response object is used to send string output for display in the browser. To save you from having to continually type Response.Write in your ASP files to display data, you can instead use the equal sign shortcut. Putting the equal sign (=) in front of the Request object is shorthand for Response.Write. For example, you could use either of the following to include the value of HTTP_USER_AGENT in your HTML document:

```
<%=Request.ServerVariables ("HTTP_USER_AGENT")%>
```

or

```
<%Response.Write
        Request.ServerVariables("HTTP_USER_AGENT")%>
```

The following example shows VBScript code using the equal sign as the shortcut for `Response.Write` and `Request.ServerVariables` to display some common server variables. Figure 13-4 shows the results of the following code:

```
<%@ LANGUAGE="VBSCRIPT" %>
<HTML>
<HEAD>
<TITLE>Server Variables</TITLE>
</HEAD>
<BODY>
<H1>Server Variables</H1>
<P>
The browser you are using is
            <%=Request.ServerVariables("HTTP_USER_AGENT")%><BR>
The remote host machine you are using is
            <%=Request.ServerVariables("REMOTE_HOST")%><BR>
The name of the server you are using is
            <%=Request.ServerVariables("SERVER_NAME")%><BR>
The port the server you are using is
            <%=Request.ServerVariables("SERVER_PORT")%><BR>
The server software you are using is
            <%=Request.ServerVariables("SERVER_SOFTWARE")%><BR>
The server protocol you are using is
            <%=Request.ServerVariables("SERVER_PROTOCOL")%><BR>
The path the server has taken is
            <%=Request.ServerVariables("PATH_INFO")%><BR>
The translated path is
            <%=Request.ServerVariables("PATH_TRANSLATED")%><BR>
</P>
</BODY>
</HTML>
```

One of the most common uses of the Request and Response objects is to retrieve and display the data a user has entered in the form. Data submitted from a form is stored as *name value pairs*. Suppose you created a form with a single input text field and set the NAME attribute to `"fname"`. The HTML code for the form might appear as follows:

```
<FORM METHOD="POST" ACTION="request_results.asp">
<P>Enter your first name: <INPUT TYPE="text" NAME="fname"
            SIZE="20"></P>
<P><INPUT TYPE="submit" VALUE="Submit">   <INPUT
            TYPE="reset" VALUE="Clear"></P>
</FORM>
```

When a user enters his or her name in the form's text input box and submits the form, the name value pairs are set. For example, if the user enters Kim and clicks the Submit button, the name value pair (`name=value`) is set to

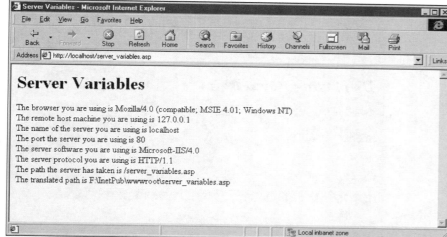

Figure 13-4:
Common
server
variables
displayed.

fname=Kim. Using Request.Form and the name used in the form, you can examine and display the value the user entered in the form. The following example shows a script command line that displays the greeting "Hello" followed by the Response.Write and Request.Form objects to display the name that the user entered in the form.

```
<FONT FACE="Verdana,Arial" SIZE=5>
<P>Hello <%=Request.Form("fname")%>.</P></FONT>
```

Figure 13-5 shows the form and the results of using the Response.Write shortcut and Request.Form object in the Active server page.

Redirecting readers with Request and Response

The Request and Response objects are also helpful when you want to send a command to the browser that causes it to connect to a different URL. For example, you might want to direct users to a certain page based on what the user input in a form. The following form example prompts the user to enter his or her age, and then runs a script named agecheck.asp that redirects the user to a page based on the age entered in the form:

```
<FORM METHOD="POST" ACTION="agecheck.asp">
<P>Enter your age: <INPUT TYPE="text" NAME="age"
        SIZE="3"></P>
<P><INPUT TYPE="submit" VALUE="Submit">   <INPUT
        TYPE="reset" VALUE="Clear"></P>
</FORM>
```

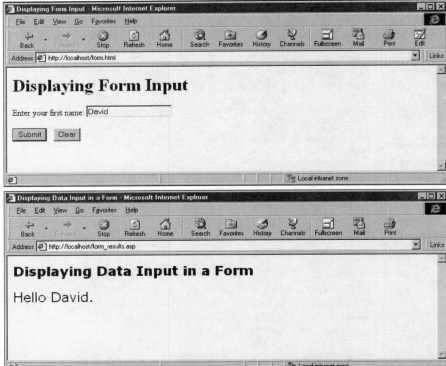

Figure 13-5:
A form and
a Web page
displaying
the data
input into
the form.

The following script (agecheck.asp), uses the Request object to check the
value the user has input in the form's input text box and the
Response.Redirect object to display a page for adults (adults.html) or a
page for minors (minors.html):

```
<%
If Request.Form("age") > 17 Then
    Response.Redirect "http://localhost/adult.asp"
 Else
    Response.Redirect "http://localhost/minor.asp"
End If
%>
```

Keeping pages current with Response.Expires

One problem you may encounter when publishing Active server pages is the
way Internet Explorer 4 caches pages. Internet Explorer 4 not only caches
pages to the hard disk, but also stores the last five pages that were viewed

in memory. This can affect the way your ASP application performs. Suppose that you are using a script to display the time in a page. A user might visit your page, jump to another site, load less than four different pages, and return to your page showing the time. Unfortunately, the time will be the same as when the user first loaded the page. This is because the Internet Explorer browser has cached the results of the ASP page in memory and doesn't request that the page be updated when the user returns. To solve this problem, you can use the Response object along with the Expires property to force the page to expire, so it will reload and show the correct time the next time the user loads the page.

The following example shows a page that displays the time and sets the Expires property of the Response object to 0:

```
<%@ LANGUAGE="VBScript"%>
<%Response.Expires=0%>
<HTML>
<HEAD>
<TITLE>Date and Time</TITLE>
</HEAD>
<BODY>
<H1>The Date and Time</H1>
<P>The date and time is <%Response.Write Now%></P>
</BODY>
</HTML>
```

The Application and Session objects

As mentioned, an ASP application is defined as all the ASP files within the virtual directory and its subdirectories. The Application object is used to share information among all users of your application. One of the most common uses of the Application object is to create a hit counter.

Because data is shared among users, the Application object includes methods that allow you to lock and unlock access to the application object. Two methods let you protect the application object: Lock and Unlock. The Lock method protects the application object so that clashes don't occur when two or more users try to change a variable at the same time. The Unlock method makes the variable accessible to other users.

The following example shows a script that creates an application object named Hitcount that displays the number of hits a page has received. The script ensures that the variable is locked when the Hitcount variable is being changed:

```
<%@ LANGUAGE="VBScript"%>
<% Application.Lock
Application("Hitcount") = Application("Hitcount") + 1
Application.Unlock %>
<HTML>
<HEAD>
<TITLE>Hit Counter</TITLE>
</HEAD>
<BODY>
<P>This page has received <%=Application("Hitcount") %>
        hits.</P>
</BODY>
</HTML>
```

To define the beginning and ending of an application as well as the beginning and ending of an individual session, ASP uses a special file named Global.asa. The Global.asa file lets you run script commands when a user first visits or exits your site (starts an ASP application) or when a session starts or ends. The global.asa file lets you trigger your script commands with the Application_OnStart and Application_OnEnd methods and the Session_OnStart and Session_OnEnd methods. The Application_OnStart event occurs only once — when the first user requests a Web page from the virtual directory. When another user requests a page from the same directory, the Session_OnStart event is triggered. If two browsers are accessing pages in the same virtual directory, both user sessions must end before the application can be closed. When all user sessions in the virtual directory have ended, the Application_OnEnd event is triggered.

Keeping track of a user can be a major problem because the IIS 4 connection is stateless. The session object lets you store information and keep track of a user as he or she jumps from one Web page to another. For example, you can create session object variables to create a "shopping cart" type of application. (A virtual shopping cart lets you store references to products that the user may want to purchase at a later time.)

The Server object

The Server object lets you interact with the Web server. For example, the CreateObject method is a Server object that lets you use server-side ActiveX components within your Web applications. In addition to creating objects, you can also have a Server object interact with the utility functions of the server; for example, you can create a Server object to control the period of time allowed before a script times out. The next section shows you how to use the Server object with some of the ActiveX components that ship with IIS 4.

Active Server Components

Active server components are programs written so you can accomplish special tasks quickly without having to start programming from scratch. As mentioned, Active server objects are built into IIS 4. Active server page components, on the other hand, are Dynamic Link Libraries (DLLs) or executable files that developers can create in any language and call using VBScript. Third-party Active server components are being published on the Web and are available for purchase, so you don't have to reinvent the digital wheel.

The components bundled with IIS 4 include Browser Capabilities, Ad Rotator, Content Linking, File Access, and Database Access. This section shows examples of how you can use the first four components. The Database Access component is covered in Chapter 14.

Determining the capabilities of the browser

Knowing whether a user is viewing your pages using Internet Explorer or Netscape Navigator can allow you to display pages tailored for the appropriate browser. The Browser Capabilities component identifies the browser that the user is currently using to view your pages. It matches the browser's user agent string to entries in a special initialization file named Browscap.ini. When the Browser Capabilities component matches a user agent string, all features listed for that browser are immediately accessible as properties of the component.

You can construct simple IF-THEN statements that determine the capabilities of the browser. For example, you could use the Browser Capabilities component to test the browser and display a text message to the user who is using a browser that doesn't support a particular feature. The following uses the Browser Capabilities component to display a table listing whether or not the client's browser supports a feature. Figure 13-6 shows the results of this example:

```
<% Set bc = Server.CreateObject("MSWC.BrowserType") %>
<DIV ALIGN="CENTER">
<TABLE BORDER=1>
<TR>
    <TD>Browser/Version</TD>
    <TD><%= bc.browser %>/<%= bc.version %></TD>
</TR>
<TR>
    <TD>Frames</TD>
```

(continued)

(continued)

```
      <TD><% If (bc.frames = TRUE) Then %> Supported
         <% Else %> Not Supported
         <% End If %></TD>
</TR>
<TR>
   <TD>Tables</TD>
   <TD><% If (bc.tables = TRUE) Then %> Supported
      <% Else %> Not Supported
      <% End If %></TD>
</TR>
<TR>
   <TD>Java Applets</TD>
   <TD><% If (bc.javaapplets = TRUE) Then %> Supported
      <% Else %> Not Supported
      <% End If %></TD>
</TR>
<TR>
   <TD>JavaScript</TD>
   <TD><% If (bc.javascript = TRUE) Then %> Supported
      <% Else %> Not Supported
      <% End If %></TD>
</TR>
<TR>
   <TD>VBScript</TD>
   <TD><% If (bc.vbscript = TRUE) Then %> Supported
      <% Else %> Not Supported
      <% End If %></TD>
</TR>
</TABLE>
</DIV>
```

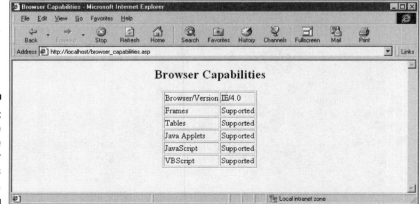

Figure 13-6:
An example
using the
Browser
Capabilities
component.

Rotating advertisements

The Ad Rotator component lets you rotate a graphic or an advertisement. It reads information regarding a graphic or an advertisement from a special text file that sets an ad image to be displayed.

To use the Ad Rotator component, you need to use the `Server.CreateObject` object as well as the `Response.Write` object with the `Ad.GetAdvertisment` variable, as shown in the following example. The text file, which in this example is named AdRotate.txt, can be named anything. This text file determines the images to display, lists a hyperlink that is activated when the advertisement is clicked, and specifies the percentage of time to show the image:

```
<% Set Ad = Server.CreateObject("MSWC.Adrotator") %>
<% Response.Write Ad.GetAdvertisement("AdRotate.txt") %>
```

The following example shows the content of the AdRotate.txt file set up to display four advertisements. Figure 13-7 shows the results of using the Ad Rotator component with this file:

```
redirect /adredir.asp
width 468
height 60
border 1
*
/images/ad01.gif
http://www.angell.com
Angell.Com
25

/images/ad02.gif
http://www.bookware.com
Bookware
25
/images/ad03.gif
http://www.authors.com
Authors
25
/images/ad04.gif
http://www.idgbooks.com
IDG Books
25
```

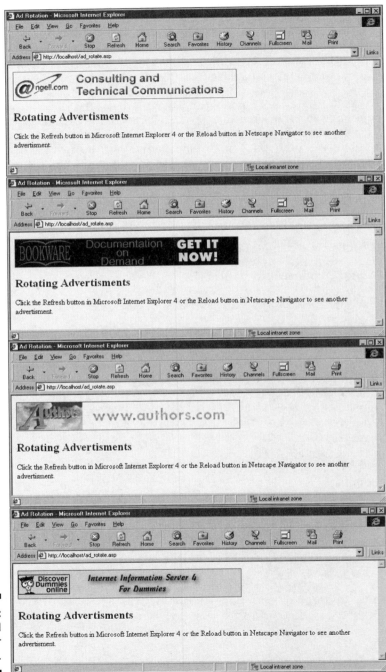

Figure 13-7:
The Ad
Rotator
component.

Linking pages sequentially

The Content Linking component is designed for publications that need to be restructured quickly, such as an online magazine. Using this components you can quickly create tables of contents or link separate Web pages, allowing them to be scrolled as a single file.

To use the Content Linking component, you need to create a text file that lists the HTML files and a description of the file that you want to link to create the publication. The filename and the description need to be separated by a tab. The following is an example of a content linking list file named nextlink.txt:

```
Topic01.html  Topic One
Topic02.html  Topic Two
Topic03.html  Topic Three
```

After you create the content list and the individual HTML files for your publication, you can use such methods as GetNextURL and GetPreviousURL to navigate the pages. Descriptions of individual pages are retrieved through the GetNextDescription and GetPreviousDescription methods. Alternatively, you can set up a simple counter with the GetListCount, and use GetNthURL and GetNthDescription to create links to pages or topics. The following shows an example of using the Content Linking component to create an easily modifiable table of contents:

```
<%@ LANGUAGE="VBScript"%>
<HTML>
<HEAD>
<TITLE>Content Linking Component</TITLE>
</HEAD>
<BODY>
<H2>Content Linking Component</H2>
<%  Set NextLink=Server.CreateObject ("MSWC.NextLink") %>
<%  count = NextLink.GetListCount ("nextlink.txt") %>
<%  I = 1 %>
<%  Do While (I <= count)  %>
   
<a href=" <%=NextLink.GetNthURL ("nextlink.txt", I)  %>  ">
        <%=NextLink.GetNthDescription ("nextlink.txt",
          I) %></a><BR>
<%  I = (I + 1)  %>
<%  Loop  %>
</BODY>
</HTML>
```

Creating and accessing files

The File Access component allows access to text files on your Web site. This component consists of two separate objects: the FileSystem object, which is used to open and close files, and the TextStream object, which is used to read and write to a file.

To open a file for access, you first create a FileSystem object. The CreateTextFile method lets you create a new file and the OpenTextFile method lets you open an existing file. After you create or open a file, you can use the TextStream object to read or write to the file. Be aware that a file should be opened for only reading or only writing, but not for both at the same time. The following example uses the File Access component to create a new file named testfile.html in a subdirectory named data, write the lines for an HTML file, and close the open file. This example also includes a link to the new file that is generated when the page loads, so you can see that the file was indeed created:

```
<%@ LANGUAGE="VBScript"%>

<HTML>
<HEAD>
<TITLE>File Access Component</TITLE>
</HEAD>
<BODY>
<H2>File Access Component</H2>
<% Set fs=CreateObject("Scripting.FileSystemObject")
Set a=fs.CreateTextFile("f:\InetPub\wwwroot\data\
            testfile.html", True)
a.WriteLine("<HTML>")
a.WriteLine("<HEAD><TITLE>File Access Component</TITLE></
            HEAD>")
a.WriteLine("<BODY>")
a.WriteLine("<P>This HTML page was created using the File
            Access Component</P>")
a.WriteLine("</BODY>")
a.WriteLine("</HTML>")
a.Close %>
<P>Check out the newly created <A HREF="data/
            testfile.html">test file</A>.</P>
</BODY>
</HTML>
```

Troubleshooting Your Scripts

Writing scripts in VBScript and JScript is a lot easier than writing programs in C or PERL, but it still demands that you use proper syntax. Misspellings or leaving out a quotation mark or parentheses causes your page to display an error message in the browser window. To help you debug scripts, IIS 4 comes with Microsoft Script Debugger, shown in Figure 13-8. Script Debugger isn't installed by default, so you need to use the Windows NT 4.0 Option Pack Setup program and add the Microsoft Debugger component. Microsoft Visual InterDev and Visual Studio 98 come with built-in script debuggers, so you don't need the IIS 4 debugger if you have one of these products installed.

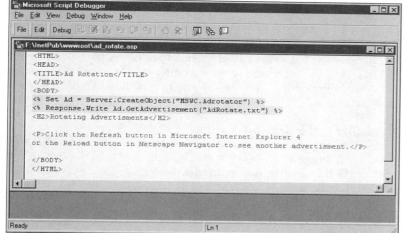

Figure 13-8:
The
Microsoft
Script
Debugger.

Remember that Internet Explorer caches pages to memory and to disk. Therefore, if you change a script, be sure you are not reloading the cached page. A shortcut to reloading a page is to press and hold down the Shift key while clicking the Refresh button. You can stop Internet Explorer from caching to disk by first choosing View⇨Internet Options. In the Temporary files group, click the Settings button, and then select Never for the Check for Newer Versions of Stored Pages option.

Server-Side Include (SSI)

A server-side Include (SSI) is a special form of server-side script built into Web servers. Unlike using CGI, ASP, and ISAPI, using server-side Includes doesn't require learning a scripting language to display information, such as the contents of a text file, the time of day, or the size of a file. IIS 4 recognizes the server-side Include as a command, which is also called a *directive*. Files that include server-side Includes must end with the file extension .stm, .shtm, or .shtml. The syntax for a server-side Include is

```
<!--#directive variable-name="variable-value"-->
```

The syntax is similar to an HTML comment tag. Using a variation of the comment tag helps ensure that the server-side Include command does not appear in the browser. The server-side Include is differentiated from a comment by the # sign.

The most common use of SSI is to include the contents of a file in an HTML page. The following example uses the SSI directive #INCLUDE to include a file named heading.html stored in the data subdirectory. The #INCLUDE directive is similar to the FrontPage Include Page component.

```
<!--#INCLUDE FILE="data/heading.html"-->
```

The SSI #INCLUDE directive lets you specify the path to a file as FILE or VIRTUAL. The FILE setting uses a path relative to the directory of the current document. The VIRTUAL setting is the full path relative to a virtual directory.

Another server-side directive is #ECHO, which can be used for displaying HTTP header environment variables, such as the date and the IP address. HTTP header environment variables are similar to the ServerVariables collection explained earlier in this chapter. #FLASTMOD displays the last modification date of a file, and #FSIZE displays the size of a file. The following example, named ssi_example.shtml, shows some common server-side Include directives added to an HTML page. Figure 13-9 shows the results of this example:

```
<HTML>
<HEAD>
<TITLE>Server Side IncludesExamples</TITLE>
</HEAD>
<BODY>
<!--#INCLUDE FILE="data/heading.html"-->
The IP address you are requesting this information from is
<!-- #ECHO var="REMOTE_ADDR"-->.<BR>
The current date is
<!--#ECHO var="DATE_LOCAL"-->.<BR>
The size of the default.htm file is
<!--#FSIZE FILE="default.htm"--> Kilobytes.<BR>
The default.htm was last modified on
<!--#FLASTMOD FILE="default.htm" -->.
</BODY>
</HTML>
```

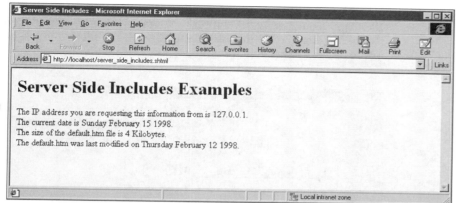

Figure 13-9:
An example
of server-
side Include
directives.

Internet Server Application Programming Interface (ISAPI)

By creating ASP pages, you are actually working with the Internet Server Application Programming Interface (ISAPI). Like the Common Gateway Interface (CGI), which is also available with IIS, ISAPI is a programming interface. To work with ISAPI, you have to use a programming language, such as C/C++ or Delphi. The ISAPI programs are compiled as Dynamic Link Libraries (DLLs). IIS 4 automatically loads these DLL programs into memory. When someone accesses your Web pages, the ISAPI program takes the user input and processes it based on what the program is designed to do. ISAPI programs perform much better than CGI scripts and don't require the overhead that CGI requires. ISAPI programs, for example, let you create programs to perform tasks such as accessing the file system or retrieving data from databases.

ISAPI applications fall into two different categories: filters and extensions. An ISAPI filter, which is transparent to the client, can be used to monitor requests, use custom authentication schemes, and translate data. For example, when a user loads an ASP file, the ISAPI filter sends the page to the Active server to process the server-side scripts before sending the page to the requesting user's browser.

ISAPI extensions are used for form processing and tasks such as retrieving data from databases. For example, you can use an extension to process data input into a form, add the input to a database, and send back a verification response to the user who submitted the form. This is similar to using a CGI script; the big difference is that instead of using a program written in PERL, you use a DLL. Extensions are also available that let you get operating system-level access.

The ISAPI Filters tab in the Web Site Properties dialog box, shown in Figure 13-10, lets you specify ISAPI filters. The table lists the status of each filter (loaded, unloaded, or disabled), the name of the filter, and the priority rating of the filter (high, medium, or low) set inside the DLL.

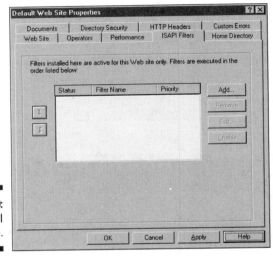

Figure 13-10:
The ISAPI
Filters tab.

The Add, Remove, and Edit buttons are used to modify filter mappings. The Enable and Disable buttons are used to modify the status of filters.

Chapter 14

Connecting Databases to Your Web Site

Creating a database-driven Web site is the fastest-growing trend on the Web. Publishing dynamic, up-to-date pages from information stored in a database is much more appealing than manually creating passive, static Web pages.

Databases are critical and inevitable building blocks for creating pages that are easy to update. This chapter explains some of the most common database technologies for IIS 4, and how to connect to an Access or SQL Server database to create updateable Web pages from database queries.

The Changing World of Database Connectivity

Don't blink. One of the fastest-changing scenes in computing is the world of database connectivity. It's easy to get lost in the sea of changing database technologies. To help give you some perspective, this section looks at what's on the way out and what's coming in as replacements. In the recent past, Microsoft supported Internet Database Connectors (IDC). With IDC, you could execute SQL statements using a file that ended with the .idc extension, and the results were merged into a special HTML Extension (HTX) file, which ended with the .htx extension.

Today, Microsoft is phasing out Internet Database Connectors in favor of Active server pages and ActiveX data objects (ADO). ADO is built into IIS 4. ADO components are replacing remote data objects (RDO) and data access objects (DAO). ADO offers advantages over these older RDO and DAO components. For example, it's much less complicated to access database records with ADO. ADO uses OLE DB to manipulate data though a database's ODBC driver. OLE DB is a new technology that goes beyond working with databases to let you access different types of data, such as an SQL database, an e-mail system, and images. Currently, OLE DB interfaces with ODBC to connect to databases. This is likely to change to OLE DB interfacing directly with databases and other types of data sources. Using ODBC, you can access any ODBC-compliant database, which includes Microsoft Access, Oracle, and Microsoft SQL Server.

Active server pages and ADO have also replaced dbWeb as the new database development technologies for the Microsoft Web platform. dbWeb was directly incorporated into Microsoft Access 97. It was designed to create database queries and connect them to database pages. Using Active server pages and ADO, you can achieve the same results as dbWeb. For example, you can build queries and automatically update HTML pages.

Another new Microsoft database connectivity product is Microsoft Remote Data Service (RDS). RDS was originally named Microsoft Advanced Data Connector (ADC). RDS is designed for developers who use Visual Basic or Visual C++ to access remote databases over the Internet. RDS is based on the new OLE DB database connectivity standard. It offers a collection of ActiveX components that connects standard ActiveX controls with OLE DB-based providers. RDS lets developers create client-side scripts or VBScript applets to access OLE DB data directly through RDS. RDS works with Microsoft SQL Server, but it doesn't have a graphical user interface. RDS is available as a free download from Microsoft's Web site at `www.microsoft.com/data/rds`.

Assessing Your Database Needs

One of the first questions you need to ask yourself is "Just how powerful a database do I need?" On the low end, you can get by with using a Microsoft Access database. On the high end, you need a professional-strength database, such as the Microsoft SQL Server. Be aware that if you want to generate pages to numerous users, you will be putting quite a strain on your system using Microsoft Access. Microsoft itself recommends that Microsoft Access be used solely for development purposes and not for production. Microsoft Access was designed as a single-user desktop database — not for server use.

The main problem with using a high-end database solution such as SQL Server is that it is very expensive — thousands of dollars for a real-world solution. Microsoft is the only major company that sets a price for an SQL server product, which is approximately $1,400 for a five-user license and $3,000 for an unlimited number of connections. Most relational database companies will have a salesperson try to assess how big your company is and your database needs before quoting you a price. A license for unlimited connections using Oracle could run well over $60,000. Besides being able to afford the SQL server, you should also consider the time it will take to create and maintain an SQL database. Working with SQL Server demands learning numerous individual commands; you aren't presented with an intuitive graphical user interface such as Microsoft Access.

Another thing to consider is the support for database tools and other servers that you may want to use with your database. For example, Microsoft SQL Server 6.5 is tightly integrated with Microsoft Site Server and with the Microsoft BackOffice family of servers. The next section explains some of the tools you can use to create and manage databases.

Tools of the Database Trade

Although FrontPage 98 includes some features for accessing and displaying data in Web pages, it isn't a full-blown client/server development environment. FrontPage 98 uses Database Regions components as a simple database query mechanism to display information from a database on the Web server. Database Regions can often satisfy simple database inquiry requirements. FrontPage implements Database Regions by adding server-side VBScript code to your Web page. To execute these scripts, you create an Active server page and the Active data objects component and access your database through an ODBC driver.

Visual InterDev is a comprehensive, integrated Web development environment that incorporates language tools and site-management capabilities. It is the tool of choice for working with databases because it is designed specifically for integrating content into Web sites with ASP, OLE DB, and Active data objects. For example, InterDev includes wizards for quickly creating connections to databases.

If you are using Microsoft SQL Server, you can use Web Server Assistant to create pages that can be automatically updated when data in a database is changed.

Microsoft Access 97 also comes with a variety of enhancements for distributing data via an intranet or the Internet as well as features allowing Access databases to interact directly with documents located on the Web. Access 97 gives you several options for creating static and dynamic Web pages from data contained in tables. The static HTML files you output are a snapshot of the data at the time you publish your files. In general, you use static HTML files for reports and datasheets that you update and distribute on a regular basis, such as weekly or monthly. These files are then integrated into your Web site as pages.

Many companies sell database solutions to help simplify integrating databases with Web sites. One product that is particularly noteworthy is Drumbeat 2.0 from Elemental Software. Drumbeat presents you with a graphical environment, so you can use drag-and-drop operations to connect to a database and create database-driven Web pages using IIS 4. This can be a tremendous time-saver, especially when working with SQL database tables that typically require you to manually enter SQL commands. You can find out more by visiting Elemental Software's Web site at www.elementalsoftware.com.

FrontPage 98 and Access 97 Database Integration

More and more organizations are publishing their databases on corporate intranets and on the Internet to offer convenient access to data. Making existing information widely and easily available offers people and companies the ability to work more efficiently. With FrontPage, you can create custom database queries on dynamic, richly formatted Web pages, providing visitors to your site with information only a mouse click away.

Integrating databases into a Web site is still surprisingly complex even when using FrontPage 98 and Access 97, and involves working with several separate programs. Although Access 97 is the most common low-level Windows database, you are not limited to using a Microsoft Access database. You can use any database with an available Open Database Connectivity-(ODBC) compliant driver to publish data on a Web site.

To work with FrontPage and an Access or ODBC-compliant database, you need to perform several steps, including the following:

✔ Create and secure a folder that will contain your database file. The folder needs to be protected, so that other users cannot browse through your database.

✔ Import your database file into your FrontPage web.

✔ Define the ODBC Data Source Name (DSN) for the database you will use for queries in a Web browser. The ODBC driver needs to be given some information to identify the type of data that will be accessed and the location of the database. This information is set up using a single name, which is the Data Source Name. The ODBC data source is created using the ODBC 32 applet in the Windows NT Control Panel.

✔ Build Structured Query Language (SQL) queries in a database-management tool, such as Microsoft Access. Queries are essential tools in any database-management system. You use queries to select records, update tables, and add records to tables. Most often, you use queries to select specific groups of records that meet criteria you specify.

✔ Create a database region. The fastest way to create a database region is to use the FrontPage Database Region wizard to submit SQL queries to an ODBC-compliant database that is accessible from the Web server computer.

✔ Create the search form and the Active server page that returns the query results to the Web browser. When a user visits your Web site and submits search criteria, the database query is run and the page is displayed in the client's browser.

Microsoft Access Web Publishing

Microsoft has equipped Access 97 with a variety of enhancements for distributing data through private Intranets or the Internet. For example, the Hyperlink field data type saves the hyperlink value in a memo field and formats the display. The Hyperlink field value may consist of the following three components:

✔ **Display text,** an optional descriptive name for the hyperlink that appears as emphasized text, using underlines and having a distinctive color.

✔ **Address,** a required reference to the location of a related document. The reference can be an Internet URL for the Web and FTP sites, a relative or fully qualified path and filename, or a file on a network server specified by UNC (Uniform Naming Convention).

✔ **Subaddress,** an optional reference to a named location in a related document, such as a bookmark in a Word or an HTML document, or a named range in an Excel spreadsheet.

Individual components of Hyperlink values are separated by the pound sign (#) as the delimiter. For example, #Microsoft Web Site#http://www.microsoft.com/ displays *Microsoft Web Site* in the text and jumps to the home page of www.microsoft.com when clicked.

Exporting tables to HTML pages

The easiest approach to creating Web pages from data is to export that data from Access 97 as formatted HTML documents. Access 97 gives you several options for creating static and dynamic Web pages from data in tables. To create a formatted Web page from the Northwind.mdb database from the Suppliers table, do the following steps:

1. **Double-click Suppliers.**

   The Suppliers table of the Northwind.mdb database opens in Datasheet view.

2. **Choose File⇨Save As/Export.**

   The Save As dialog box appears.

3. **With the To an External File or Database option selected, click OK.**

   The dialog box closes and the Save Table 'Suppliers' In dialog box appears.

4. **In the Save as Type drop-down list, select HTML Documents (*.html, *.htm).**

   Selecting HTML Documents makes the Save Formatted check box available.

5. **Click the Save Formatted check box to add a check mark.**

   By doing this, you include the Access 97 automatic HTML formatting. (The Autostart check box is also made available.)

6. **Click the Autostart check box to add a check mark.**

   Your default Web browser will now display the page when Access exporting is complete.

7. **Click the Export button.**

   The export process begins, and the HTML Output Options dialog box appears.

8. **Click OK.**

   The HTML Output Options dialog box closes, leaving the HTML Template text box empty. (Later in this chapter, you can find out how to create a base template for your Web pages.) The Suppliers.html Web page automatically appears in your browser.

9. **Scroll to the right to display the Home Page table column, and you'll notice some local and external links.**

   If you want to use the local links, you need to copy the HTML files to the directory where you stored the Suppliers.html page. Be aware that the external links have changed locations on the Microsoft Web.

The Web browser is responsible for determining much of the formatting of the table display. The browser attempts to display tables within the width of the display area when possible, making a best guess on the relative width of columns. The key to developing effective Web pages of data is designing tables that include only the fields you need to display to minimize clutter. To cater to the largest Web audience, make sure your Web page design is suitable for the 640 x 480 resolution used by older PCs and the majority of laptop computers.

Exporting a query datasheet with a template

Access 97 comes with various templates you can use for your Web data pages, but using FrontPage 98 offers more powerful options for creating and editing Web data pages. After you create an HTML template using FrontPage 98, copy it to the \Templates\Access\ folder. When the HTML Options dialog box appears, click the Browse button to navigate to and select your template.

When you specify a template in the HTML Options dialog box, the template becomes the default template for the succeeding Web pages you export. The location and name of the template file appears in the HTML Templates text box of the Hyperlinks/HTML page of the Options dialog box. Choose Tools⇨Options, and then click the Hyperlinks/HTML tab to display the HTML Template text box.

Exporting reports to HTML

You can export an Access report to HTML in a manner similar to that for table or query datasheets. Unlike static datasheets, exporting a multipage report creates multiple Web pages, one for each page of the report. You can export Access reports only to static Web pages. Office 97 includes a special template, Nwindtemp.htm in the \Office\Samples folder, specifically designed for reports.

To export the Catalog report of Northwind.mdb to a series of Web pages, using Nwind.htm to add a logo and navigation features, follow these steps:

1. **Start Access.**

2. **Click the Reports tab, and then select Catalog.**

3. **Click the Preview button.**

   The Catalog report opens in preview mode.

4. **Choose File⇨Save As/Export.**

5. **Select the To an External File or Database option, and click OK.**

   The Save Report Catalog In dialog box appears.

6. **In the Save as Type drop-down list, select HTML Files (*.html, *.htm), and click the Autostart option to add a check mark.**

   The Save Formatted check box is marked and disabled; you can't export an unformatted report.

7. **Click Export to continue.**

   The HTML Output Options dialog box appears.

8. **Click the Browse button.**

9. **Select the Nwindtem.htm template in the HTML Template to Use dialog box.**

   This template is stored in the `Program Files\Microsoft Office\Office\Samples` folder.

10. **Click OK.**

    The first page of Northwind Traders catalog appears in your Web browser. Reports are formatted as HTML tables without borders.

11. **You may notice that the images are not moved automatically. To display the images, move the image files to the folder where you created your HTML report files.**

12. **Click the Next hyperlink to proceed to the second page of the catalog.**

13. **Scroll to the bottom and click the Next button to display the third page.**

    When you export a report, the Access export feature appends Page# to the filename of the report for pages 2 and higher.

As a general rule, Access reports are the best choice for exporting large amounts of data to Web pages. You have much more control over the appearance of the Web page with exported reports than when you export a datasheet with the same content.

Creating Web Pages Using Microsoft SQL Server

Using an SQL server with IIS 4 allows numerous users to be connected to and access data from your Web site at the same time. One of the most popular SQL servers used with IIS 4 is Microsoft SQL Server. At first,

Microsoft sold a version of Sybase's SQL server and later began to produce its own versions of the SQL Server with release 6.0, after it dissolved its relationship with Sybase. The latest version, at this writing, is Microsoft SQL Server 6.5. Currently, Microsoft is developing SQL Server 7.0. Similar to working with an Access database, you use the ODBC driver to connect to a SQL database and use the ActiveX Data Object (ADO) components that come with IIS 4 to display the results on a Web page. This section explains each of the steps you need to take using NT Server, IIS 4, and Microsoft SQL Server 6.5 to configure the ODBC Data Source Name (DSN) and use the ActiveX Data Object to create a Web page using a SQL database table.

Be aware that you pay a price for the power of using an SQL server on the Web. Microsoft has separate licensing requirements that go beyond the license agreements for IIS 4, Windows NT Server, and the standard Microsoft SQL Server license. To handle unlimited connections, you need to purchase an additional license from Microsoft.

Configuring the Data Source Name

To configure a Data Source Name, first make sure you have created a SQL database table. To illustrate the following examples, I created a database table named *clients* containing the following fields: Cust_ID, First_Name, Last_Name, Address, City, State, Zip, Email, and Phone. After you have created your database table, you can configure the Data Source Name (DSN) on your Windows NT Server. The following steps explain how to configure the Data Source Name for using SQL Server:

1. **Choose Start⇨Settings⇨Control Panel.**

   The Windows NT Server Control Panel appears.

2. **Double-click the 32-bit ODBC icon.**

   The ODBC Data Source Administrator dialog box appears.

3. **Click the FileDSN tab, and then click Add to specify a new Data Source Name.**

4. **Select the SQL Server entry, and click Advanced.**

   The Advanced File DSN Creation Settings dialog box appears, as shown in Figure 14-1.

5. **After the DRIVER=SQL entry, type** Server=*your_server_name*, **and then press Enter.**

   Replace *your_server_name* with the name of your SQL Server. For the example, I entered **Server=WS1**.

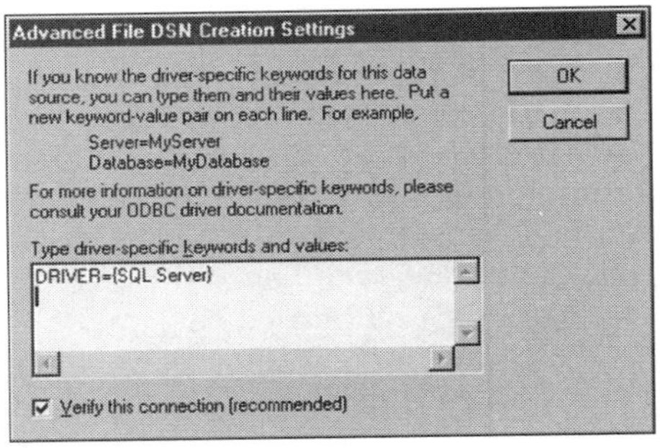

Figure 14-1:
The
Advanced
File DSN
Creation
Settings
dialog box.

6. **Type** Database=*your_database_name*, **and then click OK.**

Replace *your_database_name* with the name of the database you want
to use. For the example, I entered **Database=clients**.

7. **Click Next.**

The Create New Data Source dialog box appears.

8. **In the Data Source Name text box, type your DSN name.**

This name can be any name you want to use. In the example, I used the
clients database, and named the data source name *clients*.

9. **Click the Next button.**

A dialog box appears, showing you the settings for the new data source.

10. **Click Finish.**

The Microsoft SQL Server DSN Configuration dialog box appears, as
shown in Figure 14-2.

11. **In the Description text box, type a description, and then click Next.**

Another dialog box appears for you to enter the login ID and password
needed to connect to the SQL Server.

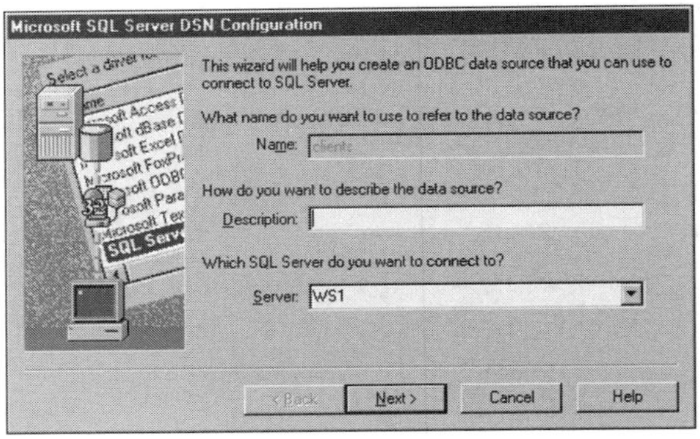

Figure 14-2:
The
Microsoft
SQL Server
DSN
Configuration
dialog box.

12. **Do one of the following:**

- If you are using the Windows NT default login and password, choose With Windows NT authentication using the network login ID.

- If you created a password for your SQL server, choose With SQL Server authentication using a login ID and password entered by the user, and change the Windows NT default login in the Login ID text box and password.

Figure 14-3 shows the Login ID set to sa (our shortcut for system administrator) and no password entered. *Remember:* Using an administrator account to test your connection is fine, but you will want to set up a different account without administrator permissions when you implement your database on a real site.

13. **Click the Next button.**

The database you entered in Step 6 should appear in the Change the default database to list box.

14. **Accept the default settings for the other options, as shown in Figure 14-4, and click Next.**

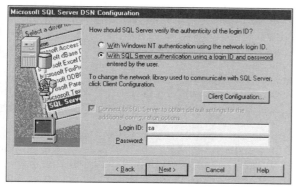

Figure 14-3: The Login ID and Password text boxes let you connect to the SQL Server.

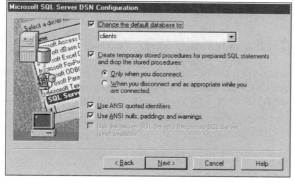

Figure 14-4: The dialog box containing the Change the default database to list box.

15. **Choose Let SQL Server ODBC Driver Choose the Translation Method.**

    Another dialog box appears with options to save long queries to a log file and log ODBC driver statistics to the log file.

16. **Click Finish.**

    The ODBC Microsoft SQL Server Setup dialog box appears, showing the current configuration settings.

17. **Click the Test Data Source button to ensure that the data source connects to the SQL server.**

    Another Window appears, informing you that the test was successfully completed.

18. **Click OK three times to close all the open dialog boxes.**

Opening the database connection

To display the page with data from your SQL database, you need to create an Active server page (.asp) containing VBScript code. Following are the beginning lines of code for the Active server page. The first line specifies that the file contains VBScript code. The next two lines create a connection object on the server and open the connection object using the parameters you set up in the data source name and your SQL Server settings for the database table.

```
<%@ LANGUAGE="VBSCRIPT" %>
Set cn = Server.createObject("ADODB.Connection")
cn.Open "FILEDSN=clients.dsn; SERVER=WS1; UID=sa; PWD="
```

The cn in this example is a variable that you can change. I used cn as an abbreviation for the word *connection*. FILEDSN is set to the domain source name you created in the preceding section. SERVER setting is the name of the SQL server you are using. UID is the user ID you set up to log on to the SQL server. PWD is the password you have set up to work with the SQL server.

Accessing the database records

After the data source connection is open, you can use the Recordset object to retrieve information from the database. The Recordset object lets you use the SQL SELECT statement to specify the records you want to display. The Recordset object is created by calling the Execute method. The SQL statement is passed as the parameter for this method:

```
Set oRs=cn.Execute("SELECT * FROM clients") %>
```

The oRs variable was created as an abbreviation for objectRecordset. You can use any SQL statements in between the parentheses to display selected fields. For example, to display only the last name (Last_Name) and e-mail (Email) fields in the clients database, you could enter the following:

```
Set oRs=cn.Execute("SELECT Last_Name, Email FROM clients")
     %>
```

You can also set criteria for displaying fields using SQL statements. The following example displays only the last name (Last_Name) and e-mail address (Email) fields if the State field is equal to CA in the clients database table:

```
Set oRs=cn.Execute("SELECT Last_NAME, EMAIL FROM clients
            WHERE clients.State='CA'") %>
```

After the records are retrieved, you can use the MoveFirst, MoveLast, MoveNext, and MovePrevious methods to navigate the records in your script. In this example, I created a table and used a Do while VBScript programming construct and the MoveNext method to display all the records in the database in table cells:

```
<TABLE BORDER=1>
<TR>
<% Do while (Not oRs.eof) %>
<%  For Index=0 to (oRs.fields.count-1) %>
 <TD VAlIGN="TOP"><%  = oRs(Index)%><BR></TD>
<%  Next %>
</TR>
<%  oRs.MoveNext
Loop %>
</TABLE>
```

The last step is to close the Recordset and Connection objects after the script has finished running, as shown in the following example:

```
oRs.Close
cn.Close
```

Putting it all together

Putting all the previous code together with the basic HTML tags, you can create an Active server page. You can create this page with any text editor or word processor using FrontPage. If you use a word processor, the file must be saved as ASCII text. Be sure to save the file with the .asp extension. For this example, I created a file named clients.asp. The following shows all the code together, and Figure 14-5 shows the results of loading the clients.asp file. Remember, to display an Active server page, you need to enter the full URL or use the localhost shortcut, for example, `http://localhost/clients.asp`.

```
<%@ LANGUAGE="VBSCRIPT" %>
<HTML>
<HEAD>
<TITLE>SQL Database and ADO Example</TITLE>
</HEAD>
<BODY>
<H2>SQL Database and ADO Example</H2>
<% Set cn=Server.CreateObject("ADODB.Connection")
cn.Open "FILEDSN=clientsnew.dsn; SERVER=WS1; UID=sa; PWD="
Set oRs=cn.Execute("SELECT * FROM clients") %>
<BR>
<DIV ALIGN="CENTER">
<TABLE BORDER=1>
<TR>
<% Do while (Not oRs.eof) %>
<%  For Index=0 to (oRs.fields.count-1) %>
 <TD VAlign=top><%  = oRs(Index)%><BR></TD>
<%  Next %>
</TR>
<%  oRs.MoveNext
Loop %>
</TABLE>
<%
oRs.Close
cn.Close %>
</DIV>
</BODY>
</HTML>
```

Verifying script permissions

Unless the directory containing your Active server page is assigned the proper permissions, it will not run. After you have created the .asp file, you can ensure that the folder containing the file is set to run the Active server page and VBScript code when the page is requested. To do this, click Start⇨Programs⇨Internet Service Manager. The Microsoft Management Console appears. Open the folders for your Web site, right-click the folder that contains the .asp file, and choose Properties. Check to make sure the

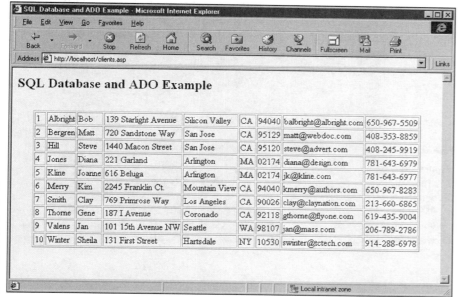

SQL Database and ADO Example - Microsoft Internet Explorer

Address http://localhost/clients.asp

SQL Database and ADO Example

1	Albright	Bob	139 Starlight Avenue	Silicon Valley	CA	94040	balbright@albright.com	650-967-5509
2	Bergren	Matt	720 Sandstone Way	San Jose	CA	95129	matt@webdoc.com	408-353-8859
3	Hill	Steve	1440 Macon Street	San Jose	CA	95120	steve@advert.com	408-245-9919
4	Jones	Diana	221 Garland	Arlington	MA	02174	diana@design.com	781-643-6979
5	Kline	Joanne	616 Beluga	Arlington	MA	02174	jk@kline.com	781-643-6977
6	Merry	Kim	2245 Franklin Ct.	Mountain View	CA	94040	kmerry@authors.com	650-967-8283
7	Smith	Clay	769 Primrose Way	Los Angeles	CA	90026	clay@claynation.com	213-660-6865
8	Thorne	Gene	187 I Avenue	Coronado	CA	92118	gthorne@flyone.com	619-435-9004
9	Valens	Jan	101 15th Avenue NW	Seattle	WA	98107	jan@mass.com	206-789-2786
10	Winter	Sheila	131 First Street	Hartsdale	NY	10530	swinter@tctech.com	914-288-6978

Local intranet zone

Figure 14-5:
The clients.asp file loaded in Internet Explorer 4.0.

Scripts radio button in the Permissions group is selected. If it isn't selected, select it now. After the Script permission is set, you can load the active server page in the browser to display the page created using your SQL database query.

Generating Web Pages with the SQL Server Web Assistant

SQL Server comes with the SQL Server Web Assistant, which lets you generate a Web page when the data in a database table changes or at a scheduled time interval. This can be a great time-saver for creating a Web site that automatically updates itself. To use the SQL Server Web Assistant to create a Web page that is updated automatically, click Start⇨Programs⇨ Microsoft SQL Server⇨SQL Server Web Assistant. The SQL Web Assistant dialog box appears, as shown in Figure 14-6.

You can then complete filling out the dialog boxes for the SQL database table you want to use and choose to generate a page when your database changes or at a scheduled time interval. Remember, you need to alter the table at least once for the HTML file to be created if you choose to have the table created whenever data in a table changes.

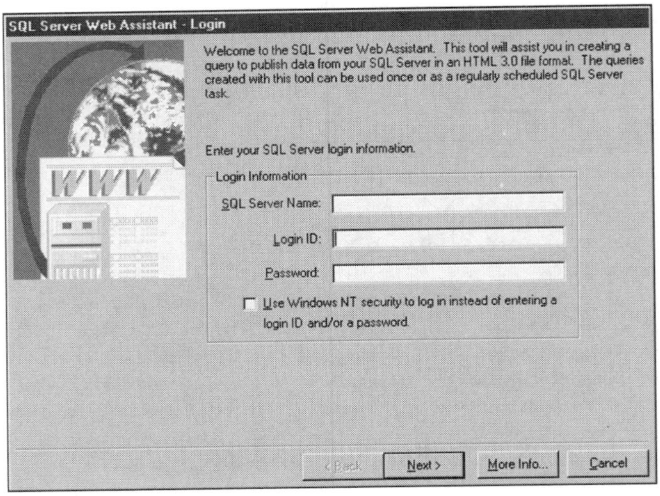

Figure 14-6: The SQL Server Web Assistant dialog box.

Chapter 15

Creating Logs and Reports

● ●

In This Chapter

▶ Choosing which log file format to use

▶ Enabling logging and creating log files

▶ Controlling log files

▶ Customizing log files

▶ Storing log information in a database

▶ Generating custom logs with ASP

▶ Creating graphical usage analysis reports

● ●

Savvy Webmasters know who is visiting their sites and what information people are viewing. By creating Web and FTP site logs, you can gain insight into the number of users visiting your site, what pages and files are being accessed most often, and the types of browsers being used to view your site. Log files and reports generated from them are powerful tools that can help you manage your sites. This chapter explains how to choose a log format and enable logging to record activity on your site. It also explains how to use the Microsoft Site Server Express Usage Import and Report Writer utilities to further examine your site by creating graphical charts and reports.

Choosing a Log File Format

One of the most confusing aspects of log files is deciding which of the available IIS log file formats to use to create your log files. Microsoft IIS can log server activity in any of the following types of log file formats:

✔ NCSA Common Log format

✔ Microsoft IIS Log format

✔ W3C Extended Log File format

✔ ODBC Logging format

This section explains each of these file formats so that you can choose the log file format that best meets your needs.

NCSA Common Log format

NCSA stands for the National Center for Supercomputing Applications. More servers use the NCSA Common Log format than any other format. Besides being a longtime standard, one of the main benefits of the NCSA Common Log format is its small log file size. The NCSA Common Log format is a fixed (noncustomizable) ASCII format. One drawback to the NCSA Common Log format is that it can be used to create logs only for Web sites, so you can't use it for FTP sites.

The NCSA Common Log format records basic information about user requests, such as remote hostname, username, date, time, request type, HTTP status code, and the number of bytes received by the server. Items are separated by spaces, and time is recorded as local time, as opposed to Greenwich Mean Time.

Microsoft IIS Log format

Microsoft's IIS Log format has been the default format for IIS until Version 4.0, which now uses the W3C Extended Log File format as the default. The Microsoft IIS Log format is a little more cryptic than other formats, but the advantage is that log files are much smaller than the other formats. Another benefit of using Microsoft's IIS Log format is that the log is stored as a comma-delimited file, meaning a comma separates each item. If you plan on creating scripts or programs using information stored in a log file, comma-delimited fields make log files much easier to parse than other ASCII log formats that use spaces for separators.

Like the NCSA format, the Microsoft IIS Log format is a fixed (noncustom-izable) ASCII format. It records more items of information than the NCSA Common Log format. The Microsoft IIS Log format includes items such as the user's IP address, username, request date and time, HTTP status code, and number of bytes received. Additionally, it includes items such as the elapsed time, the number of bytes sent to a client, and the name of down-loaded files. The time is recorded as local time.

W3C Extended Log File format

The default for IIS 4 and the most flexible log file format is the W3C Extended Log File format. The major advantage of using the W3C Extended Log File format is that it is a customizable ASCII format, which lets you choose which items to record. You can gather details about items important to you and limit the size of the log file by omitting unneeded items.

Another advantage of using the W3C Extended Log File format is that it is much easier to decipher items in the log than in other formats. The drawback is that the log files are usually quite a bit larger than files created using other log formats. Items in the log file are separated by spaces. Unlike the NCSA Common Log format and the IIS Log format, which record the local time, the W3C Extended Log File format records the time as Greenwich Mean Time.

ODBC Logging format

The ODBC Logging format allows you to log a fixed set of data fields in an ODBC-compliant database. Some of the items logged are the user's IP address, username, request date and time, HTTP status code, bytes received, bytes sent, action carried out, and name of the downloaded file. The time is recorded as local time.

To use ODBC Logging, you must set up a database to receive the data. Viewing the data in a database can be quite beneficial because you can easily sort data and create custom reports. However, using ODBC is a little more costly in space because databases are larger than ASCII text files. In addition, ODBC logs take a little more processing time because information must be sent through the ODBC driver to the database.

Enabling Logging

After you choose a log format, you can enable logging for individual Web and FTP sites. The log file is separate from the event logging accomplished through the Windows NT Server. When you enable logging, it is enabled for all the site's directories. You can, however, disable logging for specific directories. To enable IIS 4 to automatically create log files, do the following:

1. **Click Start➪Programs➪Internet Information Manager➪Internet Service Manager.**

   The Microsoft Management Console appears.

2. **Select the Web or FTP site for which you want to create a log file, right-click the site, and then choose Properties.**

   The Default Web Site Properties dialog box appears, as shown in Figure 15-1, with the Web Site tab selected.

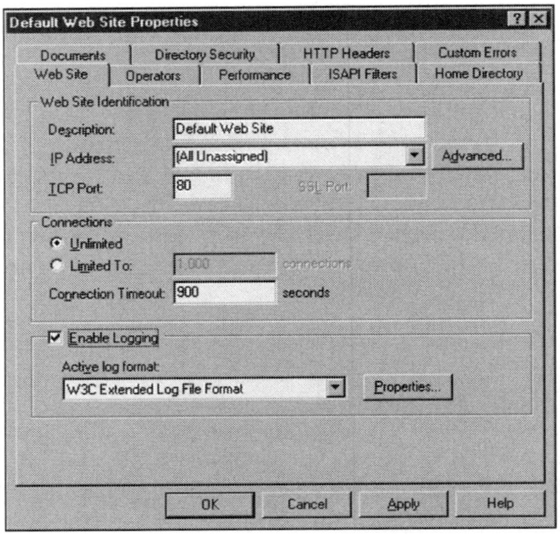

Figure 15-1:
The Default
Web Site
Properties
dialog box.

3. **Make sure the Enable Logging check box is selected.**

4. **In the Active Log Format drop-down list, select a format.**

    By default, W3C Extended Log File Format is selected, and the following fields are enabled: Time, Client IP Address, Method, and URI Stem. URI Stem is the resource accessed, such as an HTML page, a file, a CGI program, or a script. To see the available fields, you need to click the Properties button, and then click the Extended Properties tab.

5. **Click OK.**

Interpreting Log Files

By default, log files are stored in the WINNT/System32/LogFiles directory. HTTP log files are stored in the W3SVC1 subdirectory, which stands for World Wide Web Service 1, the first Web server. FTP log files are stored in the MSFTPSVC1 directory. To save space, some log files use abbreviations, so at first glance these log files can be difficult to decipher.

One of the more confusing items in a log file is the HTTP status code, which appears only as a number. Table 15-1 lists the levels of HTTP status codes to help give you an idea of what type of code the server is sending. The sections following Table 15-1 break down entries in the different log file formats to help you make sense of the different abbreviations and logging schemes.

Table 15-1	HTTP Status Codes
Code	*What It Means*
200 codes	Successful connections or operations
300 codes	Redirection, indicating data has been moved to another site
400 codes	Client error, usually resulting from incorrect syntax, unauthorized access, incapability to locate a URL, or the client timing out
500 codes	Internal server error, usually resulting from a program error, trying to perform an unsupported function, a service being unavailable, or the server timing out

Understanding W3C Extended Log files

The W3C Extended Log file begins with *ex*, followed by the date *(yymmdd)*, and ending with a *.log* filename extension. If you use a file size to store the NCSA Common Log file, the log file begins with *extend* followed by a sequence number, beginning with 01. The following shows the abbreviations used in W3C Extended Log files to identify the client and server actions:

Time	The local time
c-ip	The client Internet Protocol address
cs-method	The client server method, for example GET or POST
cs-uri-stem	The client-to-server actions, for example the HTML page, a CGI program, or a script accessed
sc-status	The server client status code

An entry in the W3C Extended Log file might appear similar to the following:

```
#Software: Microsoft Internet Information Server 4.0
#Version: 1.0
#Date: 1998-02-23 14:33:33
#Fields: time c-ip cs-method cs-uri-stem sc-status
14:33:33 205.158.247.34 GET /Default.htm 200
```

This entry states that on February 23, 1998 at 2:33 p.m., a user with the IP address of 205.158.247.34 issued a GET command to download the Default.htm file. The number 200 indicates that the request was successful.

Understanding Microsoft IIS Log files

The Microsoft IIS Log format filename begins with *in,* followed by the date *(yymmdd),* and ending with the *.log* filename extension. If you use a file size to store the Microsoft IIS Log file, the log file begins with *inetsv* followed by a sequence number, beginning with 01. The Microsoft IIS Log file format doesn't include abbreviations like the W3C Extended Log file format. Because the Microsoft IIS Log file format isn't customizable, the file will always use the same format. Not all fields will have information available for logging. For fields that are selected, but for which there is no information, a hyphen appears in the field as a placeholder. The following is a sample entry from a Microsoft IIS Log file.

```
205.158.247.34, -, 2/23/98, 19:57:09, W3SVC1, WS1,
205.158.247.34, 3275, 441, 695, 200, 0, GET, /hello.asp, -,
```

The following shows the relationship of each item in the Microsoft IIS Log sample entry:

Client IP address	205.158.247.34
Username	-
Date	2/23/98
Time	19:57:09
Service	W3SVC1
Server name (hostname)	WS1
Server IP address	205.158.247.34
Elapsed time	3275
Bytes received	441
Bytes sent	695
HTTP status code	200
Windows NT status code	0
HTTP method	GET
Target of the operation (filename accessed)	hello.asp
URI query	-

Understanding NCSA Common Log files

The NCSA Common Log file begins with *nc,* followed by the date *(yymmdd),* and ending with the *.log* filename extension. If you use a file size to store the NCSA Common Log file, the log file begins with *ncsa* followed by a sequence number, beginning with 01. A hyphen acts as a placeholder if there is no valid value for a certain item. The following shows a NCSA Common Log entry:

```
205.158.247.34 - - [23/Feb/1998:20:30:59 +0000] "POST
               form_results.asp HTTP/1.0" 200 456
```

The following shows the relationship of each item in the NCSA Common Log file entry:

Remote host	205.158.247.34
UserID	-
Username	-
LogDate, LogTime, and GMT offset	[23/Feb/1998:20:30:59 +0000]
Request	"POST /form_results.asp HTTP/ 1.0"
HTTP status code	200
Bytes sent	456

Microsoft IIS includes a command-line conversion program (convlog.exe) to convert any log file format to the NCSA format. To display the options for using this conversion program, open an Command Prompt window and enter **convlog /?** at the command prompt.

Controlling Log Files

New log entries are generated whenever any users access the server. Each entry increases the log file size. At a busy site, log files can become quite large. IIS gives you options to control the generation of log files, such as when to start a new log file and how large a log file can be. For example, you can choose to create logs on a daily, weekly, or monthly basis or you can limit a log file by size.

If you are using a time criterion, it's helpful to know that *midnight* is defined in the time zone used by the chosen log format. With the NCSA Common Log format, Microsoft IIS Log format, or ODBC Logging, midnight uses local time. With the W3C Extended Log File format, midnight uses Greenwich Mean Time.

The best way to limit the size of a log file is to create a custom W3C Extended Log file so that you save only the data you want to track.

To change the period of time that log files are generated or to control the log file size, do the following:

1. Click Start⇨Programs⇨Internet Service Manager.

The Microsoft Management Console appears.

2. Select the Web or FTP site for which you want to change logging periods or file size, right-click the site, and then choose Properties.

The Default Web Site Properties dialog box appears.

3. Click the Properties button.

The Extended Logging Properties dialog box appears, as shown in Figure 15-2.

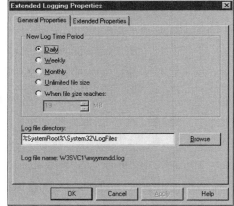

Figure 15-2:
The Extended Logging Properties dialog box.

4. Select one of the following options:

- Daily: A log file is created every day, starting with the first entry that transpires after midnight.

- Weekly: A log file is created every week, starting with the first entry that transpires at Sunday after midnight.

- Monthly: A log file is created every month, starting with the first entry that transpires after midnight on the first day of the month.

- Unlimited File Size: Data is continually appended to the log file.

- When the File Size Reaches: A log file is created when the current log file reaches the specified size.

5. Click OK.

Choosing the Unlimited File Size option appears to be an easy choice, but you may find it more difficult to track information. It is also more likely that you will use up disk space using this setting. If your server runs out of disk space when IIS is attempting to add a log entry to a file, IIS logging will shut down and the Application log of Windows NT Event Viewer will log the event. You will need to delete some files to make space. IIS logging will resume when disk space is again available.

Don't think that you can access the current log file to check your site. The current log file is not accessible while the site is running. To access the current log file, you first have to stop the HTTP or FTP site. To do this, click Start➪Programs➪Internet Service Manager, select the site, and click the Stop button.

Customizing Logs

By using the W3C Extended Log File format for a Web or an FTP site, you can create custom logs and select only the items you want to record. Only the W3C Extended Log File format lets you limit the log size by omitting un-needed items and display only the items important to you. To customize a W3C Extended Log file, do the following:

1. **Click Start➪Programs➪Internet Service Manager.**

   The Microsoft Management Console appears.

2. **Select the Web or FTP site for which you want to change logging periods or file size, right-click the site, and then choose Properties.**

   The Default Web Site Properties dialog box appears.

3. **Make sure that logging is enabled and that W3C Extended Log File Format is selected.**

4. **Click Properties.**

   The Extended Logging Properties dialog box appears.

5. **Click the Extended Properties tab, and then select the fields you want to log.**

   By default, Time, Client IP Address, Method, URI Stem, and Http Status are enabled, as shown in Figure 15-3.

6. **Click OK twice to close the dialog boxes.**

7. **Choose Console➪Exit to close the Microsoft Management Console window.**

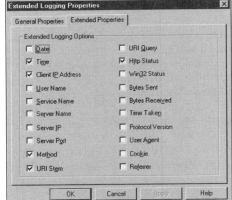

Figure 15-3:
The
Extended
Properties
tab.

Storing Log Information in a Database

To save you from having to manually convert log files into a database table, you can use ODBC Logging, which stores the log information in a SQL or an ODBC-compliant database. To store a log in a database table, you first need to create the database table with the appropriate fields for logging the data. As with any ODBC database, you need to give the database a system Data Source Name (DSN), which is a name that the ODBC software will use to recognize the database.

After supplying IIS with the DSN, you may also need to specify the username and password needed to access the database. The following steps explain how to set up a database and configure the ODBC driver for ODBC logging:

1. **Create a table with the following fields.**

   ClientHost (character), Username (character), LogTime (datetime), Service (character), Machine (character), ServerIP (character), ProcessingTime (integer), BytesRecvd (integer), BytesSent (integer), ServiceStatus (integer), Win32Status (integer), Operation (character), Target (character), and Parameters (character).

   To help you set up the database, the type of data for each field is included in parentheses after each field name. The default table name for ODBC Logging is Internetlog, but you can use any filename.

   IIS 4 includes a SQL query template file that you can run to create a database table named inetlog that will accept log entries. The template file is named Logtemp.sql. If you accepted the defaults, the directory containing the template is \WinNT\System32\inetserv\. If you want to use the default settings that IIS 4 uses, change the name from inetlog to Internetlog.

2. Click Start⇨Settings⇨Control Panel.

The Windows NT Server Control Panel appears.

3. Double-click the 32-bit ODBC icon.

The ODBC Data Source Administrator dialog box appears.

4. Click the System DSN tab (see Figure 15-4), and then click Add to specify a new Data Source Name.

The Create New Data Source dialog box appears.

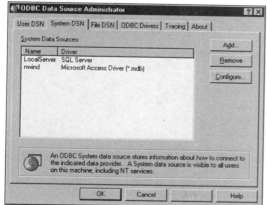

Figure 15-4:
The System
DSN tab.

5. Select the driver that matches your database software.

For example, if you are using a SQL server database table, select SQL Server.

6. Click Finish.

The setup dialog box appears for the database driver you selected.

7. Type a Data Source Name.

The fields displayed in the dialog box will vary for different types of databases. To use the default DSN setting for ODBC Logging, type HTTPLOG. If you are using Microsoft SQL Server, be sure to also fill in the name of the SQL server to which you want to connect.

8. Continue filling in the remaining dialog boxes associated with the type of database you selected.

If you are using the SQL server, be sure to fill in the Login ID and password fields to gain access to the SQL server. You can accept the defaults for the rest of the dialog boxes. Click OK to close each open dialog box.

9. **Choose File⇨Close to close the Control Panel window.**

10. **Click Start⇨Programs⇨Internet Service Manager.**

   The Microsoft Management Console appears.

11. **Right-click the Web or FTP site for which you want to use ODBC logging, and then choose Properties.**

12. **In the Web Site or FTP Site tab, make sure the Enable Logging check box is selected, and from the Active Log Format drop-down list box, select ODBC Logging.**

13. **Click Properties.**

   The ODBC Logging Properties tab appears, as shown in Figure 15-5.

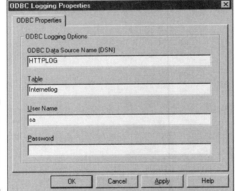

Figure 15-5:
The ODBC
Logging
Properties
tab.

14. **Type the Data Source Name and the name of the database table.**

   Be sure to also include a username and password if these are required for accessing your database. In the example, I used *sa,* which is short for system administrator. You most likely will want to use a different username and password for accessing your SQL database table, rather than using an account with administrator permissions.

15. **Click OK twice to close the ODBC Properties and the Default Web Site Properties dialog boxes.**

16. **Choose Console⇨Exit to close the Microsoft Management Console window.**

Creating Usage Reports

Microsoft Usage Import and Report Writer is included in IIS as a part of Microsoft Site Server Express 2.0. By default, Site Server Express is not installed, so to use the Usage Import and Report Writer, you need to run the Windows NT 4.0 Option Pack setup program to install Microsoft Site Server Express.

The Report Writer comes with 21 reports to help you analyze Web traffic by displaying the data in a well-designed graphical and textual format. The Usage Import program imports information from all IIS-supported log file formats. Using the Usage Import and Report Writer, you can easily pinpoint the top-requested and least-requested pages at your site. You can also easily track the number of people using Microsoft Internet Explorer versus Netscape Navigator.

Importing data

The Usage Import utility reads your log files and stores them in a relational database, which the Report Writer uses to produce your analysis reports. The first time you start the Usage Import program, it displays dialog boxes for you to identify the log file format, the server, and the log files you want to import. To import data so that you can use the Report Writer to create automatic reports, do the following.

1. **Click Start⇨Programs⇨Microsoft Site Server Express⇨Usage Import.**

   A message box appears, informing you that no Internet sites are configured in this database.

2. **Click OK to use Server Manager to configure your site.**

   The Log Data Source Properties dialog box appears.

3. **Choose the log file format you are currently using.**

   For example, to choose the default file format, select W3C Extended Log File Format.

4. **Click OK.**

   The Server Properties dialog box appears.

5. **In the Local Domain text box, type your local domain name.**

   I used bookware.com as the local domain name. You need to use your own domain name for this example to work.

6. **Click OK.**

   The Site Properties dialog box appears.

7. Enter the full URL to your Web site.

I entered `http://wsl.bookware.com`. Again, you need to use the URL that relates to your Web site for this to work.

8. Click OK.

The Log File Manager appears, as shown in Figure 15-6.

9. Select the log data source you have just created; in the Log Location text box, type the path to the log file you want to import.

Alternatively, you can use the Browse button to locate your log file. For this example, I entered `f:\WINNT\system32\LogFiles\W3SVC1\ex980227.log`.

10. Click the Start Import button, which is the right-facing green arrowhead in the toolbar.

Message boxes appear, displaying the status of importing the selected log files, followed by a message box that informs you that the import was successful and the amount of time it took to import the data.

11. Click OK to close the message box.

The Usage Import Statistics message box appears.

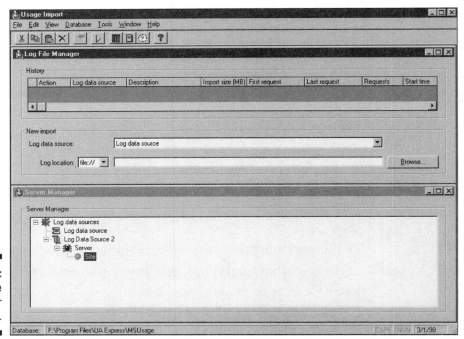

Figure 15-6:
The Log File Manager window.

12. Click <u>C</u>lose to close the message box.

13. Choose <u>F</u>ile⇨E<u>x</u>it to close the Usage Import window.

Creating reports with Report Writer

Report Writer lets you create impressive graphical analysis reports as HTML, Microsoft Word, or Excel documents. The analysis reports are based on the usage database created when you imported the log information, as shown in the preceding section. Report Writer lets you choose from numerous preconfigured reports for tracking a variety of categories. For example, you can track the browser type, the geographical regions visitors come from, the number of hits, the sites from which visitors were referred to your site, the types of requests, the frequency with which users return to your site, and who has visited your site and at what times. The following steps explain how to create a report with Report Writer:

1. **Click Start⇨<u>P</u>rograms⇨Microsoft Site Server Express⇨Report.**

   The Report Writer dialog box appears.

2. **Click OK to use the default option, From the Report Writer <u>C</u>atalog.**

   Another Report Writer dialog box appears, displaying three folders.

3. **Click the plus signs next to the file folders to display the different report files. Choose the file that matches the type of information for which you want to create a report.**

   For example, choose Browser and the operating system detail report to display the types of browsers and operating systems used to access your site.

4. **Click <u>N</u>ext.**

   A dialog box appears that lets you choose the date range to analyze.

5. **Click <u>N</u>ext to accept the default option, <u>E</u>very Request You've Imported.**

   A dialog box appears, that you can use to add custom filters to include or exclude data for analysis. The text box allows you to enter a Boolean expression to filter and customize your report.

6. **Click <u>F</u>inish.**

   A window appears, displaying the information that will be used to create your report.

7. **Click the Create Report button, which is the right-facing green arrowhead in the toolbar.**

   A dialog box appears for you to specify the file and format that you want to use to create the report.

8. **Type a filename and select a format.**

   For example, I accepted the default HTML format and entered browser.html for the filename. You can choose from an HTML, a Microsoft Word, or an Excel format.

9. **Click OK, and the Report Writer creates your report.**

   A Report Writer statistics dialog box displays the statistics of your report.

Choosing the analysis report in the HTML format automatically displays the report in your browser, as shown in Figure 15-7. If you created a Microsoft Word or Excel file, you need to start the application and load the file. The default directory for your reports is `Program Files/UA Express/Reports`.

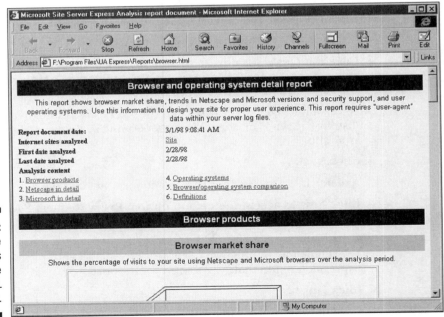

Figure 15-7:
The analysis report in the HTML format.

Part IV
The Part of Tens

The 5th Wave   By Rich Tennant

"Can someone please tell me how long 'Larry's Lunch Truck' has had his own page on the intranet?"

In this part . . .

Creating the coolest Web site in the world means nothing if no one visits it. Getting the word out about your Web site is an essential element of your Web site development process, and this part presents ten ways to market your Web site on the Internet. This part also helps you with the never-ending search for new tools and other resources to keep your Web site fresh. It includes a comprehensive resource of online and offline Web site development resources as well as a number of popular third-party tools.

Chapter 16

Ten Ways to Market Your Web Site

▶ Understanding Web marketing

▶ Writing and submitting information about your Web site to search engines

▶ Using keyword, META tags, and titles to get your Web site noticed by search engines

▶ Using links to draw in visitors from other Web sites

▶ Promoting your Web site through newsgroups and mailing lists

▶ Buying banner advertising

C reating the coolest Web site in the world means nothing if no one visits it. Getting the word out about your Web site is an essential element of the Web site development process. This chapter presents ten ways to market your Web site on the Internet.

Understand Web Marketing Is Unique

The approach to Web marketing requires managing an ongoing campaign with the objective of getting visitors and keeping them. You increase the number of visitors to your site by employing the entire spectrum of Web site promotion techniques. These techniques range from using special HTML tags in your Web pages to informing search engines of your Web site. (A *search engine* is a special Web site that a visitor can use to search for Web sites based on specific keywords.)

Internet marketing obeys the basic principles of marketing, yet it's unique because of its digital, global network context. The Web is a dynamic medium that provides marketing opportunities in the form of search engines, e-mail, newsgroups, links, and online and offline media. You can do your own Web site marketing, or if your organization has money to spend, you can outsource it to Web marketing professionals. Whatever route you take, you need to know the elements of effective Web marketing.

Before you run off to orchestrate a Web marketing campaign for your Web site, make sure your site has something to attract visitors and keep them coming back. Making your Web site attractive to users represents one of the largest commitments you'll make toward ensuring the success of your site.

Write Your Words

Getting started with your promotion efforts begins by creating a collection of keywords and documents that you'll send to search engines, site administrators, journalists, newsgroups, e-mail recipients, and others. Take some time to think about, prepare, and refine your promotional materials. The core components of your Web promotional materials include the following:

- ✔ A title for your Web site. Your Web site title should not only catch people's attention but also convey the essence of your site.

- ✔ Assemble your contact information, including a name, an e-mail address, a phone number, and a fax number.

- ✔ Develop a list of keywords. One of the most important exercises you can go through when you begin to promote your Web site is to define your keywords. Essentially, keywords are those search terms your prospective visitors enter at a search engine when trying to find information. Create your keywords from the perspective of the user. You should develop a list of 10 to 30 keywords.

- ✔ Write a description of your Web site in one sentence, in 25 words, in 50 words, and in 75 words.

- ✔ Develop a 500- to 1,000-word press release that can act as the principal source of information for a short article about your Web site.

Tap Search Engines

Search engines are possibly the most important element for Web-based marketing. A recent CommerceNet and Nielson Media survey of Web users showed that 71 percent of Web users use search engines to get to Web sites. The distant second source, at only 9.8 percent, was friends and relatives. This speaks volumes for any Web site promotion campaign you embark on. The bottom line is that penetrating search engines is the primary starting point for your Web site promotion campaign.

User access to most search engines is free because the companies that support them make their money by selling advertising space on their Web pages. All the popular search engines work in the same general way, often based on the Z39.50 protocol, a standard for database format and search utilities. Many search engines actively go out and search the Web using spiders, Web crawlers, or bots programs. They check that existing links still work and add material to their giant databases.

Table 16-1 lists the largest search engines on the Internet. You should seriously consider these sites as a minimum target for getting the word out about your Web site. Note, however, that hundreds of other specialized search engines are on the Internet.

Table 16-1	Top Search Engines on the Web
Search Engine	*URL*
AltaVista	www.altavista.digital.com
Excite	www.excite.com
HotBot	www.hotbot.com
InfoSeek	www.infoseek.com
Lycos	www.lycos.com
Megellan Internet Guide	www.mckinley.com
WebCrawler	www.webcrawler.com
Yahoo!	www.yahoo.com

Submit to Search Engines

It takes time and effort to get your Web site recognized on the leading search engines of the Web. Making your Web site attractive to search engines means you influence them to increase the chances that people who want to find your site will do so. Search engines often take weeks to add your site to their database.

Manual submission means going to the search engine site and entering your submission through your Web browser. Most search engines take submissions directly from the Web. Just go to the search engine site and look for a link or button that's labeled something like Add URL. Doing it on a one-by-one basis lets you tailor your submission for each search engine and helps you develop a relationship with the search engine company.

Checking out Web marketing demographics

A good source for Web demographics is CyberAtlas (www.cyberatlas.com), which is a service of I/PRO (www.ipro.com). This site justly defines itself as The Reference Desk for Web Marketing. An example of useful information at CyberAtlas is the ranking of the top 25 busiest Web sites.

Doing submissions manually, however, can be a very time-consuming process. A faster way to make submissions to a larger group of search engines and directories is to use a submission service or submission software to send URL submissions to multiple search engine sites. Automatic submission services place your URL at a few hundred search engines and directories on the Internet.

Be careful when choosing a search engine submission service. A number of automatic submission scams are operating on the Web.

Submit It!

Submit It! (www.submit-it.com) is considered one of the best of the automatic submission services. It provides a free service that submits your Web site information to 15 search engines, announces sites, and directories. Submit It! also provides a number of services for promoting your Web site, including announcement services, link partnering with other Web sites, mailbot (automatic mailing list management) services, and search engine monitoring.

SitePromoter

An automatic submission program essentially does what the submission services do, but instead you run the campaign. SitePromoter (www.sitepromoter.com), which lists for $99, is such a program. It lets you create your own customized entries for over 150 search engines. SitePromoter comes with all the templates you need for each search engine, so your submissions comply with each search engine's submission rules. It also generates updates that enable your listing to move up to the top of the list, and includes the Net Copywriting module to help you write effective keywords and descriptions. SitePromoter also includes online updates to all the search engines for a full year, tracking of where you are listed, and other tools for managing your own campaign.

Design Web Pages for Search Engines

Search engines use algorithms to process information about your Web site. An *algorithm* is a program that applies logical analysis to make decisions about information being processed. Most search engines see word placement and repetition as indicators of the word's importance. Some of the words a search engine finds on a Web site are considered more important than others, which means these words will make stronger matches in queries. The following are search engine guidelines to keep in mind when constructing your Web pages:

- **Word frequency in documents.** In general, the more often a query word occurs in a document, the higher the score.

- **Words in document titles.** Pages that use search terms in the title will be ranked significantly higher than documents that contain the search term only in the text. Most search engines record the title of the URL and weigh the title's contents heavily in search results. This makes the choice of words in your title extremely important.

- **<META> tag keywords.** The <META> tags in HTML documents let you place keywords in the HEAD element of an HTML document. These keywords can be accessed by spiders and other types of information retrievers visiting your Web site. Web pages that use your search terms in the keywords <META> tag are weighted more highly than text words, but less highly than title words.

- **Document length.** When the search words appear frequently in a short document, the page will be ranked higher than when the words appear in a longer document.

- **Word proximity to the beginning of the page.** Search engines usually consider words located near the beginning of the home page as more important than the same words appearing later in the text.

- **Repetition of words.** Word repetition is used as a measure of word importance by search engines. Many search engines, however, use filters to prevent Web page designers from word packing (that is, repeating the same word over and over again to skew the search results).

- **Number of other sites that link to your page.** Checking links is a way of measuring the popularity of your Web site. Search engines then use site popularity information as a determining factor in positioning a site in a search result. The more popular a Web site is, the higher the search engine ranks it.

- **Subject category of your Web site.** Some search engines remember your Web site by a subject category. For example, Yahoo! places your Web site in the hierarchical subject category that it thinks is appropriate.

For more information on search engines, check out the Search Engine Watch site (www.searchenginewatch.com/).

Define your keywords

Defining your keywords is an essential part of authoring Web pages. Keywords are those search terms your prospective visitor enters at the search engine site when trying to find specific information. You need to formulate your keywords as they would commonly be used in a search query at a search engine. The words that you rank at the top of your keyword list should be included in Web page titles, Web document text, and <META> tags.

Master <META> tags

You can help search engines find your Web documents by using the HTML <META> tag on your Web site. Not all search engines take advantage of this tag, but many do. This is an optional tag used just after the <TITLE> tag and has the following general form:

```
<META NAME="description" CONTENT="text description of your
          page">
```

Some search engines will present the text you include as CONTENT along with the title of your Web page when they present your site as a match against a search. You can also use the following:

```
<META NAME="keywords" CONTENT="a list of keywords">
```

In this case, CONTENT includes a list of words identifying your site and content, all separated by commas. You don't have to use META tags on every page of your Web site; you can add them only to key pages. Some search engines display only the first 250 characters (about 25 words) when your site comes up as a match against a search. It's up to you to make sure these first 250 characters contain the right information.

The Web Developer's Virtual Library Meta Tagging for Search Engines at www.stars.com/Location/Meta/Tag.html keeps abreast of <META> tag developments that relate to search engines.

The power of titles

The title of a page is displayed in the title bar and is coded into the Head section of your HTML documents using the <TITLE> tag. Most search engines display the title of the page in the search results, and many give added weight to title words in their ranking algorithms. For these reasons, you should make your page titles descriptive and be sure to use your heavy-hitter keywords in your titles.

Harness the Power of Links

The use of hyperlinks, more than any other feature, separates the World Wide Web from other communications media. Links (including those from search engines) represent the most common trigger for sending someone to your Web site. One of the best methods of Web site promotion involves getting your site linked from other sites across the Web. To really capitalize on the hyperlinked nature of the Web, you need to do some role reversal to think like the Web users searching for information connected to your Web site. You can link to other sites without permission, provided you're not claiming it as a section of your own site. You want to develop cross-linking, however, to get something in return. Here are some guidelines in using links as a Web site promotional campaign:

- ✔ Try to define subjects that you want to become a hit at your Web site.

- ✔ Partner other Internet sites that have potentially symbiotic relationships with your Web site.

- ✔ Use a moderate number of high-quality links that provide a high number of visitors instead of thousands of seldom-used connections.

- ✔ Check out other sites like yours that may be good places for cross-linking.

- ✔ Put yourself in your visitor's shoes, and think of as many different routes to get to your site as possible. Envision a chain of links leading backward from your site.

- ✔ Be persistent, personable, and prodding when trying to establish cross-linking.

- ✔ Contact other Webmasters through e-mail, which is the preferred approach. Write a brief comment of about 25 words to explain why you want to cross-link.

- ✔ Link to a Web site's home page, not to any of its supporting pages.

Put Your URL in Its Place

Your URL is the pointer to everything about your company. After you have your URL in place using your domain name, you need to integrate it into any existing materials your organization uses, including the following:

- ✔ Company stationery, including business cards

- ✔ All print, radio, and TV advertising

- ✔ Company voice mail and messaging systems

- ✔ Product packaging and point-of-purchase displays
- ✔ Press kits and newsletters
- ✔ Give-away gizmos, such as coffee mugs and T-shirts
- ✔ Yellow Pages and other business directory listings
- ✔ E-mail signature files

Work the Newsgroups and Mailing Lists

Both newsgroups and mailing lists can become valuable resources for publicizing a Web site. Newsgroups and mailing lists comprise communities of people who are actively engaged in discussing particular subjects. You need to package your messages carefully, however, to avoid offending these communities. Broadcast commercial messaging, called *spamming*, isn't viewed as friendly. The bottom line here is to use netiquette when working with newsgroups and mailing lists.

Thousands upon thousands of newsgroups comprise Usenet, which is distributed all over the world. Most Web surfers access newsgroups through their service provider, which actually subscribes to the newsgroups. For a listing of newsgroups, you can do a search on your ISP news server using a newsreader, or check out the Yahoo! site at `www.yahoo.com/News/Usenet/`.

Mailing lists represent the e-mail equivalent of newsgroups. After subscribing to the list, you receive e-mail messages that people post to the list. Of course, you can post to the list, too. Over 40,000 mailing lists exist. For a listing of mail lists, check out the Yahoo! site at `www.yahoo.com/Computers_and_Internet/Internet/ Mailing_Lists`.

Announce Your Site

You can submit your URL and information about your Web site to a site that specializes in announcing new sites. Typically, this process involves filling out a Web form at the announcement site. These sites provide listings and reviews of new sites and are free. Two popular announcement sites are What's New Too (`http://newtoo.manifest.com/`) and InfoSpace (`http://www.infospace.com`). The NetHappenings site (`http://scout.cs.wisc.edu/scout/net-hap/`) lets you fill out a form, and then adds the information into the NetHappenings mailing list.

Get Your 15 Minutes of Fame

Offline references to your URL from the media can yield a big jump in site visits. The press release usually represents the starting point of a successful offline promotion campaign. Target your material to the journalist and publication. Provide enough information for a busy journalist or author to write up a piece. You can use the services of a company that manages the media connection for you. It acts as a placement service for getting media coverage of your Web site. An example of this service is URLwire (www.URLwire.com). It will orchestrate a campaign for a price of between $500 and $2,000.

Buy Banners

Banners are the staple of Web-based advertising. *Banners* are graphical images that advertise products and services as well as provide a link to the sponsor's Web site. Because banners enable users to click through to the Web site, they draw visitors to the site. Banner advertising is typically sold by the impression (also referred to as a Page View or Exposure). An *impression* means that a visitor to a Web site viewed a page containing your banner ad.

You can expect, on average, that 2 percent to 3 percent of visitors who see your ad will actually click it to visit your Web site. Web ad sites typically charge a set rate for a block of impressions. Popular spots for Web banner advertising are search engines because they reach a large audience and can provide highly targeted advertising. To do banner advertising at the larger sites, be prepared to spend several thousand dollars per month. Don't, however, overlook bartering for advertising by exchanging banners.

Getting into the world of banner advertising requires knowing the rate card game. A *rate card* is a document that should provide all the information you need on ad rates, banner ad size, submission specifications, contract issues, company background, and visitor demographics. Many sites publish their rate cards as Web pages. Volume discounts, visitor information, advertising inventory, and features should all be covered in the rate card. The rate card is the starting point for pricing and negotiation. A Web advertising agency can manage your Internet-based advertising for you, but many businesses can do it themselves. You can easily create a banner ad, whereas a print ad or television ad requires a production effort involving designers, printers, and others.

The 5th Wave   By Rich Tennant

"Well, this is festive - a miniature intranet amidst a swirl of Java applets."

Chapter 17
Ten Webmaster Resources

*T*he minute you get your Web site up and running, you begin the never-ending search for new tools and other resources to keep your Web site fresh. Beyond the excellent Microsoft Web site development tools (FrontPage 98, Visual InterDev, and SiteServer), a number of third-party tools can help you create and deploy Web sites. This chapter describes the top ten resources that will be of interest to any Webmaster.

HTML and DHTML Editors

The following lists some HTML and DHTML editors worth a serious look:

Dreamweaver, at www.macromedia.com

Dreamweaver by Macromedia is a high-powered Web-authoring tool supporting Dynamic HTML that runs in both Microsoft Internet Explorer and Netscape Navigator Web browsers. It includes good support for more advanced Web publishing elements, such as adding JavaScripts. One major advantage of using Dreamweaver is that it never changes your existing code without informing you that the change must be made to work correctly.

HoTMetaL Pro, at www.softquad.com

SoftQuad is known for its adherence to the HTML standard. The latest version includes Cascading Style Sheet support. HoTMetaL Pro's Information Manager does a good job of importing existing sites. It also comes with great utilities, such as PhotoImpact's GIF Animator, Aimtech's Jamba, and DTL's DataSpot 1.2, a database-publishing package.

HomeSite, at www.allaire.com

This low-cost HTML editor is feature-rich and powerful without being overwhelming. HomeSite supports a wide variety of Web standards and extensions. Its easy-to-use interface, integration with new Web technologies (Dynamic HTML and RealAudio), and quality-control features, such as document weighing, link verification, HTML validation, and spell checking, make it a notable HTML editor.

Portable Documents

HTML can't address all the needs of online publishers. *Portable documents* go beyond HTML to include sophisticated formatting options that can also be read on all platforms. There is only one serious candidate in portable documents:

Adobe Acrobat, at www.adobe.com

Adobe Acrobat lets you create documents without sacrificing fonts and more sophisticated layout elements that are not possible using HTML. Adobe Acrobat creates files in the PDF (Portable Document Format). To view the PDF documents, the user must have Adobe Acrobat Reader, which is free for the downloading from the Adobe Web site.

Web Database Tools

Integrating databases into a Web site can be a daunting task. The following are currently the best tools for working with databases and Web pages:

DrumBeat 2.0, at www.elementalsoftware.com

DrumBeat lets you create pages automatically from databases without having to be a database hack. You can create sites from a database by simply dragging a server element onto the layout and identifying the database to use. DrumBeat automatically generates the server-side JavaScript for objects dropped into and out of a layout. The SQL Builder wizard lets you build interactive, database-driven Web sites without writing code. The DataForm wizard creates pages for searching, updating, inserting, and deleting records in ODBC-complaint databases. Microsoft liked the product so much, it took an equity stake in the company.

Cold Fusion, at www.allaire.com

Cold Fusion 3.1 is a complete rapid application development system for working with databases on the Web. Cold Fusion Studio presents you with visual tools to use any ODBC-compliant database, such as Microsoft SQL Server. It includes Crystal Reports Visual Report Writer 5.0.

Windows NT and IIS Resources

The following lists some useful resources on the Web for Windows NT Server and Internet Information Server:

15 Seconds, at www.15seconds.com

This site provides comprehensive information about Internet Information Server, including links and FAQs. 15 seconds is a resource for developers and administrators working with Microsoft Internet Solutions, with a focus on server-side solutions, such as ASP. The site includes lots of current and useful articles with information not available anywhere else.

Microsoft Internet Information Server, at www.microsoft.com/iis/

This site provides a mix of useful information and Microsoft propaganda, but it's worth checking out for IIS developments and resources. Also check out www.microsoft.com/iis/Partners/ for a listing of developers with wares designed for Internet Information Server.

Microsoft Support Online, at support.microsoft.com/

An article database for finding solutions to problems with Microsoft products.

Windows NT Resource Center, at www.bhs.com

Operated by Beverly Hills Software, this is a comprehensive resource for all things Windows NT. It includes hundreds of links, NT consultant listing, NT user groups, and the NT tech center.

Online Webmaster Resources

Here are some important sites for Web developers:

CNet's Builder.com, at www.cnet.com/Content/Builder

This is a comprehensive resource for Webmasters, Web developers, and other Web professionals. It has coverage of scripting, scripting tools, Web design, Web business, and more.

Microsoft Site Builder, at www.microsoft.com/sitebuilder

This site includes a number of useful materials for working with Internet Information Server and Web sites. Billed as a one-stop resource for Web professionals, including programmers, designers, authors, and administrators, this site is full of active server information and includes samples of VBScript and JScript.

WebMonkey, at www.webmonkey.com

HotWired's highly opinionated Web design and development site is adver-tised as a "how-to guide for Web junkies." The site lives up to its name. The site includes essays and tutorials on such topics as Web design, Dynamic HTML, stylesheets, graphics and fonts, Java, JavaScript, and multimedia.

Image Editors

Images are a large reason why the Web is so successful. Following are some of the best image editors:

Adobe Photoshop, at www.adobe.com

The industry standard for high-end graphics editing, Photoshop doesn't include a lot of special Web-publishing features. It does, however, give you top-of-the-line image-editing tools. Although it's expensive, once you've used Photoshop, you'll be hooked.

Ulead PhotoImpact, at www.ulead.com

PhotoImpact stands out as a great editor for about a quarter of the price of Photoshop. What really makes PhotoImpact worth a look are the great Web utilities that come bundled with it, including SmartSaver and GIF Animator, which are covered in the next section.

PaintShop Pro, at www.jasc.com

The king of shareware image editors, PaintShop Pro is an easy-to-use editor with an impressive number of features for creating Web graphics. At even less than the cost of PhotoImpact, PaintShop Pro is a viable alternative to Adobe Photoshop.

Image Utilities and Optimization Tools

The following are the best image special-effect utilities and optimization tools you can find:

Ulead Smart Saver, at www.ulead.com

SmartSaver is a fantastic tool for quickly optimizing GIF images. An out-standing feature is the Batch mode, which lets you specify a range of colors to generate samples for quickly picking out the smallest-quality GIF image. SmartSaver comes free with PhotoImpact and is also available as an inex-pensive standalone program.

HVS JPEG, at `www.digfrontiers.com`

This Adobe Photoshop plug-in is the ultimate optimization tool for compressing JPEG images. Compressing over 2MB files into 15K file is a designer's dream. Truly amazing.

Ditherbox, at `www.ditherbox.com`

Using the browser-safe palette can be limiting. This Adobe Photoshop compatible plug-in produces 216-color GIF images with the smallest file sizes around.

Eye Candy, at `www.alienskin.com`

Anyone who has tried creating special effects with Photoshop knows that it is a time-consuming job. Eye Candy is a Photshop plug-in that includes over 20 filters that take the drudgery out of creating special effects. Some of the effects include intricate drop shadows, carvings, and flaming text.

GIF Animator, at `www.ulead.com`

The animation and optimization wizards make this utility the critics' choice for creating animated GIFs. Animated GIF images can be optimized to less than half the size in half the time, compared to using other GIF animation tools.

Debabelizer Pro, at `www.equilibrium.com`

The industrial-strength tool for optimizing multiple image and video files, Debabelizer Pro is the master tool for converting images from one platform to another. The batch conversion features and its Web-centric features make this a powerful tool for high-end Web designers.

Scripting

Programmers are some of the most generous people on earth — or maybe just on the Web. You don't have to create scripts and applets from scratch. Here are some of the top JavaScript, ActiveX, VBScript, and Java applet resources that include scripts and applets you can download and use in your Web pages.

JavaScript

WebCoder.COM, at `webcoder.com`

A great site for learning about JavaScript. Includes the Scriptorium, which is a compendium of code. It allows quick access to simple scripts to provide a starting point for working with JavaScript.

24-Hour JavaScripts, at www.javascripts.com

A terrific site with an attitude and well over 1,300 free scripts. You must register for this site.

Cut and Paste JavaScript, at www.infohiway.com/javascript/

The Cut and Paste JavaScript site includes over 195 Java Script programs that, like the name says, you can cut and paste into your HTML documents.

ActiveX and VBScript

ActiveX.com, at www.activeX.com

The ActiveX.com site is part of CNET. The site is filled with lots of ActiveX controls, which are broken down into several groups, including Browser Enhancements, Online Applications, Tools and Utilities, Site Development, Application Development, Database Connectivity, and Control Development.

ASP Developer's Network, at www.aspdeveloper.net

ASP Developer's Network has code examples, links, ASP tutorials, ASP consultants, and more. This site also includes the Active Merchandiser program written in ASP for creating an online store.

ASP Developer's Site, at www.genusa.com/asp/

One of the best, an informative unauthorized site for all things ASP, including news, tutorials, and source codes.

ServerObjects, at www.serverobjects.com

ServerObjects develops and distributes ActiveX and Component Object Model (COM) for servers. This sites includes a number of ASP components you can purchase for running on Internet Information Server.

Windows NT ActiveXServer Bulletin Board, at www.activexserver.com

This resource-rich site is filled with technical information for ASP professionals.

Wynkoop Pages, at www.swynk.com

This site is billed as the most comprehensive independent SQL Server Resource on the Internet — and it is. The site includes a comprehensive SQL script library.

ASP Hole, at www.asphole.com/asphole/

This site provides an outstanding aggregation of content from various IIS and technology-related sites; the ultimate list of ASP resources.

Ncompass, at www.ncompasslabs.com

Ncompass provides ActiveX plug-ins and tools. This site also has ScriptActive, an ActiveX plug-in for Netscape Navigator to support VBScript scripts.

Java Applets

Like JavaScripts, VBScripts, and ActiveX components, free Java applets you can use at your site can be found at numerous sites. The following are the cream of the crop:

EarthWeb's Gamelan, at www.developer.com/directories/pages/dir.java.html

This site contains thousands of Java applet examples sorted by categories.

Sun's Java Site, at java.sun.com

Sun Microsystems' site may not be the best site for getting applets, but it's the site to visit to check out the latest news on Java developments.

Java Review Service, at www.jars.com

Jars is a well-known rating service for Java applets. This site is jam-packed with information on the latest Java applets.

The Java Boutique, at javaboutique.internet.com

A great site for locating Java applets to spice up your Web pages, it's also one of the simplest sites to use, with coding samples appearing under the running applet.

The Java Centre, at www.java.co.uk

This site provides a showcase for a number of Java applets.

Magazines

Here are some helpful Webmaster and Windows NT magazines and their related Web sites:

Web Developer magazine (www.webdeveloper.com)

Microsoft Interactive Developer (www.microsoft.com/mind)

Web Techniques (www.webtechniques.com)

Windows NT Magazine (www.winntmag.com)

Windows Magazine (www.winmag.com)

Index

(continued)

• *G* •

• *H* •

• *I* •

(continued)

IDG BOOKS WORLDWIDE BOOK REGISTRATION

Register This Book and Win!

We want to hear from you!

Visit **http://my2cents.dummies.com** to register this book and tell us how you liked it!

- ✔ Get entered in our monthly prize giveaway.

- ✔ Give us feedback about this book — tell us what you like best, what you like least, or maybe what you'd like to ask the author and us to change!

- ✔ Let us know any other *...For Dummies*® topics that interest you.

Your feedback helps us determine what books to publish, tells us what coverage to add as we revise our books, and lets us know whether we're meeting your needs as a *...For Dummies* reader. You're our most valuable resource, and what you have to say is important to us!

Not on the Web yet? It's easy to get started with *Dummies 101*®: *The Internet For Windows*® *95* or *The Internet For Dummies*®, 5th Edition, at local retailers everywhere.

Or let us know what you think by sending us a letter at the following address:

...For Dummies Book Registration
Dummies Press
7260 Shadeland Station, Suite 100
Indianapolis, IN 46256-3945
Fax 317-596-5498

BUSINESS AND
GENERAL
REFERENCE
BOOK SERIES
FROM IDG

COMPUTER
BOOK SERIES
FROM IDG